Faith, Doubt, and Reason

Faith, Doubt, and Reason

BRENT A. R. HEGE

Foreword by Paul Valliere

WIPF & STOCK · Eugene, Oregon

FAITH, DOUBT, AND REASON

Copyright © 2019 Brent A. R. Hege. All rights reserved. Except for brief quotations in critical publications or reviews, no part of this book may be reproduced in any manner without prior written permission from the publisher. Write: Permissions, Wipf and Stock Publishers, 199 W. 8th Ave., Suite 3, Eugene, OR 97401.

Wipf & Stock
An Imprint of Wipf and Stock Publishers
199 W. 8th Ave., Suite 3
Eugene, OR 97401

www.wipfandstock.com

PAPERBACK ISBN: 978-1-5326-8398-5
HARDCOVER ISBN: 978-1-5326-8399-2
EBOOK ISBN: 978-1-5326-8400-5

Manufactured in the U.S.A.   DECEMBER 17, 2019

Scripture quotations are from New Revised Standard Version Bible, copyright © 1989 National Council of the Churches of Christ in the United States of America. Used by permission. All rights reserved worldwide.

To my "Faith, Doubt, and Reason"
students at Butler University, 2008–2020
Sapere aude!

Table of Contents

Foreword by Paul Valliere ix

Preface xi

Chapter 1: Faith 1

Chapter 2: Doubt 42

Chapter 3: Reason 78

Chapter 4: The Meaning of Life 110

Conclusion: Faith, Doubt, and Reason 146

Epilogue 163

Appendix 1: "The Big Picture" 165

Appendix 2: Discussion Questions 166

Appendix 3: Brief Biographies 173

Bibliography 179

Foreword

BRENT HEGE'S *FAITH, DOUBT, and Reason* is an eloquent contemporary representation of a venerable idea in American higher education: the idea that the liberal arts and the theological tradition, far from being adversaries, can be allies in the promotion of good teaching and mature learning. A college course Professor Hege and some of his colleagues have been offering to first-year students at Butler University for more than a decade is a case in point. "Faith, Doubt, and Reason," which forms part of Butler's liberal arts core curriculum, has proved to be a productive collaboration for the students and faculty involved in it. The course does not serve any confessional purpose. Butler is not a denominational school but a secular university. Religiously committed students enjoy no special status in "Faith, Doubt, and Reason." Yet secular-minded students do not enjoy special status, either. The fact that a university is constitutionally secular does not mean that it must promote secular-mindedness. "Faith, Doubt, and Reason" aspires to challenge everyone: believers, seekers, skeptics, secularists, "spiritual-but-not-religious"—the whole spectrum.

That faith, doubt, and reason are worth thinking about is obvious enough once one recognizes that these three activities are the engines of intellectual and spiritual growth in a human being. But how should such learning be structured? The first step is to recognize that faith, doubt, and reason are interdependent. To engage one of them is to engage the other two as well. Efforts to deny this linkage—to honor one of the trio while downgrading the other two—will end by downgrading all three. As Hege puts it, faith, doubt, and reason "support one another like the three legs of a tripod; without one of the legs, the tripod collapses."

This simple but profound truth is salutary in all directions beginning with traditions of piety—Jewish, Christian, Islamic, Hindu and other. In traditions of piety, the temptation to marginalize doubt and reason in the name of faith is great. What the religiously motivated marginalizers fail to see is that only a rational being is capable of faith in the first place, so the degradation of reason for the sake of faith inevitably degrades faith as well. As for doubt—a cognate of "double"—all it means is "to be of two minds" about something, which is to say to be capable of reflecting on something, capable of seeing something from more than one angle. To banish doubt from the exercise of faith is to banish reflection on faith itself—again, a degradation.

The same sort of syndrome affects those who marginalize faith in the name of reason. Recent manifestations of dogmatism by secular progressive groups in elite liberal arts institutions exemplify this phenomenon. Secular-minded activists tend to see their own causes as supremely rational while not recognizing the extent to which their commitments involve a kind of faith. Blindness to faith combined with certainty about one's own rationality is a formula for fanaticism.

To flesh out his theme, Professor Hege takes us through some of the exercises he has presented in "Faith, Doubt, and Reason" over the years. Most of these involve reflection on paradigmatic moments in the biblical and western traditions, such as the Binding of Isaac (Genesis 22), Job's quarrel with God, Descartes' meditations on selfhood, Gretchen's tragedy in Goethe's *Faust*, Ivan Karamazov's parable of the Grand Inquisitor, and others. Hege does not presume to tell us how we should respond to these iconic stories and arguments. He is an expert teacher. He helps us to think for ourselves.

University students and faculty will find *Faith, Doubt, and Reason* a helpful read, but so will readers outside the academic world, especially members of study groups in churches and other religious fellowships. Hege addresses an important need in contemporary religion: the need for a *thinking* faith. To be sure, this is just one of several needs. We also look for a heartfelt faith, an activist faith, a charitable faith. Yet none of these can take the place of a faith that nourishes and is nourished by the *intellectual* love of God. In a world of spectacular scientific achievements, advanced technology and extraordinarily complex social and political challenges, faith communities have to do more than preach and act. They have to be able to think. As Hege shows, there are plenty of resources in our historic traditions to help us. Fine teachers like Brent Hege can also help us. And we can help each other by reading and pooling our thoughts on books like *Faith, Doubt, and Reason*.

Paul Valliere
Indianapolis, Indiana

Preface

PERHAPS NO OTHER FACULTIES are more quintessentially human, more central to our quest for meaning and significance, than faith, doubt, and reason. At the same time, perhaps no other human faculties are more consistently misunderstood, twisted, and sometimes even abused. These three concepts can lead us to meaning and joy just as easily they can cause confusion and conflict. Regardless of how we use them, they are an essential part of who we are and we can never be without them.

What, then, do these terms mean? How are they—or ought they to be—interrelated? That is the subject of this book.

We live our lives in a relentless search for meaning. Religion, theology, philosophy, literature, poetry, art, music, dance, the sciences, politics, language, human culture writ large: all have their origin and their goal in our quest to live meaningful lives in pursuit of truth, beauty, and goodness. No other species on Earth has mastered these pursuits like we have. While there are considerable debates about the meaning, proper use, and continuing relevance of faith, doubt, and reason, no one will deny their fundamental role in shaping human beings across the millennia. If, as I will argue, one of the most important features of humanity is our desire to live meaningful lives, then faith, doubt, and reason are essential elements of the human personality and indispensable guides on the human quest for meaning and wisdom.

My chief argument in this book, then, is that faith, doubt, and reason form the heart and soul of the human quest for meaning and wisdom. Without them, we cease to be who we truly are as human beings. That is a lofty claim, to be sure, and as such it requires careful analysis and support. By way of such analysis I will offer a five-part argument for the central and enduring significance of these quintessentially human qualities.

In the first chapter, I will define faith as what Paul Tillich called "ultimate concern." I will further distinguish faith and belief, the confusion of which is at the root of much unnecessary and costly misunderstanding and conflict, especially between religion and the sciences. I will also show that faith need not be restricted to religion, as faith is in fact a far broader and more fundamental human quality. Following Tillich, I will contend that faith, when properly understood, is something universally human.

In the second chapter I will explore the various types of doubt: skeptical doubt, methodological doubt, and existential doubt. I will show how methodological doubt functions in relation to finite reality and is used to create good beliefs. I will then show how existential doubt functions in relation to infinite reality and forms a permanent and necessary element of the structure of faith as ultimate concern. A test case for this claim is the problem of evil and suffering, explored with the help of the Book of Job, Fyodor Dostoevsky's *The Brothers Karamazov*, and J. L. Mackie's "Evil and Omnipotence."

In the third chapter I will consider the two types of reason: technical or instrumental reason and ontological or existential reason. Building on the analysis of doubt, I will show how technical reason relates to finite reality and, along with methodological doubt, is used to formulate strong beliefs, using René Descartes as our guide. Likewise, I will show how existential reason is the human capacity for self-transcendence, creativity, freedom, and meaning-making, all of which is related to the human capacity for faith as ultimate concern. Toward the end of this chapter I will explore Thomas Nagel's contention that life is fundamentally absurd and relate that realization to the human capacity for existential reason and our quest for ultimate meaning and significance.

In the fourth chapter, I will build on Nagel's thoughts on life's absurdity by focusing our attention on the various means and methods we use to create meaning for our lives, especially in light of our universal experience of love, fear, and death. Our companions on this journey will be Michel de Montaigne and Johann Wolfgang von Goethe, but we will conclude our reflections by returning to the ancient Wisdom Literature of the Bible, specifically the Song of Songs and Ecclesiastes, to remind us that these questions are at least as old as human civilization itself and to seek in these ancient texts wisdom and encouragement along our own quest for meaning.

In the conclusion, I will explain the necessary interrelation and interdependence of these three human faculties of faith, doubt, and reason.

To do so, I will also offer a defense of the liberal arts as a noble and indispensable aid in pursuit of a life well-lived. At a time when the liberal arts are increasingly under attack, I will make a case for their purpose, their beauty, and their many contributions to living a meaningful life that takes seriously Socrates' warning that an unexamined life is not worth living.

To do so, I will rely on my own experiences and insights gained by teaching a First Year Seminar entitled "Faith, Doubt, and Reason" at Butler University in Indianapolis, Indiana. For the past twelve years I have taught this yearlong course, open to students from each of Butler's six colleges and intended to be first-year students' introduction to collegiate academics and the liberal arts. With each section of the course limited to eighteen students, these seminars afford opportunities for close reading of texts, wide-ranging discussions, close relationships between students and instructors, and discovering and being enriched by new, challenging, inspiring questions and ideas.

The First Year Seminar "Faith, Doubt, and Reason" embraces each of these objectives and invites students to embark on a lifelong journey of growth, self-discovery, intellectual rigor, commitment to informed and just citizenship, and passion for learning for its own sake. Through reading and discussing classic texts in theology, philosophy, and literature, we ask some of the most fundamental and challenging questions of human existence: What do I take with absolute seriousness? From what do I seek ultimate fulfillment and meaning? What is true? What should I believe? What is the meaning of my life? How ought I to live a just and authentic human life?

As a Lutheran theologian, I naturally approach these questions from the perspective of the Christian theological tradition and, more broadly, the Western intellectual tradition as a whole, and therefore the course inevitably reflects a specific and limited approach to these questions. There are certainly other perspectives and other approaches to these questions that have long and noble histories and much wisdom to teach us. In this book, however, I will be focusing on the way these questions have been raised and debated in the Christian West.

The first text we read in "Faith, Doubt, and Reason" also serves as a model for my approach to the questions raised in this book. In his short essay, "Answer to the Question: What Is Enlightenment?" Immanuel Kant challenged his readers with a summons that doubled as Kant's motto for the Enlightenment: *Sapere aude!* We might loosely translate this as "Dare to think for yourselves!" Kant prized above all else the individual conscience in pursuit of truth and wisdom; to that end he urged his readers to "throw off the yoke of immaturity" and begin to think for themselves, without the sometimes-suffocating constraints of convention, tradition, or temporal or spiritual authorities. While convention, tradition, and authorities do have their place, Kant's point remains valid today: we must demand the freedom to think our own thoughts, to follow our own conscience, to seek the truth wherever our inquiries lead us, and to encourage others to do the same.

Anyone familiar with Kant's works knows that he did not mean by this that any belief is as valid as the next, nor that we are free to believe whatever we want. Kant insisted on rigorous standards for knowledge and wisdom, such that we must always be prepared to account for our beliefs and commitments and to admit when we are mistaken, for the sake of our love of the truth. Free inquiry and passion for the truth unchecked by a healthy intellectual humility can often end in disaster, as we have seen far too frequently in the course of human history. Nevertheless, Kant's commandment serves as a fitting beginning for our quest, and in these pages we will insist on thinking for ourselves. Likewise, Kant's motto hearkens back to the beginnings of the Western philosophical tradition, to Socrates' insight that the unexamined life is not worth living. We live our lives in pursuit of goals and objectives to create a meaning for our lives, but if we never take time to reflect honestly and critically on those goals and objectives, what hope is there for success in our quest to discover or create meaning in our lives? In these pages we will do that important work of reflecting on our lives and on what we take seriously, with the hope of discovering what it is that really matters in the end.

This book emerges from more than a decade of inviting first-year university students to embrace these questions and to begin their own journey toward thinking for themselves, in pursuit of living an examined life. For their final paper at the end of the first semester of "Faith, Doubt, and Reason," students interview five people on Butler's campus, asking them to define faith, doubt, and reason and to describe their interrelation. The students then compare the definitions they received in their interviews to the definitions we have developed in the course on the basis of our reading and discussion of classic texts. These papers succinctly summarize and distill a semester's worth of wrestling with some of the perennial questions of human existence and they are a joy to read. I have learned so much from my students as I also continue to wrestle with these very same questions. What better way to engage these questions more deeply than to write my own "final paper" on faith, doubt, and reason? This book is my contribution to that discussion, deeply rooted in the inspiring exchange of ideas I have been privileged to share with more than a decade's worth of Butler students.

Because everyone possesses these faculties and uses them in various ways throughout their lives, this book is intended for a general audience and not for a small group of academic specialists. As Paul Tillich mentions in his sermon on "The Depth of Existence," nothing deep and meaningful is too sophisticated for us to grasp, so we shouldn't need advanced training in theology and philosophy to make sense of faith, doubt, and reason as these faculties contribute to our quest to live meaningful lives. This book, then, can be read and enjoyed by anyone wishing to dig deeper into their lives with the help of classic texts on faith, doubt, and reason. I hope it will be especially useful in undergraduate courses and in small discussion groups in churches and beyond. Because this book is intended for a broad audience, I have dispensed with some of the typical accoutrements of academic scholarship. For example, I have done my best to keep the jargon and "inside baseball" references to a bare minimum. Attentive readers with advanced training in theology and philosophy will certainly recognize where I am indebted to specific figures and schools of thought, but such training is not required to comprehend and appreciate what follows in these pages. Likewise, for the most part footnotes are limited to texts I have directly cited. I have also purposely written the book in a conversational style rather than the more formal and technical language of the academy. Finally, instructors and small group leaders will find discussion questions for each chapter at the end of the book, along with brief biographies of major figures discussed in the book.

Just as no person is an island, no book is ever written alone. In addition to the hundreds of students whose questions, insights, and enthusiasm have sustained and energized me as a teacher and scholar, I must make special mention of two Butler colleagues, Paul Valliere and Stuart Glennan, who first designed the "Faith, Doubt, and Reason" First Year Seminar fifteen years ago. Teaching this course has been a singular honor, and I owe them both a debt of gratitude for creating the course I have most loved to teach and for encouraging me to make it my own. I owe an additional debt of gratitude to Paul Valliere for coming out of retirement to write the foreword to this book.

Susan Neville, Becky Ries, Christine Moore Smith, Rob Stapleton, Chris Bungard, Angela Hofstetter, and Bill Watts, Butler colleagues who at various times over the past twelve years have administrated and advised the FYS program and faculty cohort, are to be commended for their care and dedication to providing a rigorous and meaningful academic experience for our first-year students. I thank each of them for their vision, support, and guidance. For the past two years I have immensely enjoyed the friendship and collegiality of Chad Bauman, Bryce Berkowitz, Chris Bungard, Natalie Carter, Melissa Etzler, Antwain Hunter, Jeana Jorgensen, and Rob Stapleton, fellow FYS instructors with whom I have shared meals, conversations, classroom time, and reflection on teaching these inspiring courses.

The "Wednesday Word & Wine" book group at Bethlehem Lutheran Church in Indianapolis, led by John Todd, graciously included an earlier version of this manuscript in their reading list. I am particularly indebted to Shirley Daniels, Katie Harber, Shari Morgan, Pastor Ken Ranos, Pastor Dave Schreiber, Nancy Stephan, John Todd, and Fred Winter for pointing out errors and making suggestions for revisions to the manuscript we read together. It was a joy to learn from the entire Word & Wine group as we shared our insights on faith, doubt, reason, and the meaning of life, sustained by delicious snacks, fine beverages, and the mutual conversation and consolation of the brothers and sisters, as Luther so aptly put it.

My wife, Kate Boyd, who makes my own life meaningful and joyful beyond measure, has been a constant companion and advocate, especially when work threatens to overwhelm the deeper joys of life. She also made helpful suggestions for revisions to an earlier version of this manuscript. For her love, wisdom, inspiration, and good humor, I am profoundly grateful: "*Die Summe unseres Lebens sind die Stunden, wo wir lieben*" (Wilhelm Busch).

Finally, I dedicate this book to my "Faith, Doubt, and Reason" FYS students at Butler University from 2008 to 2020 with the first words they read in the course, before they had any idea what they were getting themselves into: *Sapere aude*! Dare to think for yourselves! I am grateful to each and every one of them for their companionship in our shared quest for wisdom. Hundreds of "FDR Veterans" are now out in the world and I hope they've continued to draw inspiration and sustenance for the journey in the good and meaningful work we did together in Jordan Hall, "beneath the Hoosier sky."

Chapter 1

Faith

WHAT DOES IT MEAN to have faith? Is faith synonymous with religion, or is faith something more basic, more fundamental to the human experience? Is faith synonymous with belief, or are they distinct concepts? Are there proper and improper objects of faith? What is the relationship between faith and science and between faith and history? Can faith be lost? All these questions and more are the topic of this chapter.

Faith as Ultimate Concern

If we look up the definition of faith in the dictionary, we will see a number of entries. Most dictionaries will define faith using the word "belief." Often faith is defined as believing something without evidence, as a type of knowledge that is gained without experimentation or proof. Other meanings of faith specifically mention religion, such as faith being belief in a higher power or faith as a synonym for a particular religious tradition, such as "the Christian faith." But do these dictionary definitions capture what faith really is?

In the 1950s, the German-American Lutheran theologian Paul Tillich surveyed the typical popular assumptions about faith and despaired that the deeper meaning and significance of faith was in danger of disappearing. Then, as now, he noticed that faith was being discussed in a variety of contexts as if everyone agreed on what they meant by using the term. But he also noticed that "faith" was being used in simplistic, shallow, and even contradictory ways, so much so that its misuse threatened to obscure the deeper meaning and power of faith altogether. He vowed to correct many popular misunderstandings and recover the meaning and power of faith by writing a short book intended for a popular audience, which he called *Dynamics of Faith*. In his introductory remarks, he explains why he felt the need to write such a book:

> There is hardly a word in the religious language, both theological and popular, which is subject to more misunderstandings, distortions, and questionable definitions than the word "faith." It belongs to those terms which need healing before they can be used for the healing of men [sic]. Today the term "faith" is more productive of disease than of health. It confuses, misleads, creates alternately skepticism and fanaticism, intellectual resistance and emotional surrender, rejection of genuine religion and subjection to substitutes. Indeed, one is tempted to suggest that the word "faith" should be dropped completely; but desirable as that may be it is hardly possible. A powerful tradition protects it. And there is as yet no substitute expressing the reality to which the term "faith" points. So, for the time being, the only way of dealing with the problem is to try to reinterpret the word and remove the confusing and distorting connotations, some of which are the heritage of centuries.[1]

Tillich wrote *Dynamics of Faith* when church attendance in the post-war years of the United States was heading for all-time highs. Yet he still discerned a fundamental misunderstanding and obfuscation of the meaning of faith, and he worried that such misunderstandings could be catastrophic in the lives of individuals, communities, and nations. Fast-forward to our own context in the beginning of the twenty-first century and the situation has not noticeably improved. Tillich's diagnosis of the problem applies just as much to our own time as it did to his. If anything, our situation is even direr, as the word "faith" has become even more contested, more misunderstood, and more abused than when Tillich wrote these words.

What, then, is to be done? Tillich proposed that it might be worth jettisoning the term altogether, if not for its deep roots and substantial permeation of the culture. We find ourselves in the same position as Tillich found himself. The word "faith" is just as firmly entrenched in our language and our culture as it was in his, so there is no getting rid of it. And that is not necessarily a bad thing. Faith is a category all its own, as

---

1. Tillich, *Dynamics of Faith*, xxi–xxii.

no other term can ever hope to capture the depth and breadth of all that "faith" conjures and connotes.

Tillich famously defined faith as "ultimate concern," as he wrote in the opening chapter of his book: "Faith is the state of being ultimately concerned: the dynamics of faith are the dynamics of man's [sic] ultimate concern."[2] But what does that mean, exactly? Every person has many concerns in their daily lives. We are concerned with our health, our relationships, our families, our homes, our bank accounts, our communities, our planet, and the list could go on and on. But there is always something that grasps us, something that demands our full attention and our total commitment, something we take absolutely seriously above everything else, something that promises to give us ultimate meaning and fulfillment. This is what Tillich means by "ultimate concern." It is that one thing we put above everything else, that one thing that orders and orients and relativizes everything else in our lives, that one thing to which we would be willing to sacrifice everything else for the sake of meaning and significance.

If we stop to think about it, it would be difficult to imagine someone *not* having this ultimate concern. To be human means to be ultimately concerned, to be committed, to be dedicated to something from which we seek meaning and value and significance. What that "something" is might be different for different people, but we all have something we take with total seriousness, something we value above all else. This is what theologians call the "subjective" side of faith (*fides qua creditur*).

But there is another side of faith: the "object" of faith, or what we have faith *in* (what theologians call *fides quae creditur*). What do we take with absolute seriousness? What is it that we commit ourselves to without any reservation? From what do we expect ultimate meaning and fulfillment? What are we unable and unwilling to do without in our lives? What is it that orders and orients and guides our lives each and every day? Whatever that is, that is the object of our ultimate concern, our faith. That is what we worship, what we praise, what we dedicate our lives to following, that to which we are willing to sacrifice everything else.

Here is where we discover the second meaning of "ultimate." On the subjective side, "ultimate" means that we take something to be the most important thing in our lives, whatever that might be. On the objective side, "ultimate" means whatever is truly highest, absolute, unconditional.

---

2. Tillich, *Dynamics of Faith*, 1.

In the world's many religious traditions, this might be called God, or YHWH, or Allah, or Brahman, or the Dao, etc. But what we take as ultimate does not necessarily have to be a deity. It can be justice, or beauty, or love, or truth, or the good. What matters on the "objective" side of ultimacy is that whatever we take with absolute seriousness and commitment is truly ultimate, which means that it is truly absolute and unconditional, that it can "handle" the "weight" we put on it, that it won't collapse when we demand meaning and value and fulfillment from it.

Idolatry

One way of distinguishing what is an "unhealthy" faith from a "healthy" faith is to reflect on the important distinction between the finite and infinite realms of reality. For Tillich, this is a crucial stage in the process of distinguishing between good and bad types of faith. The finite realm is whatever we can approach through our five senses, whatever is available for experimentation and empirical verification, whatever we can grasp and possess as provable and certain. In its Latin root, the word "finite" means "limited," whatever has clear and concrete boundaries, a beginning and an end. You and I are finite. Computers and trees and dogs are finite. Governments and political parties and churches and social organizations are finite. Wealth and success and power and prestige and careers are finite. They all have a beginning and an end. On the other hand, in its Latin root the word "infinite" means "without limits," whatever has no clear or concrete boundaries, whatever has no beginning and no end, whatever cannot be contained and constrained by time and space, whatever is absolute and unconditional. If we can grasp it, control it, understand it, manipulate it, or achieve it, then it is finite, not infinite. If it is always more than we can understand or grasp or control or achieve, then it is infinite, not finite.

When thinking about the meaning of faith, this distinction between the finite and the infinite is crucially important. Only the infinite is capable of handling the weight of our ultimate concern. Only the infinite can support the intensity of our most fervent hopes and dreams. Only the infinite can promise us ultimate meaning and fulfillment. To place that kind of weight on something finite is to court disaster. A person, an institution, an object, a fleeting desire can't possibly handle the weight of our ultimate concern. Tillich uses a serious word to describe this type of mistaken ultimate concern: idolatry. When we hear the word "idolatry" we often think of golden calves or graven images, which are the idols typically mentioned in the Bible. The First Commandment warns against idolatry: "You shall have no other gods before me" (Ex 20:3; Deut 5:7). But what does this mean for us today?

Martin Luther, the sixteenth-century Protestant Reformer, wrote about the relationship between genuine faith and idolatrous faith in his exposition of the First Commandment in his *Large Catechism*:

> To have a god is nothing else than to trust and [have faith] in that one with your whole heart . . . [I]t is the trust and faith of the heart alone that make both God and idol. If your faith and trust are right, then your God is the true one. Conversely, where your trust is false and wrong, there you do not have the true God. For these two belong together, faith and God. Anything on which your heart relies and depends, I say, that is really your God.[3]

For Luther, and for Tillich, what we take with absolute seriousness and devotion becomes our god. If faith is a universal human quality, that means that everyone has faith. The question isn't whether or not we have faith; the question is what we have faith *in*. Do we have faith in something genuinely ultimate, or do we have an idolatrous faith?

Idolatrous faith is dangerous because it means we are putting our total trust and confidence and hope in something that cannot handle that level of commitment or devotion. It means that we are placing our ultimate concern in something finite, something less than ultimate. As Tillich points out, this mistake will inevitably lead to "existential disappointment." What he means by this is that when we place our faith, our ultimate concern, in something less than ultimate, in an idol, we will inevitably experience a catastrophic loss of meaning and significance in our lives, because the finite is incapable of supporting the weight of an ultimate concern.

In our own time, there are many idols we are tempted to worship in place of the genuinely ultimate and infinite reality. We are encouraged to place our ultimate trust and confidence and hope in wealth, success, reputation, career, race, class, social status, political affiliation, nationality, or religious identification. None of these categories can support the weight of our ultimate concern because none of them is genuinely

---

3. Luther, "The Large Catechism," 386.

ultimate, infinite, unconditional, absolute. All are finite human inventions, accidents of birth, or products of our own choices and desires. The price of placing faith in these finite realities is existential disappointment: the total collapse and disintegration of our sense of self, our identity, our meaning, our dignity as human beings.

Let's take an example of a contemporary idol to see a bit more clearly how this works today. For many people in the twenty-first-century United States, a person is defined by their career. At parties, for example, often the first question we ask one another after being introduced is, "So, what do you do?" It is an easy way to determine where we stand on the social hierarchy and it can help us figure out the answers to a host of other questions we might not be comfortable asking directly (how much money they make, where they might live, what kind of house they live in and what kind of car they drive, etc.). Our careers can give us a sense of purpose and of belonging, a sense of satisfaction that comes with using our gifts and talents for meaningful work. All of this is good and healthy!

But what if our career becomes the primary way we define our value and worth as a human being? What if we become so focused on our career that we ignore other parts of our life? What if we obsess about our career to the point that we expect it to give us ultimate meaning and ultimate fulfillment? What's more, what if we actually accomplish all of our career goals? Then what? Will that prove my dignity as a human being? Will it give me everything I want? Will it make sense of the perennial human questions and concerns and trials that confront me throughout my life? At the end of my life, will I wish that I had spent even more time at work, more time on projects and assignments, more time trying to please my boss, more time climbing the corporate ladder? If I sacrifice everything for my career, will I find that my career is enough to make me whole? Even if I achieve all of my career goals, that will not bring me ultimate fulfillment, nor will it give my life lasting meaning. I will find that I've missed out on a deeper, more lasting meaning because I gave myself over completely to something temporary and fleeting, something finite.

How do we guard against these temptations to idolatry? This is a challenging question. In the Book of Exodus, as Moses is on top of Mount Sinai receiving the Ten Commandments from God, we see the Israelites worshipping a golden calf of their own construction because they so deeply desired something concrete and tangible to worship. John Calvin, another famous sixteenth-century Protestant Reformer, said that the human mind is a "factory of idols."[4] Saint Augustine, in many ways the father of Western Christian theology, once said that if we've understood it, then it's clearly not God we're talking about.[5] Throughout the history of the Abrahamic monotheisms (Judaism, Christianity, and Islam) there have been consistent efforts to acknowledge and avoid idolatry, precisely because we are so prone to worshipping idols. It's only natural because we deeply desire something we can grasp, manipulate, and control. We want to live our lives on our own terms and dictate for ourselves the meaning of our lives. But all three Abrahamic religious traditions caution us against such easy answers because idolatry always ends in disappointment and despair.

Why is it so difficult to avoid the temptation to idolatry? As many theologians and philosophers have acknowledged, we are perpetually susceptible to the temptation of easy answers. We often want nothing more than to live life on our own terms and to ignore anything that calls our deepest values and commitments into question. Even religion can become an idol, as we have seen at numerous times in our history. The distinction between faith and religion is especially important when considering the temptations of idolatry. Religions, as institutions with histories, traditions, rituals, texts, doctrines, and ethical guidelines, are human constructs, born of particular times and places. Perhaps it is natural to look to religion as a substitute for the ultimate reality to which it points us because we can fully embrace and follow the institution and its rules and norms. But precisely because we are able to fully embrace and follow the institution, religion itself cannot be ultimate.

Symbols

There is a Zen Buddhist parable about a man who insists on pointing at the moon. Every night he goes to the same place and raises his hand to point at the moon. He attracts the attention of the villagers and soon visitors arrive to see the man who does nothing but point at the moon. Before long, everyone's attention focuses on the man's hand. What are the defining features of his hand? What is the significance of his fingers, his hand's position, the place where he is standing? All the while, the man insists on doing nothing more or less than pointing at the moon.

4. Calvin, *Institutes* 1:11.8.
5. Augustine, "Sermon 117."

Scores of people descend on the man to behold his hand for themselves. The man mourns and weeps, for no one is noticing where his hand is pointing. No one is looking at the moon.

This is a powerful metaphor for the nature of religion. In this story, each religion is a hand pointing at the moon. The religion is the hand, but the whole point is the moon, the ultimate reality the hand is urging us to see. Despite the man's best intentions, the people only look at his hand. We find it difficult to look beyond the hand to regard the moon. The hand is right in front of us, easily seen and understood. The moon is much farther off, difficult to discern and almost impossible to comprehend in its totality. But the meaning of the hand is to point us beyond itself to see the moon. To translate this old story into more contemporary terms, we must ask what is represented by the hand and what is represented by the moon.

For Tillich, the significance of a story such as this is to focus our attention on how we speak about the ultimate reality (what some religious traditions call "God"). Do we speak about ultimate reality the same way we speak about the reality we can see and feel and touch all around us? Or do we need special language to speak about ultimate reality? If the ultimate reality is really *ultimate* (that is, unconditional, infinite, without limits), then that clearly means that it is unlike any part of the finite reality we experience all around us in our daily lives. And that also means that we need a special kind of language to talk about it and to express what it means to be ultimately concerned, to have faith. The language we use to do this is the language of symbols.

What is a symbol, and how do symbols function? Tillich lists six important characteristics of a symbol that help us understand how to make sense of faith as ultimate concern. First, a symbol points to something else (think of the hand pointing at the moon in the Zen parable above). Second, a symbol doesn't merely point us to another reality; the symbol also participates in the reality to which it points us. Third, a symbol opens up a dimension of reality that would otherwise remain closed off and inaccessible to us. Fourth, a symbol opens up dimensions of our own selves that would otherwise remain closed off and inaccessible to us. Fifth, a symbol cannot be randomly or arbitrarily created but emerges organically from the history, culture, and language of a specific group of people. Sixth, a symbol stays "alive" as long as it fulfills the task it's meant to do, but the symbol dies when it no longer performs that task. Let's take a closer look at each of these characteristics of a symbol.

First, a symbol points beyond itself to something else. Symbols are like arrows pointing us beyond themselves to something we might not otherwise see or grasp. The symbol is not the goal; rather, the symbol guides us toward the goal by pointing us in its direction. But symbols are not arbitrary, nor are they merely one-dimensional. This brings us to the second point about symbols: symbols also participate in the reality to which they point. A nation's flag, for example, is not just a piece of cloth to the people of that nation. Instead, the history and values and meaning of the nation are in a very real sense "contained" in the flag. This is why burning a flag is such a powerful act. It is not just burning a piece of cloth; it is an act directed against what the flag represents, what it symbolizes. For many people, burning the flag is interpreted as an attack on the nation itself. For others, burning the flag is a powerful symbolic gesture of protest and criticism of the nation itself. Symbols thus take on an aura of holiness or sacredness because they represent something far greater than the physical object or finite concept of the symbol itself.

Third, symbols have disclosive power. A symbol will give us purchase on or access to a deeper or more significant level of reality than we would otherwise be able to articulate or experience. Much like a great work of art or a moving piece of music, a symbol lays bare certain aspects of reality and meaning that we can't quite get hold of in any other way. We might experience depths of love or beauty or truth or goodness that we didn't expect to discover, or that we had no other way to articulate. Similarly, symbols also provide access to the depths of our own being by giving us a deeper and more significant sense of ourselves as we really are. That same work of art or piece of music might also reveal something profoundly true about myself that I didn't know before or that I struggled to comprehend. It might remind me of my own pain and loss or it might lift me to greater virtue or appreciation for life in all its tragic beauty in a way that nothing else can do.

The last two points are that symbols develop organically and thrive as long as they fulfill their proper disclosive function. Each community's symbols are drawn from its own history, culture, traditions, language, and worldview to open up these deeper levels of reality and of ourselves. Symbols are not invented randomly, nor can they be arbitrarily altered. Symbols, when they are doing their job, take on an aura of such obviousness and inevitability that we can sometimes forget that they are symbols. Only a cataclysmic event can destroy a symbol, because only a catastrophe can rob a symbol of its disclosive power. Imagine the catastrophe we would have to undergo in the United States to abandon the Stars and Stripes and create a completely different flag. Very likely it would require the dissolution of the United States of America and the creation of an entirely different nation. Or consider a once-powerful symbol that has ceased to function as a living symbol: Zeus, the king of the Greek Olympian pantheon of gods and goddesses. Zeus once functioned as a powerful symbol for the Greek people. Temples were built to his glory, oaths were sworn to him, animals were sacrificed to him, lives were dedicated to his honor. But how many active temples to Zeus are there in Greece today? The symbol of Zeus ceased to do what symbols are intended to do, so it died and was replaced by new symbols.

What does all of this have to do with faith? For Tillich, faith requires the use of symbols because only symbols are able to express the ultimate reality in ways that we finite creatures can understand and incorporate into our own quests for meaning and fulfillment. The language we use to describe everyday objects is insufficient to express the ultimate, infinite reality, so it's impossible to talk about the ultimate the way we would talk about a car or a tree. But at the same time, finite language is the only tool we have available to us to say anything meaningful at all. So faith uses language and concepts and images and metaphors drawn from our finite experience to say something true and meaningful about ultimate reality. A symbol or a metaphor "works" when we remember that what we're trying to express is just as much *unlike* as *like* the symbol or metaphor we're using. For example, when Christians call God "Father," implied in that analogy or symbol is that in many ways God is *like* a male human parent, but it's just as important to remember that in equally important ways God is *unlike* a male human parent. If we forget the "unlike" and assume that we mean God is literally a male human father, then we run the risk of falling into idolatry.

If we stop to look, we'll notice that symbols are all around us and that we use symbols every day of our lives, whether we are religious or not. Religions are particularly rich symbol systems, with a host of interrelated symbols to guide religious people in their lives and to frame how they live in and understand the world and their place in it.[6] To take Christianity as an example, there are a whole host of symbols in the Christian tradition that fulfill each of these functions Tillich mentions. Some of the common symbols shared by different Christian communities include God, the

---

6. For more on how symbols function within religious traditions, see Geertz, "Religion as a Cultural System."

Trinity, the Christ, the Holy Spirit, the cross, creation, the sacraments of Baptism and the Eucharist, and the list could go on and on. Each of these symbols draws on everyday language and images to say something profoundly true about reality and ourselves, but they only make sense—they only "work"—within the context of the Christian tradition.

The most basic and fundamental Christian symbol is the symbol of God. Tillich, somewhat unhelpfully, describes God as the symbol for God. But what he means is that the symbol "God," with all of its related symbols (Trinity, Father/Mother/Parent, Creator, Love, Shepherd, Judge, etc.), is the best way Christians have of expressing what is truly ultimate, what is really real, what is the most important and significant and meaningful reality, what shapes and orients and guides Christians through their daily lives. Other religious traditions have other symbols, other names, for this ultimate reality. Jews use the symbol of YHWH. Muslims use the symbol of Allah. Hindus use the symbol of Brahman. Daoists use the symbol of the Dao. Alongside or instead of traditional religious symbols, people might use the symbols of the True, the Good, the Beautiful, Justice, Love, etc. And in each case, a whole system of rituals and practices and beliefs and moral guidelines and ways of living develop that are intended to orient and shape people's living in the world with the help of those symbols.

Myths

In many religious traditions, including Christianity, stories are told that expand on the meaning of the symbol to provide guidance and orientation in life and to allow the symbol to perform its function in ever more complex and mutually reinforcing ways. In Christianity these stories have been collected in the text known as the Bible. The Bible contains many different types and genres of texts, so much so that it's better to think of the Bible as a library rather than as a single book. Among other things the Bible does, it tells stories about God interacting with the world, appearing to and sometimes speaking to human beings, engaging in debates and decisions about daily life or historical events, giving commandments and summoning commitment and loyalty, and other similar activities. These stories place God into a human framework and often help people relate to and better understand God and God's desires for our shared life together. For theologians like Tillich, these stories can best be described as myths.

A word of caution is in order here. To our twenty-first-century ears, "myth" doesn't sound like the right word to use to talk about God or the Bible. In our contemporary US-American culture, if something is a myth that usually means that it's not true, that it's fiction, that it's made up. But in theology and religious studies, "myth" means something quite different. In its technical sense, a myth is a story about a deity interacting with finite creatures in the finite realm. In this sense, a myth is a story that expresses something deeply and profoundly true and meaningful about human existence, the world, or ultimate reality, but in the form of a symbolic or metaphorical story about divine-human interactions, rather than an account to be taken literally.[7]

A good example of a non-religious myth is the myth of Santa Claus. In its contemporary US-American version, Santa Claus is an elderly white man with a full white beard and big belly, dressed in red and white fur, who lives at the North Pole, where he has a workshop of elves who make toys for the world's children. On Christmas Eve Santa flies through the sky on a sleigh pulled by reindeer and stops at each home, climbs down the chimney, and places the presents under the tree and in the stockings hanging over the fireplace for the good children whose names he has checked twice on his list. He will often eat cookies and drink some milk left for him by the children, and sometimes he will also find carrots or apples for his reindeer. Santa Claus never ages and will never die. He is virtually omniscient and has the ability to alter the laws of physics in order to accomplish his task every Christmas Eve.

Like all myths, the myth of Santa Claus has evolved over time to meet the needs of the context in which the myth continues to have power and resonance.[8] Over the years, Santa morphed from a "jolly old elf" into someone more recognizable as a typical human being. He eventually added a ninth reindeer, Rudolf. In most places he no longer brings coal or switches for naughty children but delivers presents to all, without judgment. The stories about him continue to proliferate, thanks to a booming industry in Christmas-themed artwork, advertising, songs, stories, films, and television specials. But at its core, the myth of Santa Claus endures because it evokes powerful images and values that parents want to pass on to their children: generosity, goodness, kindness, compassion,

---

7. For an introduction to the use of "myth" in a variety of contemporary academic contexts, see Segal, *Myth: A Very Short Introduction*.

8. For more on this evolution of the myth of Santa Claus, see Bowler, *Santa Claus: A Biography*.

innocence, mystery, and wonder. These values and ideals are profoundly true, despite the fact that Santa Claus doesn't literally exist.

Santa Claus is an instructive illustration of another truth about myths and symbols, namely that it is often devastating when the spell is broken and we recognize for the first time that these stories are myths and symbols rather than literal facts. Many of us remember quite vividly when we first learned that Santa Claus doesn't exist as a real, flesh-and-blood person. Perhaps the questions piled up and proved too difficult to answer convincingly, or perhaps a classmate at school or a friend or family member let us in on the secret. Either way, the loss of naiveté that comes with learning the truth about Santa Claus can be devastating, which reinforces the power and potency of symbols and myths.

When children reach a certain age, they naturally begin to ask increasingly challenging and skeptical questions about Santa Claus. How can he really visit all the children of the world in one night? How do the reindeer fly? If people have been to the North Pole, why has no one seen Santa's workshop? What does he do when a home doesn't have a chimney or a fireplace? How does he get past the alarm system? Why didn't he give me that gift that I really, really wanted? I was so good this year! Often, parents will create ever more elaborate explanations to assuage their children's doubts until, inevitably, the stories no longer make literal sense and the illusion shatters.

Something similar happens with all myths and symbols, including properly religious myths and symbols. Tillich draws a distinction between an unbroken myth and a broken myth, as well as a related distinction between natural literalism and reactive literalism. An unbroken myth is a myth that is not recognized as a myth, meaning it is simply taken literally as a factual statement about finite reality. Santa Claus lives at the North Pole and flies in a sleigh drawn by flying reindeer. George Washington chopped down the cherry tree. A serpent slithered out onto a tree branch and had a conversation with Adam and Eve, the first human beings. Moses parted the Red Sea so the Hebrews could cross to safety on dry land. Jesus walked on the water to comfort his frightened disciples. The stories simply mean what they say, literally. But questions will inevitably arise about these stories, either through our own questions or through exposure to other, more critical perspectives. At this point the myth is "broken" and it is recognized as a myth. Now two responses are possible. We can accept these stories for what they are and learn to appreciate them as myths expressing something profoundly true and meaningful in symbolic, metaphorical language, or we can refuse to accept this and insist on taking the stories literally, repressing any doubts or questions that might shatter the illusion. In the latter case, we are engaging in what Tillich calls reactive literalism, which is an interpretive strategy that knows, deep-down, that we are engaging in a reading that can't withstand honest questions and criticisms.

Reactive literalism has many causes and justifications. Perhaps we simply can't accept a new way of thinking about the stories that have shaped and guided us for so long. Perhaps our doubts and questions frighten us and we prefer the comfort that reactive literalism supposedly provides us. Perhaps those in authority over us discourage us from asking too many questions. Perhaps we fear what else we might have to rethink if we give up even some of our previous assumptions. Perhaps it's a combination of some or all of these reasons. For Tillich, it's vitally important to respect the boundary between natural and reactive literalism. Natural literalism is a normal, healthy stage in the development of faith and religious commitment. Religious people often learn the stories of their traditions as children and are profoundly influenced and shaped by these narratives. No one should be forced into abandoning their assumptions against their will. At the same time, however, it is inevitable that questions will arise, and these questions should not be ignored or discouraged. This is a natural stage on the journey from what theologians sometimes call "first-order" to "second-order" theology and it is a sign of a healthy, maturing faith.

Reactive literalism, however, is a different matter. Once the myth is "broken," it is impossible to go back to that first-order naiveté and resume a natural literalism. To insist on taking literally what we now know is a myth or a symbol is to sacrifice our reason and to suppress the doubts and questions we rightly have, with sometimes dire consequences. Many of the conflicts and controversies in our culture between religion and science, for example, can be explained by an insistence by some religious people on a reactive literalism. The refusal of some Christians to accept the overwhelming scientific evidence for evolution and a universe that is billions of years old is a good example of reactive literalism and its dangers. Because of this overwhelming evidence, it is no longer possible to take the creation narratives of Genesis literally as scientific fact. This does not mean that these narratives are not true, only that they are true as myths, as narratives that express in symbolic language something deeply and profoundly true and meaningful about God, the world, and humanity. If we take them literally, however, we are forced to choose between faith and reason, thereby splitting our personality by putting two parts of ourselves into conflict. A split personality is not a healthy personality. Such reactive literalism can also have significant consequences for our public life, as we see in attempts to influence public education policy to "teach the controversy" between creationism and science.

Often those who persist in reactive literalism will insist that they do so in order to safeguard God's ultimacy and to protect the integrity and truthfulness of the Bible. But Tillich offers an interesting counterargument to these claims. By suggesting that God interacts with and intervenes directly in the finite realm, we are actually making God something less than God. If God is truly ultimate and infinite, Tillich suggests, then God cannot be contained by or limited to the finite. Literalism, he says, "deprives God of his [sic] ultimacy and, religiously speaking, of his majesty. It draws him down to the level of that which is not ultimate, the finite and conditional. . . . Faith, if it takes its symbols literally, becomes idolatrous!"[9]

Similarly, to insist on the factual accuracy of every passage of the Bible is, again according to Tillich, to misunderstand the purpose of the Bible and to make it an idol (there's even a word for this common mistake: bibliolatry). If we insist on making the Bible itself ultimate, on refusing to read it honestly and critically as a faithful witness to human wrestling with the reality of God, we put the Bible in God's place. We can cherish and honor the Bible, but we should not have faith in the Bible, because the Bible is not ultimate. Tillich, who was a Lutheran pastor and theologian, is drawing on a description of the Bible proposed by Martin Luther, who said the Bible is like the manger in which we find the Christ child. The Bible is a vessel containing or pointing us toward the ultimate, but it is not ultimate in itself. To put it another way, the Bible is like the finger pointing at the moon.

Here we come back once again to the important distinction Tillich makes between the infinite and the finite. Faith relates to the infinite, that for which we yearn but can never hold as a possession. As St. Augustine once said, "Our heart is restless until it rests in you."[10] The finite realm, on the other hand—the material world all around us—is not the sphere of faith. Rather, the finite realm is the sphere of belief. One of the most

---

9. Tillich, *Dynamics of Faith*, 60.
10. Augustine, *Confessions*, 3.

common misunderstandings of faith (you'll even find it in some dictionaries) is that faith is believing in something without evidence. For some people, faith might even mean believing in something despite strong evidence to the contrary. But faith and belief are not synonyms. In fact, they're not even all that closely related. To summarize, faith refers to the infinite, while belief refers to the finite.

Beliefs

What, then, is a belief? A belief is an assertion or acceptance of the truth of finite facts that are supported by sufficient evidence. I believe that the sun will rise tomorrow in the east. I believe that bears are bigger than bees. I believe that if I jump out the window I will fall to the ground. All of these beliefs are good beliefs because they are supported by evidence sufficient to make them facts. Bad beliefs, on the other hand, are beliefs that are not supported by the facts. I might believe that the sun will rise in the west tomorrow, but that would be a bad belief. I might believe that cows stand on two legs and talk to one another when we're not looking, like they do in the classic *Far Side* cartoon, but that would be a bad belief. I might believe that the Earth is only 6,000 years old because the Bible (supposedly) says so, but that would be a bad belief. All of these are bad beliefs because they're not supported by the evidence available to us.

There is an equally important distinction between a belief and an opinion. A belief must be supported by evidence because beliefs are related to facts. An opinion, on the other hand, is about our personal preferences or attitudes or emotions, not facts. It is a fact that Brussels sprouts are a member of the cabbage family, but it is my opinion that they are delicious (it's very likely that you disagree!). It is a fact that Jimi Hendrix had many hit songs, but it is my opinion that he is one of the greatest rock guitarists of all time. I am entitled to hold pretty much any opinion I like, but I am not entitled to believe anything I want. I might not like the fact that there are mosquitos, but that doesn't mean I can refuse to believe that they exist and that they can pose a threat to my health. I might wish that Santa Claus were a real person, but I have no right to believe that he exists. There is a crucial distinction between beliefs and opinions that we must always bear in mind: beliefs must be based on facts, while opinions are based on personal preferences and attitudes.

But back to beliefs. How do we formulate good beliefs? A particularly helpful essay on this topic is "The Ethics of Belief," written by the English mathematician and philosopher William Clifford toward the end of the nineteenth century. In this essay, Clifford describes the method used to formulate a good belief and the precise criteria that must be met before we can believe something, framing the entire process in explicitly *moral* terms. He begins his essay with a story about a ship owner who had organized a trans-Atlantic voyage for passengers aboard his ship. The ship was old and he wasn't sure it was seaworthy, so there was a decent chance the ship wouldn't survive the voyage. Nevertheless, he took the passengers' money and the ship set sail. He rationalized his decision, thinking that even if the ship went down he would receive a hefty insurance check. The ship did reach its destination safely, but was the ship owner justified in letting the ship make the voyage at all?

Clifford points out several important issues in this hypothetical story. First of all, the ship owner had serious doubts about the seaworthiness of his ship, but he ignored those doubts and let the ship sail anyway. Second, whether or not the ship safely completed its journey is ultimately irrelevant. The ship owner had no right to allow the ship to sail if he had doubts about its seaworthiness and its safety. What should the ship owner have done? According to Clifford, he had a moral obligation to investigate his doubts, which means that he was duty-bound to have the ship checked out from top to bottom before allowing it to set sail. He had no right to let the ship sail and merely hope that it would make the journey safely. In other words, he had a moral obligation to acquire sufficient evidence that the ship was seaworthy before believing it would survive the trip.

This brings us to the first important point about beliefs. As Clifford writes, "It is wrong, always, everywhere, and for anyone, to believe anything upon insufficient evidence."[11] We have an obligation to investigate matters and determine the evidence before we can believe something. Our desires or our hunches do not amount to sufficient evidence; just because I really *want* something to be true doesn't make it true. We must do the hard work of investigation and analysis of all available evidence, and until we do that work we have no right to believe something.

The most important tool we have for determining what to believe is doubt. If we have doubts, we should embrace them because doubts are a

---

11. Clifford, "The Ethics of Belief," 77.

warning sign that what we want to believe might not be true. We often ignore our doubts because they make us uncomfortable or because they would require too much effort to assuage. It's far easier just to risk it and hope for the best, but that is a profound abdication of our moral duty, according to Clifford. As he puts it, "Where it is presumption to doubt and to investigate, there it is worse than presumption to believe."[12]

Why is this a moral issue? For Clifford, what we believe is a moral issue because our beliefs are never just our own privately held opinions. What we believe will always influence our actions in the world and we will naturally pass on our beliefs to others through our words and our deeds. A bad belief can have a ripple effect, especially if those bad beliefs confirm what we want to be true. For example, if I believe that by mixing bleach and ammonia I can have the cleanest house in the neighborhood, I will be sorely mistaken and I will very likely end up in the hospital. Bleach is a good cleaning solution. Ammonia is also a good cleaning solution. Put them together and we create chloramine vapors, which will very likely cause nausea, edema, and even seizures. If we ignore our responsibility to research the facts and we just share our new cleaning tip with our followers on social media, we will end up with a public health crisis on our hands.[13]

This is obviously an extreme example, but you can certainly think of many other examples of where bad beliefs have trickled down to thousands of gullible people because no one took the time to think critically about what they were being asked to believe. For example, for centuries most Western people believed that anyone who was not white was intellectually, physically, and spiritually inferior to white people. Rather than investigate this belief, they simply passed it on, generation to generation, with devastating effect. More recently, a large number of US-Americans believe that climate change is a hoax, despite overwhelming evidence to the contrary. The results of ignoring that evidence, of stifling those doubts, are already proving to be catastrophic for our planet. Beliefs are never a matter of personal preference; they always have public, real-world implications. We have a moral duty to investigate the facts and to

---

12. Clifford, "The Ethics of Belief," 96.

13. Here I'm shamelessly stealing from an episode of the animated sitcom *King of the Hill*, S10E02, "Bystand Me," in which Peggy Hill encourages her newspaper readers to mix bleach and ammonia for a failsafe cleaning solution. As might be expected, hilarity ensues.

determine to the best of our ability what is true and what is false before we believe anything and act on those beliefs.

Before we panic and assume that we must personally investigate every new piece of evidence we encounter, Clifford goes on to say that there are certain situations where we're justified in trusting someone else to aid us in determining what is true and false. When formulating a good belief, we have four options available to us. (1) We can personally investigate the evidence, (2) we can rely on our experience, (3) we can rely on the "constancy of nature," or (4) we can trust the experts. We've already discussed the requirement to investigate the evidence ourselves, and we'll have more to say about this in the chapters on doubt and reason. So let's take the remaining three options in turn.

Experience is a powerful tool in our intellectual toolbox. We can trust our experiences when we can be reasonably sure that the situations we encounter are similar to experiences we or others have encountered in the past. For example, I don't have to wonder each time I take a step whether the ground beneath my feet will support my weight. A lifetime of experience has confirmed that the ground is solid and that I can step on it without falling through. But where my experience is lacking (when, for example, I encounter an animal I've never seen before), it's in my best interest to be wary and to pay special attention to the details of this specific situation before deciding how to act. If I'm in a new place and encounter an unfamiliar animal (let's say I meet an armadillo for the first time), I would be wise not to assume that it's friendly or harmless until I learn more details. Eventually I'll conclude that armadillos are relatively harmless and I don't need to be too worried. But if I encounter a Cape buffalo for the first time, I would soon discover that I need to keep my distance and avoid any sudden movements or aggressive signals.

There are other situations where I might be in a new context, but I can trust that nature has certain laws and patterns that I can trust, regardless of the specific place I find myself. Say I'm visiting a new country and I want to wash my hands. My experience tells me that water is safe to touch (generally speaking), but it's still the case that I've never been to this particular place before. Do I first have to ask a scientist to test the water to ensure that it's safe before I wash my hands? No, I can trust that water in one part of the world is basically the same as the water I'm used to using at home. Regardless of the place I find myself (Indianapolis, Prague, Lima, Accra, Kuala Lumpur, Sydney), water is always H2O. I don't need to test whatever comes out of the faucet every time I travel beyond my home to determine that it's really water. This is what Clifford means by the "constancy of nature." This also applies to human nature, which Clifford believes is more or less constant across time and space. Human beings will always have certain positive and negative aspects of their nature (a tendency toward cooperation and bonding, coupled with a competing tendency toward selfishness and aggression), so that we can trust that human beings are fundamentally the same, despite their very real cultural differences.

So far, all of this seems to be fairly obvious. Obviously gravity is a constant, as is the chemical composition of water. But what happens when we can't do our own investigating and we can't rely on the constancy of nature or our own experience? What happens when we're dealing with something beyond our own capacity to investigate and understand? At this point, Clifford says we must rely on experts. There will be many situations where we're dealing with something beyond our experience and expertise, but that doesn't mean that we're helpless. There are very likely people who have devoted their lives to understanding the topic we're concerned about. These people have amassed the experience and expertise through years of careful study and engagement with the topic and we're justified in trusting their analysis as long as they really are experts in that field and they're telling the truth as far as they know it.

How does this work in real life? To take just one current example, climate change is a hotly contested issue right now. According to Clifford, if we want to know the truth about climate change, we have two options: we could spend the time and effort needed to become experts on climatology ourselves, or we could trust others who already have that expertise. Almost all experts on the climate agree that climate change is happening and that humans are largely responsible for the rapid changes in climate we are currently witnessing. Depending on our own ideological perspective, the fact that there is overwhelming consensus on this matter could be validating or threatening, but for Clifford our personal ideological convictions are irrelevant. Ideology does not change the facts. We might have strong feelings about climate change, but that doesn't change what's actually happening. And to figure out what's actually happening, we should trust people who have devoted their lives to studying and understanding climate change. An overwhelming majority of scientists agree, based on the evidence, that climate change is happening and that humans are largely responsible.

At this point, we have to ask two questions. Do these experts know what they're talking about? And are they telling the truth as far as they know it? If we can answer "yes" to both of these questions, then we're obligated to believe them. If we're not sure on one or both counts, then we have an obligation to continue to doubt their conclusions. As it stands right now, we have no reason to doubt that climatologists are lying, and we have every reason to trust them and their expertise. This means, then, that we have a moral duty to believe that climate change is real, that it is largely caused by human beings, and that it is a grave crisis that must be addressed by potentially drastic measures.

Faith, Belief, and the Bible

So far, so good. You might even be asking yourself, "What does all of this have to do with religion?" It's a good question, and it certainly does have a lot to do with religion. Let's take another example to see how this relates to religion. There is overwhelming scientific evidence that the universe is approximately fourteen billion years old and that the planet Earth is approximately four and a half billion years old, with *Homo sapiens* emerging approximately two hundred thousand years ago from earlier hominid species that have long since gone extinct. All of this is settled fact, based on clear and indisputable empirical evidence. There are some Christians, however, who insist that this cannot be true because it seems to contradict a particular reading of the Bible. According to this group of Christians, the Bible must be read as a scientific textbook with reliably accurate information about the origin of the universe and of the human species. If we read the Bible this way, we must conclude that God created the universe approximately six thousand years ago and created the first human beings *ex nihilo* ("out of nothing"), fully formed and, presumably, without belly buttons! Which version of our origin story are we to believe?

What we're dealing with here is a question that cuts to the very heart of the matter we're pondering in this chapter. Is the Bible a textbook of reliable facts about history and science, or is it a book about faith, using a variety of genres and types of language (including myths and symbols) to get its points across? Does the Christian faith require accepting every single word of the Bible as literal fact, or can the Christian faith engage with the best contemporary knowledge of the world, even when taking the Bible seriously as sacred scripture? Here the distinction between faith and belief and between the infinite and finite realms is especially important. Faith is related to infinite reality and uses the language of symbol and myth to explore questions of ultimate meaning. Belief is related to finite reality and uses the language of facts and the sciences to determine what we can know with certainty about the world. It is a category mistake for faith to insist on a certain reading of the facts, despite the evidence. The evidence is as clear as it can be that we live in a universe that is billions of years old and that our human species is the product of millions of years of evolution. That is non-negotiable. So why do so many Christians vehemently reject the clear evidence?

One reason for the conflict is a misunderstanding of the status and function of the Bible. If we assume that in order for the Bible to be trustworthy in matters of faith it therefore must be literally true in every factual detail, we must reject the findings of contemporary science because in some important respects those findings are incompatible with the biblical narrative. But if we read the Bible as a collection of many texts using a variety of genres, including myth and symbol, to point us toward the ultimate, infinite reality through the language of symbol, story, and metaphor, there is no need to assume there is a conflict between faith and science.

Faith and Science: Genesis

The creation narratives in Genesis (yes, there is more than one!) are ground zero for this frequent conflict between faith and science. According to biblical literalists, who tend to conflate the two creation narratives in Genesis 1 and Genesis 2 into one account, the creation narrative in Genesis is an accurate scientific description of the origins of the universe and of human beings in particular. To say otherwise, they argue, would be to call the truth and trustworthiness of the entire Bible into question. So literalists will often insist that God created the universe in six days, that God created Adam out of the dust of the Earth and created Eve out of Adam's rib, and that God then gave dominion over all the Earth and its creatures to the first human couple. Based on a certain reading of biblical genealogies and other dating strategies, some literalists (but not all) argue that the universe is approximately six thousand years old.

All of this is non-negotiable for many literalists because it is what, to them, the Bible clearly says. This means, then, that any scientific evidence we might have that contradicts these conclusions must be rejected out of hand, no matter how convincing it otherwise might be, simply because it contradicts this particular, predetermined reading of the Bible. This means that accepted scientific theories such as the Big Bang and the evolution of species (including our own) through natural selection must be rejected as false, despite overwhelming empirical evidence supporting both theories. Literalists must therefore choose between faith and science.[14]

But what if we read these creation narratives in a different way? What if we read them carefully and notice that the two creation narratives in Genesis are actually quite different? What might that mean for how we interpret them? If they really are different, what were the ancient editors of the Bible thinking by including both of them at the beginning of the Bible, right next to each other? Wouldn't they want to be consistent? That's a good question, and the answer depends on how we read and interpret these two creation narratives. If we read them as scientific accounts of the origin of the universe and of the human species, then we find ourselves in a difficult situation. These two stories simply don't add up, so we're forced to distort the stories and ignore important details to make them agree with each other. Let's take a closer look to see what we're dealing with in the first chapters of Genesis.

The first chapter of Genesis begins at the very beginning, when God began to create the heavens and the earth. At that point, the earth was "a formless void and darkness covered the face of the deep, while a wind of God swept over the face of the waters" (Gen 1:2). Notice that there are already "things" here, before God began to create. There is earth, there is water, and there is God. Nothing was formed yet, which is to say that what is there at the beginning is chaos. In the first chapter of Genesis, God creates by speaking, and what God does by speaking is to separate one thing from another, to bring order to the chaos. First, God speaks light into being, separating light from darkness, day from night. Second, God separates the waters above from the waters below, creating sky and oceans. Third, God separates dry land from the waters and creates vegetation. Fourth, God creates the sun and moon and stars. Fifth, God creates all of the animals that swim in the waters and fly in the sky. Sixth, God

14. For more on the theological assumptions and implications of this view, see Hege, "Contesting Faith, Truth, and Religious Language at the Creation Museum."

creates everything that creeps and crawls and walks upon the dry land, including human beings. God says, "'Let us make humankind in our image, according to our likeness.' . . . So God created humankind in [God's] image, in the image of God [God] created them; male and female [God] created them" (Gen 1:26–27). After each day of creation God surveys what God has made and pronounces it good. On the sixth day, when God had finished creating the universe, God pronounced it very good. Then God rested on the seventh day.

In the second chapter of Genesis, we have a very different story of creation. The first clue we have that this is a different story is that a different word for "God" is used. In Genesis 1, the word is *Elohim*, which is the generic word for a "god" in Hebrew (and, interestingly enough, in the plural!). In Genesis 2, the word is YHWH, which is a word that devout Jews will never pronounce, as it is God's proper name. Instead of pronouncing it, when Jews are reading scripture they will say *Adonai*, which means "my lord." In everyday speech, Jews will say *HaShem*, which means "the name." In English translations of the Bible, YHWH is often rendered as "Lord" (with small caps) to acknowledge the Jewish tradition of substituting *Adonai* for YHWH.

The second clue we have that this is a different story is that in the second chapter of Genesis there are no days of creation, as in Genesis 1. Instead, Genesis 2 suggests that creation happens all on one day (Gen 2:4b). The second chapter of Genesis also begins with the creation of the man, rather than placing the creation of human beings at the end of the creative process. The Lord forms the man out of dirt and breathes the breath of life into his nostrils. There's a pun here in Hebrew, as the word for human, *adam*, is very close to the word for ground or earth, *adamah*: we are literally "earthlings"! Then the Lord plants a garden and places the man in it, giving him the fruit of every tree for food. Every tree, that is, but one: the tree of the knowledge of good and evil. The Lord notices that the man is alone and quite likely lonely, and "It is not good that the man should be alone; I will make him a helper as a partner" (Gen 2:18). So the Lord creates all of the animals and brings them to the man to name them, but the man doesn't find any of the animals particularly suitable to be his partner, so the Lord puts the man to sleep, takes a rib from his side, and forms a woman to be his partner. And that is the end of creation, according to the second chapter of Genesis.

Immediately we can see stark differences between the stories. Genesis 1 is rigidly structured, with clearly marked days and references to all of the essentials: light, water, earth, sun and moon, plants, all the animals, and human beings, each created on their own day and each blessed as good. In Genesis 2, no days are mentioned, and the order of creation is noticeably different: the man is created first, then the animals, and then the woman is created from the man. There is no mention of the creation of earth and sky and ocean, sun and moon, light and darkness. We can assume, then, that those things were already there, or at least that the authors of Genesis 2 aren't particularly interested in where they came from.

There are also significant differences in how God/the Lord creates in both stories. In Genesis 1, God creates by fiat, merely by speaking things into existence. There is in Genesis 1 what later theologians will call an "infinite qualitative distinction" between God and creation. In Genesis 2, however, the Lord creates by playing in the dirt, like a kid in a sandbox! The Lord is intimately involved in creation, just as the man is intimately connected to the dirt out of which he was formed. If God in Genesis 1 looks like a king issuing proclamations from afar, the Lord in Genesis 2 is more like a gardener or a loving parent, nurturing and caring for what the Lord has made with a hands-on involvement in creation. Later in the second creation story we read that the Lord even enjoys taking walks in the garden to soak up the cool evening breezes! It's hard to imagine the royal and rather aloof God of Genesis 1 doing anything like that.

What accounts for these significant differences between these two creation stories, placed side-by-side at the very beginning of the Bible? Why didn't the ancient editors of the Bible just pick one story and stick with it? For starters, an important difference between them concerns the contexts in which they were written and who wrote them. It's important to point out here that the Bible is arranged thematically, not chronologically according to the date the texts were written. So just because something comes earlier in the Bible doesn't necessarily mean it was written earlier. In fact, some of the oldest texts of the Old Testament are found in the Prophets (e.g. Isaiah, Amos, and Micah), toward the end of the Old Testament. Second, many of the stories of the Bible began as oral traditions and were only written down much, much later. Later still, they were edited and collated into what we know as the Old Testament and, later still, the New Testament, until finally being collected into the book Christians call the Bible. This process of editing and collating wasn't completed until the fourth century CE, over a thousand years after the first texts were written.

So what is the origin of these two creation stories? The older of the two, by far, is actually the second story, in Genesis 2. It was written by an author (or group of authors) known in biblical studies as "J" (German for *Jahweh*, or YHWH) because these "J" texts always call God YHWH.[15] It is very likely that Genesis 2 is based on a much older oral tradition, as we can see just by reading it. Imagine beginning this story with "Once upon a time" and you'll see that it reads very much like a fairy tale. Also, the Lord in this story is much more intimate, more relatable, and more anthropomorphic (looking and acting and talking like a human being) than the God of Genesis 1. The second creation story is also a local story, only concerned with the area to the immediate east of the Mediterranean Sea; it doesn't mention the creation of the sun and moon and stars or the heavens or the earth or anything much beyond the area of the Tigris and Euphrates in present-day Iraq. The first creation story is much more universal (pun intended) in scope, as it tells the story of the origin of everything that exists in the entire universe. God, in the first creation story, is far more powerful and even distant, much like a king. But the deeper meaning of Genesis 1 becomes clearer once we understand who wrote it and why.

Genesis 1 belongs to a group of texts biblical scholars call "P," for the priestly tradition. The authors and editors of the "P" texts were priests and scribes, the religious elite of the nation of Israel, and they almost always used "Elohim" for God because "YHWH" was far too holy to be pronounced or written down. One of the features of the P texts is a focus on order and ritual, which is natural for priests to be concerned about. The P texts were written during and immediately after the catastrophic destruction of the Jerusalem temple and the exile of the religious and political elite of Israel to Babylon (in present-day Iraq) in the sixth century BCE. Without the temple, the regular patterns of worship and sacrifice could not continue, and it was as if the entire world had crashed down all around them. Everywhere they looked, they saw chaos. When we read Genesis 1 in light of this tragedy, it starts making a lot more sense. In Genesis 1, God creates by bringing order to chaos. The days of the creation mirror the days of the week, with the Sabbath on the last day, just like in the temple and in the religious life of pious Jews. And if we place the days of creation side-by-side, we can see another pattern emerging:

15. This shorthand for the authors of the Pentateuch comes from what biblical scholars call the Documentary Hypothesis; for more, see Friedman, *Who Wrote the Bible?*

Day 1: light	Day 4: sun and moon and stars
Day 2: water and sky	Day 5: fish and birds
Day 3: land and vegetation	Day 6: plants and animals and human beings

Day 7: rest

When we read the text in this way, we can see that the pattern is almost architectural: first the spaces are created, and then God creates the things that will fill those spaces: sun and moon and stars fill the light and darkness, birds and fish fill the sky and seas, plants and animals and human beings fill the earth. God surveys all that God has made and sees that it is very good indeed, and on the seventh day God rests, much like a king sitting down on his throne. In other words, according to the authors of Genesis 1, the entire universe is God's temple! Even though the physical temple in Jerusalem was destroyed and everything seems to be overwhelmed by chaos, P is reminding the people that God is still in control, that there is order amidst the chaos they're experiencing at the moment, that the entire universe all around them is good and sacred and holy, that they are never far from God, even when they're exiled in a strange land.

How much of this deeper meaning is lost if we insist on reading these texts like a science textbook, especially when we know from contemporary science that this isn't at all how the Earth and its species came to be? The first two chapters of Genesis are a wonderful object lesson in the importance of recognizing the difference between faith and belief and between myth and fact. If we read these stories as factual accounts of the origin of the universe, as matters of belief, we will have to perform increasingly complicated intellectual gymnastics to make the stories fit together, and we will have to ignore or reject much of what scientists have to teach us about the world around us and about our own human origins. But if we read these stories as myths that are meant to teach us something deeply and powerfully true about God, the world, and ourselves, about what it means to live meaningfully in the world conceived as the product of God's own creative will, about what it means to be formed from the earth and to return to it, about what it means to see the world as God sees it, as "very good," and to live accordingly, about what it means to regard every human being as made in the image of God and to treat them as bearers of God's own image, we will have a far richer understanding of these texts and what they have to teach us even today, without having to choose between faith and science. Faith uses the language of myth and symbol to express truths about ultimate, infinite reality and about the meaning of human existence, while science uses the language of fact to express truths about finite reality.

Faith and History

Science is one particularly prominent area where many religious people believe there is a conflict with faith. But there are also frequent misunderstandings of the relationship between faith and history. For many Christians, faith must be supported by historical facts, especially by historical facts recorded in the Bible, in order to be true. When historians call some of these historical events recorded in the Bible into question, many Christians reject the conclusions of historical scholarship because they believe these conclusions conflict with their faith. For example, if it could be proven beyond a shadow of a doubt that Moses did not part the Red Sea, some Christians would believe that their faith is now a shattered lie because the Bible contains a factual error. As a result, many Christians are tempted to ignore historical research, especially when it conflicts with what they believe to be true about the Bible. According to theologians such as Tillich, this is another prominent example of misunderstanding what faith is by confusing faith and belief. Just as faith should not be threatened by scientific research, faith also should not be threatened by historical research because both scientific and historical research are concerned only with facts and belief, not with faith.

Just as scientists deal with observable empirical reality with the help of the scientific method, historians also use specific methods to analyze and interpret the past. At the most basic level, the historical method tries to reconstruct what happened in the past with the help of documents, artifacts, eye-witness accounts, patterns, continuing effects of events, and the uniformity of physical laws and of human nature. One important difference between the scientific method and the historical method is that, unlike scientific experiments, historical events cannot be repeated and studied in a lab. But that doesn't mean that all history is guesswork. It simply means that historians rank their confidence that a particular event actually happened on a scale of probability. If there is significant corroborating evidence concerning a particular event—the signing of the

Declaration of Independence, for example—then historians can be quite confident that this event really happened and they can tell us a lot about what transpired in Philadelphia, Pennsylvania, in 1776. Where there is little or no documentary evidence or few or no artifacts that would confirm that a specific event happened, historians use other tools to determine whether or not an event likely happened in the past. For example, there is no documentary evidence outside the Bible that Moses parted the Red Sea to allow the Israelites to escape Pharaoh's army. In that case, historians must rely on other tools, such as the uniformity of physical laws, to determine whether or not such an event is likely to have happened. In this case, it's very unlikely that such an event happened because we have no reason to believe that seas can suddenly part into two halves, with dry land in the middle sufficient to allow thousands of people to walk across the sea to the other side. Any historian worth her salt is going to be quite suspicious about this story's historical accuracy.

Another important feature of historical research is that, just like scientific research, the conclusions historians draw from their research are always open to revision if new evidence arises. For a long time there was strong evidence that that Earth was stationary and the sun, moon, and stars all revolved around the Earth. Pre-modern people were right to believe that the sun revolved around the Earth because that's what the evidence suggested. But eventually the evidence pointed to a different conclusion: that the Earth revolves on its own axis while also revolving around the sun. Because of this new evidence, we changed our belief. The same principle applies to historical research. As long as the evidence supports a certain historical belief, we are justified in believing it; but if new evidence arises, we have a duty to investigate it and to revise our beliefs accordingly if need be.

Now imagine that someone bases their faith, their ultimate concern, on a particular historical event. For a while, the available evidence might confirm the historicity of that event, or at the very least not contradict it or render it impossible. But suppose new evidence arises that calls that event into question. If this person has placed their faith in this event, it's very unlikely they will be willing to take the new evidence seriously and revise their commitments. More and more evidence mounts that makes it extremely unlikely that this event ever happened. Now this person is caught in a dilemma. They have made this event central to their faith, their ultimate concern. New evidence will destroy that faith, but ignoring the evidence will require them to sacrifice their ability to reason, which is a central feature of our human personality. They will continue to have nagging doubts and questions that will destabilize their commitment, whether or not they choose to acknowledge those doubts and questions. It's quite likely that they will double down on their insistence that what they believe is true, in spite of overwhelming evidence to the contrary. Before long, they will ignore anything that might call their commitments into question and they will begin to lose their grip on basic facts and common sense.

This is another illustration of the importance of recognizing the key differences between faith and belief. History, like science, deals with finite reality, with facts. This is the realm of belief, not faith. As Clifford reminds us, we have a moral duty to support our beliefs with sufficient evidence, and this applies equally to scientific and historical beliefs. Just as the origin of the universe and of the human species is a matter of belief, which should be decided by scientists, the historical events recorded in the Bible are likewise a matter of belief, which should be decided by historians. If faith is truly faith, our total commitment to the infinite, ultimate reality, then we shouldn't be bothered by historical investigation of specific episodes recounted in the Bible. If historians conclude that Moses never parted the Red Sea, that should have no effect whatsoever on genuine faith, because genuine faith isn't concerned with specific historical details, which are matters of belief, not faith. Two stories in the New Testament can illustrate this point for us quite clearly. The first story concerns the birth of Jesus, and the second concerns his death by crucifixion.

The Birth of Jesus

Every Christian is familiar with the stories of the birth of Jesus. Mary and Joseph were engaged and one day Mary is visited by an angel who tells her that she is pregnant with the Son of God. Joseph isn't sure he wants to go any further in this relationship, but he's visited by an angel in a dream who convinces him not to abandon Mary. Caesar Augustus calls for a census of all his subjects, so Joseph and Mary set out for Bethlehem, Joseph's ancestral hometown. When they arrive they find that there is no room for them in any of the inns, so they end up spending the night in a stable, where Mary gives birth to Jesus. That same night, there are some shepherds tending their flocks in the fields outside Bethlehem. Suddenly an angel appears to them and shares the news that the Savior has been born in Bethlehem, and the sky is filled with angels singing their praises of the newborn baby. At first, the shepherds are terrified because it's not every day that angels appear out of nowhere! But they get over their fear and they go to Bethlehem to worship the baby Jesus. Meanwhile, far to the east, wise men are studying the heavens and they discover a star that they hadn't noticed before. Consulting their star tables, the three wise men conclude that this star is announcing the birth of a famous king, so they set off on a long journey to the west to worship the baby. When they arrive in Jerusalem, they encounter King Herod, who tells them he also wants to worship the baby. But an angel appears to the wise men in a dream and warns them that Herod wants to kill the child, who is a threat to his rule. The three wise men follow the star to Jesus and they offer him gifts of gold, frankincense, and myrrh. After they worship, the three wise men head back home by a different route to avoid Herod's wrath. Furious, Herod orders that all male children under two years old are to be tracked down and killed. Mary and Joseph learn of this plot and escape to Egypt, saving the infant Jesus' life.

This story is so familiar to Western people that we often fail to notice the details, nor do we pay much attention to where these stories are found in the New Testament. Each year at Christmas we see manger scenes with all of the main characters: Mary, Joseph, Jesus, a stable, a star, an angel, three wise men, animals, etc. But what are the biblical roots of this familiar and beloved story? When we look at the gospels, what we find can be quite surprising.

Of the four gospels in the New Testament, only two of them mention the birth of Jesus. Mark, the earliest gospel, begins with Jesus as an adult being baptized by John the Baptist in the River Jordan. John, the latest gospel, begins at the very beginning of the universe with a hymn to the Word that was with God and is God, through whom all things came into being; John only mentions that this same Word became flesh and dwelt among us, but otherwise he gives no details. Only Matthew and Luke include anything about the birth of Jesus, and they tell two very different stories.

In the first chapter of the Gospel of Matthew, after Matthew provides a genealogy of Jesus, we learn that Mary and Joseph are engaged but not yet married, and Joseph learns that Mary is pregnant. Joseph's first instinct is to break off the engagement because he is certain that he is not the father of this baby. But one night an angel appears to Joseph in a dream and reassures him that she has become pregnant by the Holy Spirit and that the child will be the Savior. Joseph awakes from the dream and marries Mary, at which point she has her son and names him Jesus.

In the second chapter of Matthew's gospel, Jesus has been born in Bethlehem, in the kingdom of Herod, and we also learn that wise men in the East have come to Jerusalem asking Herod where they can find this child, whose birth was foretold by a star they have observed from their home country. Herod immediately recognizes that this child is a threat to his rule, so he tells the wise men that he also wants to worship the child, hoping they will lead him right to the infant Jesus. The wise men follow the star to the place where the child was born and they enter the house and worship him with gifts of gold, frankincense, and myrrh (these gifts symbolize royalty, priesthood, and death, respectively). An angel clues them into Herod's nefarious plot, so they leave for home by another route. An enraged Herod decrees that every male child under two years old in his kingdom shall be put to death. But an angel appears to Joseph and warns him of Herod's plot, so Joseph packs up the family and escapes to Egypt. Not long after, Herod dies and an angel again appears to Joseph to give the "all-clear" signal, so Joseph, Mary, and Jesus return to Israel, eventually settling in Nazareth in order to steer clear of Herod's son, who is causing more trouble in Bethlehem.

As we can see, this story prominently foregrounds Joseph as the main driver of the plot (Mary is almost an afterthought). Wise men from the East arrive and pay homage to the child, bringing symbolic gifts, but we never learn how many wise men there are, and we never learn their names (the three wise men named Caspar, Melchior, and Balthazar, that latter of whom is often depicted as an African, are much later inventions). There is no mention of a census, no mention of a journey from Nazareth to Bethlehem, no mention of a crowded city, no mention of a manger, and no mention of shepherds.

Looking now at the Gospel of Luke, we see a very different story of the birth of Jesus. In the first chapter of Luke, after a general introduction to the work, we eventually meet Mary, a young woman, alone in her room, being visited by the angel Gabriel, who announces to her that she will be visited by the Holy Spirit and will become pregnant with the Son of God, whom she shall name Jesus. Mary accepts the terms of the deal and, after visiting her cousin Elizabeth, who is pregnant with John the Baptist, she pronounces the famous Magnificat. In the second chapter, Caesar Augustus in Rome has decided to conduct a census of his realm, which includes Israel. Every male must return to his ancestral home to be counted in the census. Joseph, currently living with his fiancée Mary in Nazareth, must return to Bethlehem in Judea, as Joseph is of the house of David, and David's ancestral home is Bethlehem. While they are in Bethlehem, Mary goes into labor and Joseph searches for a suitable place for her to have her baby. There is no room for them in the inn, so she gives birth to her son and lays him in a manger. At the same time, an angel appears to a group of shepherds tending their flocks in the field and announces to them that the Savior has been born in Bethlehem. The shepherds hurry off to Bethlehem to worship the child and they depart to tell everyone they meet about what they have seen.

As we can see, this story prominently foregrounds Mary as the main driver of the plot (Joseph is almost an afterthought). There is a precarious journey from Nazareth to Bethlehem because of an imperial census, and shepherds arrive to worship the child at the prompting of an angel who appeared to them in the field where they were tending their flocks. There is no mention of dreams, or of King Herod, or of a star, or of wise men, or of gold, frankincense, and myrrh, or of a journey to Egypt.

What accounts for the significant differences between the stories? Are the authors, as some Christians claim, simply emphasizing different parts of the same coherent narrative, or are these really just two completely different stories? It all depends on how we understand the relationship between faith and history. If we assume that faith must be grounded in historical facts, then we have a good reason to want these stories to harmonize so that no contradictions remain. But if we accept that faith speaks the language of myth and symbol, then we can let these stories be what they are: two unique narratives about the birth of Jesus that have two different stories to tell to two different audiences. Let's take a closer look at each story to see what happens when we read them as myths rather than as historical accounts.

From the beginning of Matthew's account it's clear that we're dealing with an event of geopolitical significance. King Herod is a prominent figure in this story, as are the illustrious wise men of the East. Angels appear to Joseph in his dreams to clue him in on the plot, and Joseph negotiates these events with aplomb, eventually whisking his family away to Egypt only to return in triumph to Israel. Sound familiar? It should! Who else went down to Egypt and then brought his people back to settle in Israel? That's right: Moses. The wise men from the East bring symbolic gifts to remind us that we're not dealing with an ordinary child here. Gold (royalty), frankincense (priesthood), and myrrh (death) each in their own way predict what will happen to this child. Jesus will be the King of the Jews, the royal High Priest offering himself as the ultimate sacrifice to God, buried with myrrh, only to rise again as the victorious Lord. His entire life and ministry is foreshadowed in the gifts these wise men bring to worship the child.

In Luke's version of the story we're dealing with a very different situation. In Luke's version, Mary and Joseph are rural nobodies, buffeted about by imperial forces beyond their control. Caesar wants a census, so Joseph packs up his family and heads out on a long and dangerous journey from Nazareth to Bethlehem. When they finally arrive in Joseph's hometown, there's nowhere for them to stay. They are outcasts, homeless, with no one to welcome them. Someone graciously offers them lodging with the animals, so Mary gives birth and lays her child in a manger. An angel of the Lord appears to shepherds, not the most prestigious occupation in the ancient world (translate "shepherd" to "parking lot attendant" and you'll have a good idea of where shepherds stood on the ancient pecking order), urging them to hurry into Bethlehem to worship the Savior of the world, born to two nobodies, lying in a feed trough. There are no kings or wise men or lavish gifts in Luke's story. There's just a family of frightened migrants on the margins of society, trying their best to get by.

We can see these themes enlarged and amplified in the rest of their respective Gospels. In Matthew, Jesus is often presented as a new Moses, bringing a new Law to the people. He is often presented as royalty, as fulfilling ancient Jewish prophecy, as bringing to fruition all that was promised long ago in the ancient scriptures. In Luke, Jesus is often presented as one who identifies with those on the margins, the poor and the forgotten and the oppressed, as bringing God's blessings especially to the last and the least. Everything Jesus will do throughout his life and ministry is contained in these two very different birth narratives, written for two very different communities of early Christians, each with their own assumptions, needs, and hopes.

The authors of these gospels were not writing history or biography, as we understand these genres today. They were telling a story, weaving a narrative rich with symbolism and allusions that would be crystal clear to their audience. For these evangelists, the power of the story itself was far more important than getting the historical details right. We see this same theme again at the end of the gospels, when Jesus is crucified.

The Crucifixion of Jesus

The crucifixion is one of the very few events of Jesus' life recounted in all four gospels, so it's especially important to notice the similarities and differences in the accounts of the last days of Jesus. All four gospels agree that Jesus was arrested, tried, and sentenced to death by crucifixion, a common practice for dealing with criminals in the Roman Empire. As this is a central moment of the story of Jesus, it's perhaps not surprising that the crucifixion plays a prominent role in all four gospels. But if we look more carefully at each gospel, we see that even here there are significant differences. Each of the gospels recounts the crucifixion from its own perspective, but here we'll focus on one detail in particular: the date of Jesus' crucifixion. It's perhaps not all that surprising that different authors would emphasize different details in their recounting of this most important event in Jesus' life, but surely they would all agree on the day of the week that Jesus was crucified. Or do they?

Matthew, Mark, and Luke are sometimes called the Synoptic Gospels, "synoptic" coming from a Greek word meaning "seen together." The first three gospels share many of the same stories and sayings of Jesus, often in the same chronological order and sometimes even verbatim.[16] This is especially clear when looking at Matthew and Luke, who, in addition to drawing on Mark's gospel, also share a common source called "Q" (from the German word *Quelle*, meaning "source"). John, on the other hand, is in many ways unique, in that John recounts many stories and sayings of Jesus not told in the other three gospels, and even those that he does share with the other gospels are often placed in a different chronological order or with significant differences in the details. But let's focus our attention on the crucifixion of Jesus, one of the few events recounted in all four gospels.

In the synoptic gospels (Matthew, Mark, and Luke), the descriptions of the arrest, trial, and crucifixion of Jesus vary in some of the details, but one thing all three stories share in common is the date of the crucifixion. For something so important to the Christian faith, obviously all of the gospels would agree on the date Jesus was crucified. And indeed, all three synoptic gospels agree that the day before he was crucified Jesus ate a final Passover meal with his disciples, after which he was arrested.

---

16. For a helpful resource that arranges the three synoptic gospels side by side, see Throckmorton Jr., *Gospel Parallels: A Comparison of the Synoptic Gospels.*

> On the first day of Unleavened Bread the disciples came to Jesus, saying, "Where do you want us to make the preparations for you to eat the Passover?" (Matt 26:17)

> On the first day of Unleavened Bread, when the Passover lamb is sacrificed, his disciples said to him, "Where do you want us to go and make the preparations for you to eat the Passover?" (Mark 14:12)

> Then came the day of Unleavened Bread, on which the Passover lamb had to be sacrificed. So Jesus sent Peter and John, saying, "Go and prepare the Passover meal for us that we may eat it." (Luke 22:7–8)

In the synoptic gospels, the drama begins on the Day of Unleavened Bread, also called the Day of Preparation, which is the day the Passover lamb is sacrificed in preparation for the beginning of Passover that evening. In the synoptic gospels, Jesus is arrested after he eats his last meal with his disciples. In the Christian liturgical tradition, Jesus' last meal and arrest are commemorated on Maundy Thursday. According to the synoptic gospels, Jesus' last meal with his disciples is a Passover Seder, which means that he is crucified on the first day of Passover (remembering that Jewish days begin at sundown). Now let's look at the Gospel of John:

> Now it was the day of Preparation for the Passover; and it was about noon. [Pontius Pilate] said to the Jews, "Here is your King!" They cried out, "Away with him! Away with him! Crucify him!" Pilate asked them, "Shall I crucify your King?" The chief priests answered, "We have no king but the emperor." Then he handed him over to them to be crucified. (John 19:14–16)

In the synoptic gospels, Jesus eats his last meal with his disciples and is arrested at the beginning of the first day of Passover (Thursday evening), which means he's crucified on Friday. This is commemorated in the Christian liturgical tradition on Good Friday. In John's gospel, however, Jesus is arrested, tried, and crucified all on the same day, the Day of Preparation for the Passover (Thursday). In other words, John's gospel has Jesus being crucified a day before he's crucified in the synoptic gospels. In our own time, we would expect historical accounts to agree on the timeline of events. We would expect that journalists and biographers concerned with getting the facts straight would at least agree on the date and time of major episodes. This would be like some historians saying that the Declaration of Independence was adopted on July 4th and others saying that it was adopted on July 3rd. So what gives here? Why does John have Jesus crucified a day earlier than Matthew, Mark, and Luke? For an answer, we need to look at the beginning of the Gospel of John.

The first "speaking role" in the Gospel of John belongs to John the Baptist, who is preparing the way for Jesus. After the prologue of the Gospel of John (John 1:1–18) we see John the Baptist standing with two of his disciples when Jesus walks by. John says, "Look, here is the Lamb of God!" (John 1:36). Fast-forward to the end of John's gospel, when Jesus is about to be crucified. He has just endured a long interrogation session before Pontius Pilate, the Roman governor, and he has been sentenced to death by crucifixion. "Now it was the day of Preparation for the Passover; and it was about noon.... And [Pilate] handed him over to them to be crucified" (John 19:14, 16). In John's gospel, Jesus is crucified on the Day of Preparation, a day earlier than he is crucified in the synoptic gospels. What accounts for this discrepancy in the dates? As we just saw, in John's gospel the first "speaking role" goes to John the Baptist, who announces that Jesus is the "Lamb of God." At the end of John's gospel, Jesus is crucified on the Day of Preparation for the Passover, at the exact moment when the lambs are slaughtered for the Passover feast. For John, Jesus is the Lamb of God who is slaughtered for the sins of the world, so John's gospel has Jesus crucified at the exact same time as the lambs are slaughtered for the Passover feast. The synoptic gospels have Jesus crucified on the following day, the first day of Passover, after the lambs have already been slaughtered.

If we assume that the gospels are meant to be accurate biographies, we're left with a rather serious conundrum, because obviously Jesus can't be crucified on two different days. One of the stories has to be wrong. But if we approach the gospels as "sermons" or myths rather than as historical accounts, we learn a different lesson. The Gospel of John has a theological point to make, a point that the author feels is more important than getting the specific historical details right. The Gospel of John wants to emphasize the deeper meaning and significance of Jesus as the Lamb of God who takes away the sins of the world, so the author of John bookends the story of Jesus with this imagery of the lamb. The first speaking line of the gospel focuses on Jesus as the lamb, and toward the end of the gospel we see Jesus being crucified at the same time as the lambs are being sacrificed for the Passover feast. For John, the theological point is more important than historical accuracy. John doesn't care that his story doesn't line up exactly with the details of the synoptic gospels, because the meaning of Jesus' crucifixion is more important than the chronological details. The symbol of the lamb, the innocent sacrifice, is more important than the precise date of the crucifixion.

The synoptic evangelists give one date for the crucifixion and John gives a different date. If historical accuracy were our main concern, we would find ourselves with a serious problem here. But historical accuracy is not the chief concern of the evangelists; rather, the evangelists are far more concerned with making a theological point. Clearly the editors of the New Testament are also more concerned with the theology than the history, otherwise they wouldn't have allowed this obvious contradiction to remain in the New Testament. There's no way around it: John has Jesus crucified on a different day of the week than the synoptic evangelists. If we were primarily concerned with historical accuracy, this would be a scandal and we should do everything in our power to harmonize these accounts. But the New Testament suggests a different approach, one that is focused on the deeper meaning of the story rather than its historically-verifiable details. John wants us to focus on the symbol, the metaphor: Jesus as the Lamb of God. John doesn't particularly care that his chronology doesn't line up exactly with the chronology of the synoptic gospels, because that's not the point. The point is the deeper meaning and message of the story, and that meaning resonates regardless of the historical details.

A Critical Faith

Our foray into biblical criticism has illustrated some important points about how religious language works. The Bible itself is more interested in the big picture, the symbolic and metaphorical themes, than in providing historically-verifiable details and empirically-validated facts. If we expect the Bible to provide accurate details that will hold up against historical and scientific analysis, we will in many cases be sorely disappointed. But the chief purpose of the Bible is not to provide these historical and scientific details. Rather, the Bible gives us the big picture by telling meaningful stories to draw us out of our narrow assumptions and self-interest, to draw us into a world of myth and symbol and narrative, speaking to our deepest yearnings and desires, irrespective of our insistence on the facts. Facts certainly have their place, and we know where to find those facts. But the Bible is not primarily concerned with facts. The Bible is concerned with myth and symbol and narrative, with *theology*, with the deeper relationship between human beings and God. The Bible speaks primarily to faith, not belief.

Our meditation on these biblical stories reminds us of an important truth about faith: faith is a matter of what concerns us ultimately, of what we are willing to stake our lives on, of what we look to for meaning and value, of what guides and orients our lives, of what has grasped us and won't let us go. Stories are far more capable than facts of checking all of these boxes because stories have the power to transcend time and place. Most of us who look to the Bible for meaning and guidance have virtually nothing at all in common with the ancient Mediterranean world, yet we still draw meaning and hope and comfort and guidance from the stories that were told and recorded centuries ago. But today we stand on the other side of the Enlightenment, with its insistence on facts and evidence. This means that we will often assume that something must be factual in order for it to be true, and this must especially be the case when we're talking about faith, the most important thing of all. But this isn't really how our ancestors thought about faith or truth, and we would do well to remember that stories can be every bit as true as facts. Oftentimes stories and symbols can even reveal deeper truths than facts can ever hope to match.

When we're dealing with beliefs about finite reality, we need to be sure that the facts all line up, that they can be verified by rigorous testing and verification. But when we're dealing with faith in an infinite reality, we're on different ground. When we're dealing with faith, we're dealing with the world of myths and symbols and images and metaphors, something closer to poetry and art than to science and mathematics. The stories that touch the deepest parts of ourselves speak to us across the centuries and across cultures because they reveal to us something deeply true and meaningful about the human condition and our yearning for meaning and wholeness in our lives. These stories that guide us are often the first stories we hear on our parents' laps and they give us a framework for interpreting and understanding everything that we experience and learn as we make our way through the world.

As we grow up, we begin to think more critically about these stories and we naturally start to question some of the details. We might wonder whether certain parts of the stories really happened, or we might question whether the stories provide the overarching framework of meaning and significance for our lives that they are intended to provide. At some point it's natural for us to question what it is that actually gives us meaning and value, what we individually take as ultimately significant. Perhaps we've learned something new about science or history that calls some of our religious assumptions into question. Or perhaps we experience a tragedy that shatters the security and the certainty of our religious ideas and convictions. And in moments like these it's natural to wonder if we might be losing our faith. But is faith something that can be lost?

This is an important question that gets at the heart of the meaning of faith, specifically the important distinction already mentioned between the subjective act of having faith (*fides qua creditur*, "the faith which believes") and the object of our faith, or what we have faith in (*fides quae creditur*, "the faith which is believed"). Both "sides" or "poles" are necessary for faith, but they are not the same thing. Faith as the act of ultimate concern, as committing our entire being to something beyond ourselves and our finite concerns, is the subjective act of faith; it is one of the things that makes us human because to be human is to be ultimately concerned with the meaning of our lives and to seek ultimate fulfillment. On the other "pole" is what we put our faith in, which is the objective side of faith, and this will be different depending on the person or the tradition that shapes and guides us. The *act* of faith is the same for everyone: it is ultimate concern. But the *object* of faith will be different for everyone because different people, cultures, and traditions use different symbols to express the ultimate reality.

So what happens when someone worries that they've lost their faith? According to theologians like Tillich, what is happening in this situation is that the symbols we use to express our ultimate concern are showing signs of strain or are beginning to seem as if they are no longer capable of providing that orientation and meaning that we seek. What was once an absolute certainty and an unquestionable reality suddenly feels deflated, impotent, or even unreal and false, and this is often experienced as a crisis, as a profound loss. Sometimes this crisis is temporary and we regain our confidence in the old symbols, but sometimes these symbols die for us and we need to discover new symbols to express our ultimate concern. We still have faith (the subjective act of ultimate concern), but the symbols (which express the object of our faith) evolve or are replaced. It is precisely the power of symbols that makes this experience feel so catastrophic for so many people who go through it, so much so that it is often called a "dark night of the soul."

But if we're honest with ourselves, we've all experienced something like this at one point or another, to varying degrees. In genuine faith we are dealing with the ultimate, infinite reality, which will always finally remain a mystery to us. We cannot know the ultimate reality like we know the finite world around us (this is one of the reasons why we shouldn't use "faith" and "belief" interchangeably). Given the ultimate mystery that lies at the heart of faith, it is only natural for us to have moments of doubt. Doubt is often denigrated as something negative or dangerous, but it's important for us to think clearly and honestly about the important role that doubt plays in our lives and in our quest for meaning. In the next chapter we'll take a closer look at doubt and try to reclaim it as a necessary and healthy part of our human experience.

Chapter 2

Doubt

Like faith, doubt is a concept that is frequently misunderstood and often maligned in our contemporary US-American society. To confess that we have doubts is often embarrassing or frustrating, something we rarely like to admit and something we wish we could overcome. But might we be misunderstanding or underestimating the many roles that doubt plays in our lives? What, after all, is doubt? How does it function? What causes us to doubt? How does doubt relate to faith? To belief? Might doubt actually be a good and healthy thing? All these questions and more are the topic of this chapter.

Types of Doubt

If we look up "doubt" in a dictionary, we see broad agreement on what doubt is: a feeling of uncertainty, a lack of conviction, a lack of confidence or trust, not believing something, etc. We notice immediately that doubt has overwhelmingly negative connotations, that it's characterized as a lack or a hesitation. Given these meanings of doubt, people would certainly be justified in wanting to avoid doubt! But is that what doubt really is?

Yes and no. Paul Tillich suggests that there are actually three types of doubt, each of which plays a specific role in a specific context. The type of doubt we most typically see defined in the dictionaries is what Tillich calls methodological doubt, while the other types of doubt he identifies (neither of which is typically mentioned in the dictionary definitions) are skeptical doubt and existential doubt. Skeptical doubt in its pure form is so rare that we don't need to spend much time on it here. Tillich defines skeptical doubt as an attitude according to which there is no truth and no meaning to anything at all. In other words, skeptical doubt, consistently held, is a form of nihilism. But skeptical doubt contains within it something of a paradox, for the assertion that nothing is true is itself a truth claim, a belief in the truth of something: namely that there is no truth. In other words, pure skeptical doubt is ultimately contradictory and rarely sustainable over a lifetime. That leaves us with the two main types of doubt: methodological doubt and existential doubt.

Methodological Doubt

The dictionary definitions of doubt focus on its methodological mode. It is called "methodological" because it is doubt used as a method, as a technique or process for discovering facts and formulating beliefs. As such, methodological doubt only deals with finite reality. The scientific method is a wonderful example of methodological doubt in action. First we ask a question and formulate a hypothesis. Then we test our hypothesis through experiments and analysis. Once we've done that, we can determine if our hypothesis was true or false. Say I want to determine if my car keys will float in water. That is the question, or the methodological doubt. My hypothesis is that my keys will not float, so now I must test that hypothesis by putting my keys in water. I discover that my keys do not float in water, but sink right to the bottom. First I had a methodological doubt, then I devised an experiment to discover the facts of the matter, and now I know that it is a fact that car keys do not float in water.

Methodological doubt plays a vital function in our daily lives. Any time we have a question about the facts or we are uncertain of what to believe, we use methodological doubt to determine the facts and decide what to believe. For example, if we read a claim online that sounds fishy, we certainly shouldn't just believe it because it sounds good and then share it with all of our friends so that the misinformation spreads like a virus. Rather, we should recognize that we have doubts about the truthfulness of this claim and then investigate it thoroughly before deciding whether or not to believe it. There are entire websites devoted to just this work of testing the truthfulness of online claims and rumors, and here Snopes is the gold standard.[1] If we take a closer look at Snopes's method

---

1. http://www.snopes.com

for determining the reliability of a whole range of claims we see a clear example of how methodological doubt works.

First, the claim is stated in its original form, along with any information the Snopes authors have about its origin and backstory. Then the claim is analyzed using basic common sense. Does this story sound fabricated? Does it sound too good to be true? Are there telltale signs of a hoax? Next, the authors dig through several reliable sources for information regarding the topic of the original claim. These sources can include newspapers, television news programs, academic journals, statements by reputable researchers or other experts, eyewitness accounts, audio or video recordings, scientific data and statistics, etc. If these sources corroborate the original claim, then Snopes declares the claim true. If these sources indicate that the claim is false, then Snopes declares the claim false. If these sources determine that certain parts of the claim are true while others are false, then Snopes declares the claim a mixture of true and false. Finally, if there is not enough information to determine with enough confidence if a claim is true or false, then Snopes declares the claim undetermined or unverifiable.

This is the basic process of methodological doubt, used for everything from the simplest questions to the most complicated scientific hypotheses and everything in between. Every belief we hold about finite reality has been won using methodological doubt. Without it, we would have no knowledge about anything at all. In the last chapter we met William Clifford, the author of "The Ethics of Belief." Clifford was a champion of methodological doubt, which he understood to be indispensable in our search for truth and knowledge. But Clifford doesn't stop there: he frames belief and doubt in pointedly *moral* terms. We have a moral duty to take our doubts and questions seriously because belief is such a powerful, essential part of our individual lives and our social relations.

Methodological doubt and belief are moral concepts because beliefs always inform our actions, which have an impact far beyond our own individual mental lives. To take an extreme example, for hundreds of years in the United States it was a widely held belief that people with dark skin were intellectually, emotionally, spiritually, and physically inferior to people with light skin. This belief justified myriad horrors perpetrated against enslaved Africans and Native Americans, including physical exploitation, torture, spiritual and mental abuse, sexual assault, destruction of families, and many more atrocities, all enshrined in the institution of chattel slavery. It never occurred to the majority of white people that there was anything wrong with this belief; it was as self-evident to them as the sun coming up in the east every morning. This belief in white supremacy was justified by several intersecting layers of support: a warped interpretation of the Bible and of Christian theology, pseudo-scientific claims, cultural imperialism, political ideology, and financial greed, among many others.

But none of it was true. Race is a cultural construct with no basis in biology, the result of nothing more than different levels of melanin in the skin: that's it. Had enough people stopped to question the truth of these assertions of white supremacy and the inferiority of people of color, a horrible injustice could have been averted. There was no legitimate reason for people to believe that slavery was justified as a good and natural institution, and a healthy use of methodological doubt would have demonstrated that slavery was immoral and unjust.

But we are rarely, if ever, entirely objective in our thinking and acting. Our beliefs and assumptions and thoughts and actions are always influenced by several factors, some of which we are aware of, but many of which we might not even recognize or acknowledge. Methodological doubt serves an important function here as well. By recognizing the fallibility and inevitable limits of human knowledge and perspective, we can try to account for those limits when formulating our beliefs and determining our actions. While it's impossible ever to be completely objective, we can still do our very best to recognize and account for our biases and assumptions as best we can. Methodological doubt helps us to ask these questions before we investigate a matter and to bear those implicit assumptions in mind when we set out on our search for truth.

Descartes' Method of Doubt

Someone who was fearless in his search for truth was René Descartes, generally considered to be the father of modern Western philosophy. Descartes was obsessed with discovering the truth: something—anything—that he could believe with absolute certainty, beyond a shadow of a doubt. Descartes spent his early life studying with the Jesuits, a Roman Catholic monastic order founded by Ignatius of Loyola, who was also the author of a book called *The Spiritual Exercises*, a series of meditations on God, Christ, and the Christian life. Divided over four "weeks," the

Exercises takes readers on an intense journey of meditation and prayer intended to discern the will of God and to conform their lives to Christ.

Descartes was surely familiar with the *Exercises* from his school days, but he gave them his own unique twist. Rather than seeking the will of God and the imitation of Christ, Descartes decided to sit down and write his own *Meditations on First Philosophy*, divided over six "days," to determine what, if anything, he could know with absolute certainty and conviction. When he stopped to think carefully about his own beliefs about himself, the world, and God, he realized that everything he believed rested on untested assumptions that could be called into question. It turns out that he didn't really know anything for certain and everything he thought he knew could be doubted. This simple realization stunned Descartes and threw him into something of a panic, so he resolved to sit down and think through everything he believed, to submit it to unflinching scrutiny and criticism until he could find something certain to believe. Early in the book he describes his reasons for undertaking these exercises and the method of doubting he will use to discover the truth:

> Several years have now passed since I first realized how numerous were the false opinions that in my youth I had taken to be true, and thus how doubtful were all those that I had subsequently built upon them. And thus I realized that once in my life I had to raze everything to the ground and begin again from the original foundations, if I wanted to establish anything firm and lasting in the sciences. . . . Yet to bring this about I will not need to show that all my opinions are false, which is perhaps something I could never accomplish. But reason now persuades me that I should withhold my assent no less carefully from opinions that are not completely certain and indubitable than I would from those that are patently false. For this reason, it will suffice for the rejection of all of these opinions, if I find in each of them some reason for doubt. . . . [B]ecause undermining the foundations will cause whatever has been built upon them to crumble of its own accord, I will attack straightaway those principles which supported everything I once believed.[2]

What Descartes is describing here is something like a massive demolition project. He has spent his whole life living in a "house" constructed of his beliefs about himself, the world around him, and God. As with any old house, there are inevitably going to be problems that need

---

2. Descartes, *Meditations*, 13–14.

to be addressed to keep the whole house from caving in. If things get bad enough, we realize that we have to tear the whole house down and start over again from scratch, from the original foundations. Otherwise we're just slapping some paint on a teetering pile of kindling waiting to collapse. What Descartes realized is that his whole "house" is just such a teetering pile of kindling, and the only way to deal with that is to tear the whole thing down to the foundation and start over. The "house" in our analogy is our entire structure of beliefs. The best way to tear down a house is with a wrecking ball, and in our analogy the "wrecking ball" is methodological doubt.

Descartes settles in behind the controls of the wrecking ball and starts swinging. When we think about what we know for certain, usually we start with our own existence. Obviously we exist, or we wouldn't be worrying about any of these questions in the first place. But how, exactly, do we know that we exist? Descartes realized that we usually assume that we exist because we have clear sensory perceptions of our own bodies and of the world around us. I feel myself sitting in my chair as I type on my computer. I see the trees blowing in the breeze outside my window. I smell the flowers my wife brought in from the garden. I taste the coffee I'm sipping as I type. I hear my dog playing with her squeaky toy on the other side of the room. So far so good, right?

Not so fast. Haven't I had dreams where I've experienced all of these sensory perceptions just as vividly as I'm experiencing them now? What's to say that I'm not having a dream right now where I think I'm experiencing things that are really nothing more than figments of my imagination? Almost two thousand years before Descartes, in fourth-century BCE China, the Daoist master Zhuangzi wrote a short story reflecting on a dream he had. He dreamt he was a butterfly, happily flitting about the flowers in a garden. Then he woke up, but suddenly he had no idea what to think. Was he Zhuangzi, a human being who dreamed he was a butterfly? Or was he a butterfly having a dream that he was a human being named Zhuangzi? How can we really know? What's to say that my entire life isn't just an elaborate dream, or, to borrow from the thoroughly Cartesian film trilogy, *The Matrix*, what if everything I think I'm experiencing is just an elaborate computer program designed to deceive me? What if none of this is really real? Then what? How can I know that I really exist?

When we sit with that question for a while we'll soon find ourselves curled up in the fetal position on the floor, slowly rocking back and forth while our brains leak out our ears. It turns out that it's very difficult to prove anything at all! Here Descartes is launching a full-frontal attack on a dominant philosophical school of his day (and ours) known as Empiricism. Empiricism's basic premise is that everything we know is derived from our sense perception and experience of the world around us. As we saw earlier, common sense tells us that this is how we come to true knowledge because this is our default answer to questions such as "How do you know that you're really sitting here right now?" We answer with reference to our sense perceptions, without even really thinking about it. But Descartes' dream argument is enough to cast suspicion on the reliability of our sense perception to give us accurate information and certain knowledge.

As if that's not already enough, Descartes goes even further. Let's grant that we can't always trust our sense perceptions to give us accurate information and knowledge because we might be dreaming. But even when we know we're awake we find that we're not much better off in our quest for absolute certainty. If I trust my sense perception absolutely, I will quickly find that it tricks me all the time. Based on sight alone, I would be correct in assuming that the sun is a tiny little yellow ball that moves across the sky every day in a predictable pattern. Then there are the moments when freaky things happen that I can't quite explain. Most of us have had the experience of hearing our name being called and turning around to answer, only to discover that no one is there. Most of us have also had the experience of feeling eyes on the back of our head, only to discover that we're completely alone. When we were children, many of us went through "haunted houses" at Halloween that included stations where we put our hands into a closed box to feel "eyes" and "guts" and other gross, creepy things, only to discover afterwards that the eyes were grapes and the guts were cooked pasta.

We turn around and see that there is no one there looking at us or calling our name. We learn in science class that that sun is several times larger than the Earth and that the Earth is actually revolving around the sun. All of this should serve to remind us that we can't always trust our senses to give us a completely accurate picture of reality all by themselves. We can be, and often are, deceived by our senses about the true nature of things. And for Descartes, anything that can fool us even once can never be trusted absolutely. So sense perception cannot be our infallible guide to sure and certain knowledge.

Let's grant Descartes that much. Each of us has had experiences where our senses have proven deceptive. But aren't there other truths out there that we can trust absolutely, beyond a shadow of a doubt? Surely mathematical truths are true regardless of the trustworthiness of sense perception, right? Whether or not we can trust our senses, 2+2=4, always and forever. A square has four sides, always and forever. These are incontrovertible facts, yes? Believe it or not, Descartes doesn't think so, at least not without some doubt. We assume that these mathematical assertions are true because we assume that we can trust the basic nature of reality as constant and trustworthy. But why do we assume that? Do we have good reasons to assume anything of the sort?

For Descartes, assumption is a very dangerous game to play. As Descartes was a good Roman Catholic, he turned to God for answers. The Christian tradition presupposes that there exists a good and perfect God who created everything that exists, including mathematical and geometrical constants, and therefore we can rest assured that two plus two always equals four and that a square always has four sides. But how do we really *know* that such a good and perfect God exists? What if that's not what's going on at all? What if, instead of a good and perfect God, there is an Evil Genius who has created an entire world of lies and falsehoods just to deceive us about every single thing we think might be true? How can I trust even arithmetic and geometry when I don't know for certain that this sensible and intelligible world all around me wasn't created for the sole purpose of messing with my mind?

Descartes insists that we can't know that for certain, at least not yet. If we're going to doubt everything, then that really means *everything*, even the existence of the material world, even the existence of my own self, even the existence of God. If we can't trust that we ourselves exist, and if we can't trust that the external world exists, then we also can't trust that a good and perfect God exists, which means that even rational truths like mathematics and geometry are susceptible to methodological doubt.

Here ends Descartes' first meditation. He doesn't seem to have a leg to stand on, having just called into question anything and everything he ever thought was true. So where does that leave him? It leaves him with even more questions. He describes the sensation he's feeling as being caught in a whirlpool, unable to touch bottom and unable to swim to the surface. He feels like he is drowning in doubt. But he pushes on because he's convinced that eventually he will find solid ground, something firm and certain to believe. He hasn't given up on his method!

Now that Descartes has succeeded in demolishing the "house" of his beliefs with the "wrecking ball" of methodological doubt, there is nothing left standing. He's torn down the house and it's time to see what's there in the foundation. After we've questioned everything, what can we still know for certain? This is a crucial moment in Descartes' *Meditations* and everything hinges on what he does next. What he realizes is that, even when he's doubted literally *everything*, there's still someone there to do the doubting, to ask the questions. Pushed to the limits of doubt, he asks the final question: *Do I exist?* He stops to think about this for a moment and, always loyal to his method, he doubts his own existence. He thinks to himself, "I do not exist." But that makes no sense. How can the question be raised if there's no one there to ask the question? Let's try again: "I do not exist." No, that can't be true. Surely I must exist to doubt my own existence. But suppose I'm being deceived by the Evil Genius. "I don't exist, but I'm being tricked into believing that I do exist by the Evil Genius whose only goal is to deceive me at every turn." Even here, I must exist because I can't be deceived if I don't exist. No matter what I do, no matter what question I ask, no matter what Evil Genius might be deceiving me, in every single case there must be an "I" there to be deceived, to ask the question, to express the doubt. No matter how hard I try to deny it, I must exist in order to think the thought or even to doubt it in the first place.

And at last we arrive at the phrase that made Descartes famous. *Cogito, ergo sum*: "I think, therefore I am." Actually, he never says that in the *Meditations*,[3] but he does say something similar: "'I am, I exist' is necessarily true every time I utter it or conceive it in my mind."[4] No matter how strenuously I deny it, no matter how many ways I doubt it, no matter how much I question it, I simply must exist in order to question my own existence. Even an Evil Genius bent on deceiving me can't make it so that I don't exist, because I must exist in order to be deceived. I am. I exist. I am real. This is the incontrovertible truth Descartes discovered by wielding the wrecking ball of methodological doubt. This is the one truth that cannot be denied, no matter how hard we try. I am a thinking thing, and as long as I am thinking, I exist.[5]

---

3. He says this precise phrase in the *Discourse on Method*.
4. Descartes, *Meditations*, 18.
5. Philosophers and theologians are notorious joke tellers (or is that tellers of notoriously bad jokes?), so naturally there are jokes about Descartes. This is my favorite Descartes joke: Descartes walks into a bar and has a drink. When Descartes has finished his drink the bartender comes over and asks if he'll have another. Descartes

Volumes have been written on the strengths and weaknesses of Descartes' use of methodological doubt and the conclusions he reached by means of that method. Many first-rate thinkers agree with his conclusions, and many first-rate thinkers insist he went off the rails and sent the subsequent history of Western thought down a path that we are only now finally abandoning, and good riddance. Regardless of how we appraise his conclusions, Descartes shows us how vitally important methodological doubt is for our commitment to know the truth about things, and how doubt is something to be embraced rather than feared. Descartes was fearless in his use of doubt and he showed us the way to use doubt as a method for discovering the truth about the finite world around us. We will see more of Descartes in the next chapter, where we'll see how he uses reason to begin to rebuild the house he tore down with the wrecking ball of methodological doubt.

It should be obvious by now that methodological doubt and belief are completely incompatible. We have no right to believe something if we still have doubts about the facts, as both Clifford and Descartes go to great lengths to convince us. Methodological doubt is the first step on the way to formulating a belief, but once we get to the belief all of our doubts should be settled and answered; if not, then we have more work to do. But do belief and doubt have the same relationship as faith and doubt? Are faith and doubt also polar opposites, so that we only have a strong faith when we've laid all our doubts to rest? Many people today assume that this is precisely how the relationship between faith and doubt should be: if we have doubts it means that we don't have faith, or at least it means that our faith is weak and vulnerable. And that must mean that having a good, strong faith means not having any doubts; it should mean having absolute and unassailable certainty.

A Doubting Faith

Kallistos Ware, a bishop of the Orthodox Church in England, has said that "It is not the task of Christianity to provide easy answers to every question, but to make us progressively aware of a mystery. God is not so much the object of our knowledge as the cause of our wonder."[6] This reflection succinctly captures the essence of the relationship between faith

says, "I think not," and disappears.

6. Ware, *The Orthodox Way*, 14.

and doubt. If, as Tillich has said, faith is the state of our being ultimately concerned, and if the object of our ultimate concern is truly ultimate, infinite, and unconditional (what Christians call "God"), then we will never have knowledge of God like we have knowledge of finite objects. This is because faith and belief refer to two different realities and this is why those terms should not be used interchangeably. Unlike belief, faith will always include doubt because with faith our questions are never settled, no matter how much research or investigation we might do. There will always be more questions, more than we can ever possibly know or understand. As Augustine once put it, "If you've understood it, it's not God."[7]

While beliefs are constructed using methodological doubt, faith relates to a different type of doubt, which Tillich calls "existential doubt." If methodological doubt asks questions such as "What are the facts?" and "What should I believe?" existential doubt asks questions like "Is the object of my faith really ultimate?" and "What does this mean for my life?" We should try to be as objective as possible when determining what to believe, but in faith we can never be totally objective because we are personally, existentially committed, involved, and concerned with our faith. In faith we seek to commit ourselves totally to the source and ground of being, of reality itself, for the sake of ultimate meaning and fulfillment. In something so important we would hope that we could know for certain that what we're committing ourselves to is really what we think it is, that it's worth it, that it can handle the weight of our faith and our hope, that we're not making a big mistake. But (and here's a big "but") we can never have that kind of certainty and security when it comes to faith, because the ultimate (e.g. God) is so much more than we can ever hope to understand. This is why faith is always a risk, a leap into the unknown, and why theologians like to use words like "trust" and "hope" when discussing faith.

Perhaps this is why John Calvin called the human mind "a factory of idols." We really don't like not knowing something, especially when what we don't know is the most important thing of all! There is no bigger question than the meaning of life, the meaning of *my* life, the meaning of it all. Everyone asks that question at some point, and each of the world's religious traditions has created complex texts, rituals, doctrines, and guidelines to assist people on their journey toward meaning. And yet, we so often obsess about the texts, the rituals, the doctrines, because

---

7. Augustine, "Sermon 117."

we're able to get a handle on them and possess them in a way that gives us some sense of control and comfort. Sometimes we even take these human creations to be ultimate in and of themselves, precisely because we can understand them and control them. And that, of course, is idolatry. And one common cause of our tendency toward idolatry is our deep discomfort with doubt.

Unlike methodological doubt, which should be laid to rest before we determine what to believe, existential doubt is a permanent, indeed necessary element of faith. To put this another way, existential doubt is a defining feature of the very structure of faith. As Tillich put it, "If faith is understood as the belief that something is [factually] true, doubt is incompatible with the act of faith. If faith is understood as being ultimately concerned, doubt is a necessary element in it. It is a consequence of the risk of faith."[8] Faith is a risk because we can never have adequate knowledge of the object of our faith; we can never know for certain that what concerns us ultimately is really ultimate, can really handle the weight of our ultimate concern. This risky, uncertain faith shouldn't discourage us, however. In fact, if we discover that we've stopped asking any questions or having any doubts about our faith, that's a pretty good sign that we're slipping into idolatry. This doubt can never be overcome because it is a permanent element in the structure of faith. It can, however, be accepted and even embraced. Tillich again:

> [Existential doubt] does not question whether a special proposition is true or false. It does not reject every concrete truth, but it is aware of the element of insecurity in every existential truth. At the same time, the doubt which is implied in faith accepts this insecurity and takes it into itself in an act of courage. Faith includes courage. Therefore it can include the doubt about itself.[9]

The Binding of Isaac: Faith or Fanaticism?

There are numerous examples of this dynamic relationship between faith and doubt in the Bible. Abram/Abraham is a classic example, so much so that the nineteenth-century Danish philosopher and theologian Søren Kierkegaard called him the "Knight of Faith." When we first meet Abram he is living in the city of Ur when God calls to him and commands him to

8. Tillich, *Dynamics of Faith*, 21.
9. Tillich, *Dynamics of Faith*, 23.

leave his home and follow God to the land of Canaan, which God promises to Abram and his descendants. Abram drops everything and follows God into the unknown. Later, God appears to Abram and tells him that he and his wife, Sarai, will have a son, despite Abram and Sarai being in their late 90s. Abram is so taken aback by this pronouncement that he falls on his face and laughs at God, and in a separate episode Sarai also laughs at God's news that she will bear a son. God has the last laugh, so to speak, when Sarai bears a son and names him Isaac, which, in Hebrew, means "he will laugh."

The paradigmatic illustration of faith and doubt in the Abraham story is the in/famous Binding of Isaac in Genesis 22, when God commands Abraham to take Isaac to the top of a mountain and offer him as a burnt offering to God. Thousands of pages have been written on this story from every conceivable angle and there will certainly be thousands more pages written about it, because it is a famously challenging and controversial text that invites endless analysis and commentary. I myself have read this story dozens of times and it seems like each time I read it I come to a different conclusion about Abraham and God. What is it about this story that invites such conflicted interpretations?[10]

By way of a brief summary, Abraham and Sarah have finally had the son God promised to be their heir. The next thing we know, God calls to Abraham and tells him to take Isaac to a distant mountain, kill him, and offer him as a burnt offering to God. Abraham packs up his things and sets off with Isaac and two servants to the mountain God has shown him. It's a three-day journey, which should give Abraham plenty of time to think about what God has asked him to do. But we don't hear Abraham's inner monologue; we just watch the group trekking across the desert toward the mountain in silence. When they arrive, Abraham tells his servants that he and Isaac will go up the mountain alone: "We will worship, then we will come back to you."

When they get to the top of the mountain, Isaac looks around and notices there's no lamb for the burnt offering. He asks Abraham where the lamb is and Abraham responds that God will provide a lamb. Then Abraham takes Isaac and ties him up, lays him on the altar stacked with wood, and raises the knife to kill his beloved son. At that moment an angel calls out to him and commands him to stop, "for now I know that you fear God and have not withheld your son, your only son, from me."

10. An excellent survey of the various ways this story has been interpreted across the centuries is Goodman, *But Where Is the Lamb?*

A ram suddenly appears in the thicket and Abraham sacrifices it instead of his son. Then God repeats the earlier blessings of Abraham, to be the father of many nations with descendants as numerous as the stars in the sky and the sand on the seashore. This is the last time God and Abraham ever speak to one another, and the next time we see Sarah she has just died.

What sense can we make of this story, enshrined in the Bible but still shocking and even horrifying? Some commentators see it as a rejection of child sacrifice, while others see it as a foreshadowing of the crucifixion of Jesus, the Son of God. Still others see it as the ultimate test of Abraham's faith in God. Kierkegaard famously imagined several versions of the story and determined that it was a story about Abraham's willingness to suspend his ethics for the sake of his radical commitment to God.[11] There might be some truth to all of these interpretations, and there are probably other interpretations that have merit, too. But what does this story have to do with the relationship between faith and doubt?

At first glance, it looks like Abraham doesn't have any doubts at all when God asks him to kill his son. He simply follows orders and raises the knife to kill his son. But if we take a closer look at the story, we can see some hints that maybe Abraham actually did have doubts, which would be consistent with his relationship with God from the very beginning. At several points in Abraham's journey with God he had doubts: he doubted that he would have a son, he doubted that God would protect him and Sarah when they were traveling in foreign lands (Abraham even lied to two different kings and said Sarah was his sister so they wouldn't kill him and take Sarah as a concubine), and he questioned God's decision to kill everyone in Sodom and Gomorrah without stopping to check if there were any righteous people in the cities. And God listened! In each of those instances where Abraham doubted God, God came through for him and delivered on God's promises. So when God commands Abraham to kill Isaac, Abraham has a lifetime of experiences with God as trustworthy and true to God's word.

Now God is asking Abraham to kill his son, his pride and joy, the culmination of his very existence and meaning. Two things could be happening here. The narration at the beginning of Genesis 22 gives readers a clue about God's thinking by telling us that God is testing Abraham. But what is the test, exactly? God could be testing Abraham's ultimate

---

11. Kierkegaard, *Fear and Trembling/Repetition*.

loyalty: is it to God or to Isaac? Or God could be testing Abraham's willingness to continue questioning God, as he has done time and again. On the flip side, Abraham could also be testing God. God had always come through for Abraham before, and God had promised that through Isaac Abraham would be the father of many nations. That can't happen if Isaac is dead! Because God and Abraham are partners in a covenant, each with their own sworn obligations to the other, Abraham could be testing God's commitment to him, just as God is testing Abraham's commitment to God.

If we look closer at the details of the story, we can tease out some of Abraham's motivations for going through with this shocking act. When the party arrives at the foot of the mountain, Abraham tells his servants that he and Isaac will go worship and then "*we* will come back to you." Perhaps he's lying to keep everyone calm and not tip them off on what's about to happen. Or perhaps he really means that both he and Isaac will come back because he trusts that God won't make him go through with killing his son. When Abraham and Isaac are alone on top of the mountain, Isaac asks where the lamb is for the burnt offering, and Abraham tells him that God will provide a lamb. Again, perhaps Abraham is lying to keep Isaac calm, or perhaps he really trusts that God will provide an alternate sacrifice rather than letting him go through with killing Isaac. The moment of truth, when he raises the knife above his head to kill his son, could be the ultimate test of God, to see whether God keeps God's promises. We can think of this almost like a game of chicken, seeing who will blink first. It turns out that God blinks first and tells Abraham, through an angel, to lower the knife now that God knows that Abraham fears God. Abraham knows that God keeps God's promises, and God has seen that Abraham trusted that God would not make him kill his son. Abraham reasoned through his past experiences with God and continued to question what type of God he was dealing with, both of which are signs of a strong and healthy faith.

We shouldn't let this interpretation numb us to the fact that this is a genuinely horrifying story, one that can easily be misused to justify all sorts of barbaric acts. In fact, two recent stories in the news bear this out. In one newspaper article, a woman in suburban Chicago received a phone call from her estranged husband, a former pastor, informing her that the world was about to end and the children needed to be prepared to "meet Jesus." So the woman dressed her daughters in white and attempted to poison them before stabbing one of them.[12] In the other newspaper article, a Florida woman heard a sermon on Genesis 22 and went home to the two children she was babysitting and drowned one in the bathtub and tried to kill the other child and then herself. In a suicide note she described being moved by the pastor's sermon on Genesis 22 and wanting to be like Abraham, but "God never told me to stop."[13]

What distinguishes these recent events from the story of the Binding of Isaac? There are several differences, but, most importantly, these recent events really happened, while Genesis 22 is a biblical myth. But beyond that, neither woman ever stopped to think about what they were doing, never entertained any doubts, and never wondered if what they were doing was good or right. They crossed over the line that separates faith from fanaticism, which dictionaries define as "unreasoning zeal" or "irrational devotion." Faith divorced from doubt and reason can easily become fanatic, with often devastating, tragic results. Commentators will continue to disagree on the interpretation of the Binding of Isaac, with some understandably dismissing it as a tragic example of fanaticism, violence, and even child abuse. I'm certainly sympathetic to those readings and I sometimes end up there in my own reading of the story. But there are some hints and clues in the details of the story that can lead us to a different conclusion, especially when we remember that this story is a myth intended to teach us something deeper than the superficial plot points, something about faith as ultimate concern. What should be clear to us, though, is that this story is by no means an invitation to attempt murder, even if we think God wills it.

A healthy faith includes doubt as a necessary element. This doesn't mean that the doubt is always on the surface, that we're always aware of the doubt that is built into the structure of our faith, but there will be moments when that doubt erupts to the surface and reminds us that we don't have all the answers, that our faith is always a risk. One of the most common catalysts for this eruption of doubt to the surface of our faith is the experience of suffering.

---

12. https://chicago.suntimes.com/news/police-mom-said-she-was-going-to-kill-her-three-children-so-they-could-meet-jesus/

13. https://www.rawstory.com/2014/05/florida-woman-accused-of-killing-2-year-old-while-re-enacting-bible-story/

Job's Suffering Faith

Perhaps the most famous story of suffering, faith, and doubt in the history of world literature is the Book of Job in the Old Testament. Written in the style of a legend or what we might today call a fairy tale, the Book of Job is notoriously difficult to translate and there are conflicting interpretations of just what is original and what are later additions to the text. Putting these fascinating textual questions aside, what is clear is that the Book of Job addresses perennial human questions of faith, doubt, loss, suffering, and meaning, told from the perspective of a man named Job.[14]

The book opens in classic fairy-tale style: "There once was a man in the land of Uz whose name was Job. That man was blameless and upright, one who feared God and turned away from evil." Job has a wife, seven daughters and three sons, thousands of livestock, and many servants. He never misses an opportunity to offer appropriate worship to God on his own behalf and also on behalf of his family. He is, as the prologue tells us, "the greatest of all of the people of the east" (1:1–5).

Meanwhile, in the courts of heaven, God is having a conversation with the heavenly beings when the Satan appears. Before going any further it's important to point out that this is *not* the Devil of later Christian tradition, the embodiment of evil and all that is utterly opposed to God. In the Book of Job, the Satan (whose name means "the Accuser" in Hebrew[15]) works for God as something like God's prosecuting attorney. It's the Satan's job to bring to God's attention anyone who might need to be punished. God asks the Satan if he is aware of God's servant, Job, who is blameless and upright. The Satan is aware of Job, but he doesn't think that Job is good for any particularly noble reasons; rather the Satan thinks Job is good simply because God has always blessed him with good fortune and happiness: "Does Job fear God for nothing? Have you not put a fence around him and his house and all that he has, on every side? You have blessed the work of his hands, and his possessions have increased in the land. But stretch out your hand now, and touch all that he has, and he

---

14. For an updated version of the Book of Job, with quite different questions and conclusions, see MacLeish, *J.B.: A Play in Verse*, which won the Pulitzer Prize for Drama in 1959 as well as a Tony Award. William Blake, the English poet and painter active at the turn of the nineteenth century, produced a lovely edition of the Book of Job with his own watercolors of several scenes from the book, reproduced in *Blake's Illustrations for the Book of Job*.

15. To remind us that we're not talking about the Devil here, I will always use the phrase "the Satan" when discussing the character in the Book of Job.

will curse you to your face" (1:9–11). So God gives the Satan permission to destroy all that Job has, only the Satan may not harm Job himself. Essentially, God and the Satan have made a bet about Job: the Satan thinks Job has faith in God only because everything in his life is wonderful and he's #blessed, while God thinks Job will still have faith in God even if he experiences loss and suffering. In this bet we see distilled a classic question of the motivations of faith and worship: do we love God only because of what we get out of it, or do we love God for God's sake, no matter what, because God is the ultimate reality from whom and in whom we have our very being?

Back on Earth, Job is enjoying another #blessed day when messengers begin arriving. Job's oxen, donkeys, and camels have been stolen, his sheep have been killed, his servants have been murdered, and all ten of his children have died in a freak accident. Job's response is to praise God: "Naked I came from my mother's womb, and naked shall I return there; the Lord gave and the Lord has taken away, blessed be the name of the Lord" (1:21).

The scene returns to the heavenly courts and God and the Satan have the same conversation about Job and make the same bet. God chastises the Satan, reminding him that Job "persists in his integrity, although you incited me against him, to destroy him for no reason" (2:3). The Satan, unmoved in his insistence that Job will crack, reminds God that Job himself still hasn't suffered directly. Yes, he has lost his fortune and his possessions and his children, but if God would only allow the Satan to go after Job himself, then the Satan is sure that Job will curse God and the Satan will win the bet. So God relents, again, and allows the Satan to inflict pain and suffering on Job, but the Satan must be careful not to kill him.

We return to Job, who is now covered from head to toe in painful sores and is sitting on an ash heap scratching himself with a broken piece of pottery. For the first time in the story we meet Job's wife, who has had enough of all of this: "Do you still persist in your integrity? Curse God, and die" (2:9). But Job is unmoved: "Shall we receive the good at the hand of God, and not receive the bad?" (2:10). Apparently this was more than Job's wife could take, because she disappears from the story, never to be seen again.

Meanwhile, three of Job's friends—Eliphaz the Temanite, Bildad the Shuhite, and Zophar the Naamathite—pay a visit to Job because they have heard of his terrible misfortune. As they approach Job they immediately recognize his great distress and they tear their robes and throw dust on their heads, weeping aloud. They then sit with him on the ground for seven days and seven nights, "and no one spoke a word to him, for they saw that his suffering was very great" (2:13). The references to weeping, tearing robes, throwing dust, and sitting for seven days all point to traditional mourning rituals, as if Job had died. But there is another way of looking at these acts, as the three friends know full well that Job is not actually dead. They see that their friend is experiencing intense suffering and they recognize that nothing they can say or do will stop the pain and make it better. Instead, they simply sit down with their friend to share his suffering, to let him know that he's not alone. In the lingo of pastoral care this is often called a "ministry of presence," meaning that sometimes the most meaningful gesture we can make for someone in grief is simply to be with them, to let them know they're not alone in their pain. Job's friends offer this tender ministry to Job in one of the most poignant scenes in biblical literature.

Unfortunately, though, Job's friends can't keep their mouths shut and it turns out that they're itching to explain to Job everything he did wrong to justify God's punishment. The bulk of the Book of Job features a series of speeches by the friends and Job's responses. It is important to remember that we readers know more of the story than the three friends do, as we know that Job really has done nothing wrong, that his suffering is gratuitous or, even worse, all meant to settle a bet between God and the Satan. The friends each in their own way represent traditional Hebrew thought about suffering and what is often called theodicy, which is the attempt to justify God's power and goodness in light of the evil and suffering that inflicts humanity seemingly at random. Each of the friends insists that Job must have done something wrong because in their theology good things happen to good people and bad things happen to bad people. Therefore, the only conclusion to be drawn from Job's suffering is that he must have sinned. God is fair and just, so suffering must be punishment for wrongdoing. Each of the friends offers a different possible meaning for Job's suffering. Perhaps Job is secretly a sinner and is rightly being punished, so he must accept his punishment as the price of justice. Or perhaps Job is being punished for the sins of his children rather than for anything Job himself has done. Or perhaps Job's punishment is intended to strengthen his faith in and dependence on God, so Job should be grateful for the opportunity to suffer for a greater purpose that will make all the pain worth it in the end. Or perhaps God is teaching Job humility and he should submit to God's plan for his life, even when it includes gratuitous suffering.

Job himself takes a different angle on the problem, however. Job vehemently disagrees with his friends' insistence that he must have done something wrong to deserve his suffering, and we know that Job is correct. Job also rejects the notion that any rewards he might receive in the future could make his current suffering somehow turn out to be "worth it." That's easy to say when you're not the one experiencing the suffering, but Job is in the midst of horrendous pain and misery, right now. Easy answers and sanctimonious platitudes aren't cutting it for Job. But Job does still share his friends' assumption that God is just. In a series of increasingly angry and hostile speeches, Job shouts and rages at God. Sometimes he feels as though God has abandoned him and that there is no goodness in the world. At other times he feels as though God is actively stalking him, like a hunter stalks their prey, and he wishes God would just leave him alone so he can die and end his pain. He wishes he had been stillborn. He wishes God would mercifully kill him rather than toying with him like a cat with a mouse. He wishes he could find the peace of Sheol, the shadowy existence in the underworld after death. As he gets more and more despondent he even begins to question God's justice as he reflects on the many instances of righteous people suffering while the wicked prosper. The unfairness of it all leads Job to despair and beg for death. But God will not put him out of his misery and Job continues to suffer. What bothers Job more than anything is that God appears to be unjust because Job knows he has done nothing wrong and yet still he suffers. It doesn't make any sense. If he did something wrong then he would accept his suffering as just punishment, but to accept meaningless suffering is too much for Job to bear.

Job begs God to explain why this is happening, and in his speeches he uses technical legal language typically reserved for bringing a lawsuit in a court, demanding that God be held liable for wrongfully causing Job's pain and suffering. The friends have had enough at this point and they are convinced that Job has gone mad. Any feelings of sympathy or solidarity with Job in his suffering are gone, and they implore him to stop digging a deeper hole for himself in his raging against God. But Job is unmoved, convinced that he is right. If only God would show up, they could finally work out what exactly is going on. Surely God will explain everything so that it all makes sense!

And then, amazingly, God does show up. "Then the LORD answered Job out of the whirlwind: 'Who is this that darkens counsel by words without knowledge? Gird up your loins like a man, I will question you, and you will declare to me" (38:1–3). God then proceeds to explain to Job what it's like to create and govern the universe, describing in loving detail the depths of the sea, the patterns of weather and the seasons, the life cycles of animals, and the delicate balance and tragic beauty of a world revolving on the axis of death and life. Rather sarcastically, God periodically stops to ask Job if he also knows all these things, as Job clearly thinks that the universe should make perfect sense to him as a human being. Job already realizes that he's punching far above his weight class here and tries to call off the meeting, but to no avail. God's just getting started.

"Will you even put me in the wrong? Will you condemn me that you may be justified? Have you an arm like God, and can you thunder with a voice like [God's]?" (40:8–9). In God's second speech, God delivers another rousing reflection on what it's like to be the creator of the universe, this time focusing on two particularly fearsome animals: Behemoth and Leviathan (perhaps a hippopotamus and a crocodile, respectively), each of which utterly terrified the people of the ancient world, and for good reason. God takes great pride in being the creator of these mighty and dangerous creatures whose strength far surpasses any human attempts to domesticate or control them. God describes them like we might describe our favorite pets, in intimate and even loving language, which only serves to highlight the immense distance between God's power and Job's smallness. Interestingly enough, at no point in either of God's speeches does God ever mention human beings, human civilization, or human concerns, except to point out how helpless and insignificant human beings are when compared to God's mighty and mysterious works of creation.

At first glance, God gives a curiously unsatisfying response to Job's incessant raging and his desperate demands that God give a clear justification for Job's suffering. Instead of revealing the economics of suffering or the grand divine plan for each human life or the secrets of divine wisdom and justice, God describes creation in its bewildering and awesome diversity. God displaces Job and, by extension, all of humanity from the center of the universe. In response to Job's questions about his very particular experience, God sings hymns of praise to all of creation. Job wants justice, but God seems to suggest that if there is justice in the universe, it's certainly not the type of justice that makes sense to human beings. It looks like we might not be the crowning glory of creation after all, that God has other things on God's mind.[16]

Job seems to get the message: "Therefore I have uttered what I did not understand, things too wonderful for me, which I did not know" (42:3b). And then come two famously difficult verses to translate in the climax of the entire book. The New Revised Standard Version translates verses 5–6 as follows: "I had heard of you by the hearing of the ear, but now my eyes see you; *therefore I despise myself, and repent in dust and ashes*" (emphasis mine). But there are other possible translations of this perhaps deliberately enigmatic verse 6, translations that completely change the meaning of Job's response. We could translate verse 6 instead as "Therefore I reject it and am consoled for dust and ashes." Or we could translate it as "Therefore I reject and foreswear dust and ashes."

In the first translation (from the NRSV), it would appear that Job ultimately agrees with his friends, that he has sinned and therefore must repent. In the second translation, it's unclear exactly what Job is rejecting, but it could be that he is rejecting the rumors he had heard about God and God's ways now that he has seen and heard God for himself. In the third translation we sense that Job has given up his mourning and has accepted that he will never understand why he was suffering. The first translation seems the least good option, especially when we continue on to verse 7, where God addresses Job's friend Eliphaz: "My wrath is kindled against you and against your two friends, for you have not spoken of me what is right, as my servant Job has." Here God clearly rejects the friends' arguments that Job must have sinned and is being justly punished by God, and with that rejection it also appears that God is rejecting the entire notion that people suffer because they have sinned or to strengthen their faith or to teach them a lesson. This is what Job's friends have been saying all along, and God is angry with them for assuming that they can know the mind of God. Job, on the other hand, has spent the entire book

---

16. One clue to dating the Book of Job is its parody of some of the Psalms; one passage in particular gives us additional insight on the author's views of the place of human beings within the universe. Psalm 8:4–5 reads, "What are human beings that you are mindful of them, mortals that you care for them? Yet you have made them little lower than God, and crowned them with glory and honor." Then we read Job's satirical response to the Psalmist: "What are human beings, that you make so much of them, that you set your mind on them, visit them every morning, test them every moment? Will you not look away from me for a while, let me alone until I swallow my spittle? If I sin, what do I do to you, you watcher of humanity? Why have you made me your target? Why have I become a burden to you?" (Job 7:17–20).

questioning and raging against God, doubting God's justice and God's goodness. And God says that Job was the only one who got it right!

At the end of the book, God restores Job's fortune and gives him new children, so that everyone lives happily ever after. But does this ending make sense within the context of the entire book? The central argument of the Book of Job seems to be that sometimes people suffer for no reason, that bad things can and do happen to good people, and that this is simply part of what it means to be human. By restoring Job's fortune and family at the end of the book, the author seems to be contradicting the central message of the book by suggesting that if we just endure our suffering we will eventually be rewarded. Some scholars believe that this epilogue was added at a later date by an editor who was uncomfortable with the theology being espoused in the original book.[17] This appended restoration story seems to wrap everything up in a nice neat bow and reassure readers that good things will eventually happen to good people, that life is fair after all. But there is another possible interpretation of the epilogue that is more consistent with the message of the book: perhaps Job is being rewarded precisely for his daring to doubt, for showing the audacity to be angry with God and to demand justice, even if he is ultimately disappointed. Perhaps God is rewarding Job for having the courage and the passion to confront God. How often do we confront issues of injustice and unfairness in the world or in our own lives? How often do we struggle to reconcile the reality of pain and suffering with a good and loving God? How often do we feel compelled to rage against God for creating and governing a world that refuses to make sense to us? And how liberating might it be to realize that this is exactly what we should be doing? That this righteous anger, this passionate doubt, is the proper response to injustice and suffering and despair, compelling us to throw ourselves wholeheartedly into the mysteries of the world, to love our fellow human beings deeply and without reservation, to pursue justice and righteousness in spite of seemingly insurmountable obstacles, even when we don't have all the answers and we don't know how it will all work out?

---

17. Notice, too, that God never mentions the bet with the Satan, which seems to suggest that the bet is also an addendum to the speeches forming the heart of the book. Surely God would have mentioned the bet to Job, especially because Job appears to have won the bet for God! But God never mentions the bet, nor does God ever mention the Satan's arguments in God's speeches. This is a good indication that the bet is from a different textual tradition and not originally related to the speeches that form the heart of the Book of Job.

The Book of Job is famous for its lack of easy answers or comforting conclusions. Some of the passages can shock us once we understand what is going on in the text, once we recognize that the Book of Job is a powerful critique of simplistic theologies of suffering and a necessary reminder that human beings are not God and cannot possibly know the mind of God. It is also a wonderful example of a passionate, mature, gritty faith. At the beginning of the book, Job doesn't spend too much time thinking about God in any real depth because everything is going well in his life. He worships God and loves God, but his relationship with God seems to be rather superficial. But by the end of the book, once he has experienced tragedy and loss, once his initial picture of God collapses and he's forced to go deeper, he discovers a far richer, more robust picture of God than he ever dreamed possible. He shouted and wept and raged against God, but he never gave up on God, and he finally realized that God was right there with him all along.

Job is a helpful reminder that doubt and even anger can be signs of a strong and healthy faith, as counterintuitive as that sounds, because God was always Job's ultimate concern. An analogy can be instructive here. When we have a fight with someone, which fight is more intense and heated: a fight with a total stranger or a fight with a loved one, like a sibling or a parent or a partner or a best friend? For most of us, we fight the hardest with those we love the most. We don't care enough to fight with a total stranger (unless we just like fighting for its own sake, in which case we have bigger problems!). We fight with those we love because we care, because we are passionate, because those relationships matter to us, and because we trust that a fight won't break the deep and lasting bond between us. This is what it was like between Job and God. Job always trusted that God was there and that God was listening, even as he shook his fists toward the sky and heaped up scorn on God. And when God showed up and responded to Job, even though God didn't answer any of Job's questions, the simple fact that God was there through it all was enough for Job.

Job never lost his faith in God, but Job's beliefs about God changed dramatically from the beginning to the end of the book. This is another helpful reminder to us about the difference between faith and belief. What we believe about God is a good and necessary way of fleshing out and describing and clarifying our faith in God, but our beliefs about God (what theologians call "doctrines") are not identical with our faith. Beliefs and doctrines can and do change all the time, for all sorts of reasons.

But a change in doctrine doesn't mean that we've lost our faith; it just means that the old ways we had of thinking and talking about and making sense of our faith no longer work. That's precisely what happened to Job. He used to think that bad things happened to bad people and good things happened to good people and that the world was inherently just and fair. But a powerful experience shattered those beliefs and he was forced to construct new beliefs, new doctrines about God, the world, and human life. Doubt is a powerful tool once we understand its function and use within faith, as the Book of Job so aptly demonstrates. And perhaps nowhere else in the Bible is doubt so praised and even celebrated than in the Book of Job.

Ivan Karamazov's "Euclidian Mind"

Job lived to change his mind about God and, as the ending of the Book of Job relates, he died "happy and full of days" (Job 42:17). But what happens when someone doesn't survive their suffering? What sense can we make of God and faith when the suffering is so intense and relentless that it utterly destroys a person? This is the theme of another classic meditation on the problem of evil and suffering, Fyodor Dostoevsky's novel, *The Brothers Karamazov*. For our purposes here we're particularly interested in the relationship between two of the Karamazov brothers, Ivan and Alyosha, specifically a conversation they have about the horrifying suffering of innocent children and what that suffering might teach us about God, human nature, and the world.[18]

Ivan Karamazov is a cynical, tortured young man who more than anything else wants the world to make sense, and he turns away from traditional Russian ways of life to embrace the modern Western European worldview of the Enlightenment for answers. His brother, Alyosha, is a novice Orthodox monk, earnest if a bit innocent and naïve about the ways of the world. They meet in a tavern to catch up on their lives and their conversation soon turns to the problem of evil and suffering. Ivan enjoys toying with his brother by calling Alyosha's deepest beliefs and commitments into question, and Ivan has come prepared with a collection of news clippings about the suffering of children. Ivan wants

---

18. The relevant chapters for our discussion are helpfully contained in an excerpt of the novel published separately as *The Grand Inquisitor and Related Chapters from "The Brothers Karamazov."*

to know how anyone can live in a world where innocent children suffer so gratuitously and needlessly, and he almost relishes the opportunity to share these gory examples with his brother, at least partly in an attempt to destroy Alyosha's faith.

Ivan tells the story of a little girl whose respected parents regularly beat her and sometimes lock her in the outhouse at night, smeared head to toe in human excrement. The little girl has no idea why her parents are treating her so cruelly, and she weeps alone in the dark, fetid hole, crying her meek tears to "dear, kind God" to save her. In another story, Turkish soldiers take perverted pleasure in torturing babies in front of their mothers, by throwing them up in the air and catching them on their bayonets or by putting a pistol in a baby's face and making it laugh before blowing its brains out. Other soldiers have refined a method of humiliation and torture where they nail prisoners to fences by their ears and leave them overnight before executing them in the morning. In a particularly horrible story, a young serf on a rural manor is playing with the lord's favorite hunting dog and accidentally injures the dog's paw with a rock. The lord of the manor sees his favorite dog limping and asks what had happened. He then brings the boy and his mother out into the courtyard, has the boy stripped naked, and commands the child to run before setting his hounds loose. The dogs rip the boy to pieces in front of his mother.[19]

Ivan wants to know what kind of world this is where such cruel and awful things can happen to small children. He insists on limiting his stories to children because children are innocents who in no way deserve these terrible fates. What kind of God would create a world where these things happen? And what moral responsibility do we have in such a world? We sometimes dismiss these stories as "bestial cruelty," but that, Ivan says, does a profound disservice to beasts, because no animal would ever think to devise elaborate cruelties to torture a victim just to humiliate them, like solders nailing prisoners to fences by their ears. Only human beings can be "artistically cruel." And by calling these crimes "bestial" it ultimately relieves us of the responsibility to confront the darkest parts of human nature that allow us to perpetrate such horrors on our fellow human beings. Decades later, the Soviet Russian novelist and dissident Aleksandr Solzhenitsyn suggested that "the line dividing good and evil

---

19. In the course of his research for the novel, Dostoevsky collected these and similar stories from contemporary newspapers. Each of these things really happened.

cuts through the heart of every human being."[20] Ivan is laser-focused on this line, wondering why it is there in the first place and what we can do to keep ourselves from crossing that line again and again and again.

Ivan poses each of these questions to Alyosha, who is more interested in listening to his brother than in answering his questions. Ivan wants to know what hope there is of justice in a world such as this. In traditional Christian teaching, all will eventually be made right and whole in heaven, but Ivan can't imagine that any future harmony would wipe away the moral stain of a boy being ripped apart by dogs in front of his mother. Even if his mother forgives his torturer, that doesn't erase the boy's suffering. No "heavenly glory," no future harmony, no final accounting will ever make up for the senseless suffering of that little boy ripped apart by a cruel lord's dogs, even if that lord were to spend eternity suffering in hell for his crimes.

Ivan eventually arrives at one of his main points: if the devil doesn't really exist, but human beings created the devil, then human beings obviously created the devil in our own image, for only human beings can be as savagely, brutally cruel as the acts we typically associate with the devil. We can't handle the implications of owning that level of cruelty and evil of which we're all capable, so we project it outside ourselves onto "the devil," relieving us of the responsibility to confront and eradicate the evil residing deep in our own hearts. We don't want to acknowledge Solzhenitsyn's line that runs straight through our own heart, so we will do anything to avoid the implications of our capacity for profound evil and indifference to the suffering of others.

Ivan has one last card to play, as he confronts Alyosha with the hypocrisy of worshipping the God who created such a world. Ivan proposes a thought experiment to his younger brother, the novice Orthodox monk: if he could create an entire universe free of pain and suffering, but that one little girl weeping alone locked in an outhouse must suffer so for eternity, would he do it? Alyosha admits that he would not.[21] For Ivan, there is no satisfactory answer to the question of suffering, especially the suffering of innocent children. Adults, he poses, deserve whatever happens to them because "they've eaten the apple" (Gen 3) and know better. But children don't know better. Children are innocent, and it's

---

20. Solzhenitsyn, *The Gulag Archipelago*, 75.

21. For an updated version of this scenario, see Le Guin, "The Ones Who Walk away from Omelas."

the suffering of children that most viscerally upsets us for precisely this reason, regardless of how we might interpret the doctrine of original sin.

For Ivan, the world must make sense or he will go mad. He admits that his understanding has significant limitations thanks to his weak, "Euclidean" mind, but surely there must be justice, some reason for all of this senseless suffering. He just can't imagine what that reason might be, and he doesn't want to accept the reason even if he can figure it out. It's the baseness, the pettiness, the meanness of humanity that threatens to drive him mad, and he reminds Alyosha that if the devil doesn't exist, human beings would have to create the devil in our own image, just to make some sense of the evil we see all around us. But even granting the existence of the devil wouldn't solve the problem because the suffering would continue, and we would still live in a world where innocent people suffer and die all the time. For Ivan, the problem here isn't God, but the world God made. Ivan accepts that God might have a plan or might have some way of redeeming all of this suffering, but that's not enough for him because he wants justice now, and if he's dead, he wants to be raised from the dead so he can see this justice for himself. But he's not holding his breath, and eventually he decides that the only morally defensible solution to this problem is to "respectfully return [God] the ticket": suicide.[22]

In the thought-world of Dostoevsky's novel, Ivan represents a nihilistic worldview that Dostoevsky satirizes and rejects as incompatible with the Russian soul and with the Christian faith. For Ivan, it is paramount that everything make sense to his "Euclidean mind." He wants justice as *he* understands it, right now. And when things don't work out that way, he wants to "return his ticket" because he can't bear to live in a world where things don't make sense. It's ultimately not the suffering itself that enrages him; it's the lack of straightforward answers. Unlike Job, Ivan has no prior commitment to God, in fact no genuine faith at all: he is committed above all to his own understanding and his own righteous indignation. The one thing Ivan never considers in his almost sadistic recounting of his stories of children's suffering is what he himself might *do* about it. His anger is not ultimately directed toward the actual suffering of the children; rather, his anger is directed at its incomprehensibility. The children are little more than props in his arguments against the injustice of the world and he uses them cynically to attack Alyosha's own faith.

---

22. For a brilliantly witty character study of Ivan, see Vicchio, *Ivan & Adolf: The Last Man in Hell*.

At the beginning of his conversation with Alyosha in the tavern, Ivan mentions how difficult he finds it to love people. Loving humanity in general is easy, or so he says. But loving individual people, loving one's neighbor here and now, he finds virtually impossible. And here is the key to Ivan's troubles: he can't bring himself genuinely and selflessly to love another flesh-and-blood human being. Humanity in the abstract—the *idea* of humanity—Ivan can love. But a unique, individual human being standing across from him face-to-face, here and now, that person Ivan is incapable of loving genuinely and selflessly.

Later in the novel we see Dostoevsky's implicit response to Ivan's arguments in the story of Father Zosima, Alyosha's elder at the monastery. Where Ivan finds it impossible to love another human being and instead focuses on satisfying his own desire for understanding and an abstract sense of justice, Fr. Zosima reverses this and insists that the key to a meaningful human life in the world is generous, selfless love for all creatures, what the New Testament calls *agape* love. To ignore the suffering of another creature because their suffering does not make adequate sense is ultimately to contribute to their suffering, and to wait until everything makes sense means never to relate authentically to another human being. For Fr. Zosima, the only meaningful response to evil and suffering is compassionate love ("compassion" literally meaning "suffering with"), which alone has the power to transform and redeem both the victim and the perpetrator of evil and suffering. Here Fr. Zosima offers a profoundly Christian response to Ivan's Enlightenment skepticism and despair. Just as Christ emptied himself of power and divinity to suffer even death on a cross for the sake of human beings (Phil 2), Christians are called to empty themselves of pride and self-importance, to love the neighbor unconditionally, never stopping to ask whether our neighbor is worthy or deserving of love. Our neighbors—whoever they are—are worthy and deserving of love simply because they are human beings created in God's image, just like you and me.

In both the Book of Job and *The Brothers Karamazov*, serious questions are raised about the nature of evil and suffering and the character of God in light of human suffering. For many people, these are precisely the questions that threaten to overpower faith and hope and they are instructive examples of the important role existential doubt plays in faith. Oftentimes there is a strong temptation to insist on an answer to these questions that resolves the tension, such as "Everything happens for a reason" or "It's just God's will." These can indeed be comforting responses to experiences of suffering or loss, but if we push them to their conclusions they tend to lead us into untenable positions, either by minimizing the reality of evil and suffering or by saying things about God that most Christians would not want to say. Sometimes these answers are accepted without much careful thought, but sometimes they are used deliberately to silence doubts that arise when what we believe about God and the world no longer makes sense of our lived human experience.

God's Power, God's Goodness, and the Problem of Evil

We have these doubts for a reason, and we ought to embrace them rather than ignore or suppress them, even when they make us deeply uncomfortable. In a classic essay, "Evil and Omnipotence," Australian philosopher J. L. Mackie addresses these questions head-on and exposes perhaps fatal flaws in typical Christian solutions to the problem of evil and suffering. Mackie embraces the questions raised by the problem of evil and follows them to their logical conclusions, wherever they might lead. The chief question he considers is how evil can exist when God is supposedly omnipotent (all-powerful) and omnibenevolent (all-good). For the sake of clarity, Mackie further defines omnipotence has having unlimited power to do whatever an omnipotent being wills to do, and he further defines omnibenevolence as always desiring to eliminate evil. An omnipotent God should have the power to create and sustain a world without evil in it, and an omnibenevolent God should want to do just that. And yet it is painfully obvious that evil does exist. Mackie is asking a question as old as the Book of Job, but the questions are framed in even starker terms by the Scottish philosopher David Hume in the eighteenth century in his book, *Dialogues concerning Natural Religion*: "Is [God] willing to prevent evil, but not able? Then is he [sic] impotent. Is he able, but not willing? Then is he malevolent. Is he both able and willing? Whence then is evil?"[23]

Over the two millennia of the Christian tradition, theologians have offered numerous potential solutions to this dilemma, but Mackie critiques four of the most common proposed solutions: there can be no good without evil, evil is necessary as a means to good, the world is better with some evil in it than with no evil, and evil is due to human free will. Mackie argues that each of these proposed solutions has fatal flaws that

---

23. Hume, *Dialogues concerning Natural Religion*, 63.

fail to safeguard the truth of all three propositions: God is omnipotent, God is omnibenevolent, and evil exists.

The first two arguments are closely related and can be analyzed together: there can be no good without evil, or evil is necessary as a means to good. These are two of the most common proposed solutions to the problem of evil and the argument is a simple one: just as we can't perceive dark without light or cold without heat, and just as we can't get in shape without the exertion of hard physical exercise, we have no way of perceiving, appreciating, or achieving the good without evil. If there were no evil in the world, we would have no conception of the good because it would just be the way things always are, something like the old joke of a fish never knowing that it's wet. The presence of evil provides a necessary contrast that allows us to recognize and appreciate the good, so that the good moments are more intense and enjoyable because we can compare them to experiences of evil and suffering. The second solution suggests that the presence of evil provides the initial impetus to achieve the good so that without evil there would be no possibility for the good to exist.

These arguments do make sense to a point, but when we push them we can see that they can easily lead us to some unsatisfying and sometimes even horrifying conclusions. For example, if we accept the first solution we would have to say that God allows genocide, rape, torture, murder, cancer, etc., to happen so that we can appreciate the good things in life. The tragic death of a family in a car accident would happen so that I can learn to have a deeper appreciation of my own family and my good fortune at not dying in a car accident. If we accept the second solution, we would have to say that genocide, rape, torture, murder, cancer, etc., must exist so that good things can happen as a result. For example, according to this argument, God allows cancer to exist so that researchers and physicians are compelled to do their research to improve the quality of human life and also so that all of us can become more compassionate toward cancer patients and more committed to philanthropic causes dedicated to eradicating cancer. In both cases, there is ultimately no reason to resist these evils because they are necessary for the good. Both of these solutions fail to safeguard God's omnipotence and omnibenevolence because an omnipotent God could create goodness itself and also our awareness of goodness without also having to create evil, and an omnibenevolent God would want to eradicate evil, not purposely build it into the structure of the world. So these first two solutions fail on both counts.

The third solution, that the world is better with some evil in it than it would be without evil, is a bit more nuanced but also fails when we push it to its conclusion. In this solution, human beings are able to develop higher moral and spiritual capacities by resisting evil and responding to suffering than we could ever hope to develop without this struggle. For example, if we were bullied as a child, we might develop a more expansive sense of compassion, kindness, and friendliness. Or if we see news reports of hurricanes or droughts or fires or mass shootings, we might be inspired to donate money or blood or time to relief efforts. This argument also makes sense to a point, but what the solution fails to acknowledge is that, just as there are higher-order moral and spiritual capacities, there are also higher-order evils to counterbalance them. A first-order moral capacity might be kindness, which responds to meanness. But a second-order evil such as vindictiveness can overpower kindness, which in turn requires a second-order moral capacity, such as self-giving love. Then a third-order evil such as sadism can counter that second-order moral capacity, and so on, *ad infinitum*. In theory, there will always be a commensurate evil to counteract any good, and we have ample evidence of this in the annals of human history. Furthermore, this third solution also fails to safeguard God's omnipotence and omnibenevolence, because an omnipotent God should not need higher-order evils to create higher-order goods, and an omnibenevolent God should not want to encourage the existence of evil for any reason. A common rejoinder to this critique is to claim that God *could* prevent evil and suffering, but God *allows* it to happen anyway for some inscrutable reason. This response affirms God's omnipotence, but it fails to safeguard God's omnibenevolence, because an omnibenevolent God would never allow evil to exist for any reason, no matter what good might result in the end.

The final solution Mackie critiques is perhaps the most common way of attempting to reconcile God's omnipotence and omnibenevolence with the existence of evil. This solution proposes that evil is not God's responsibility at all, but ours. Instead of blaming God for creating a world with evil and suffering as necessary and inevitable, this solution proposes that evil and suffering are due to the misuse of human freedom. God created human beings with free will and we choose to misuse our freedom to do evil, which inevitably results in suffering. The key to this argument is that it offers a more nuanced defense of God's omnipotence and God's omnibenevolence while acknowledging the reality of evil. God is omnipotent, but it is the nature of freedom to be beyond controlling;

otherwise we would be little more than puppets or robots, not genuinely free agents. God is omnibenevolent, but God cannot intervene in free human choices to prevent evil, even if God wants to do so. Human freedom, if it is genuinely free, must be beyond anyone's control, even God's. We alone bear the responsibility for the consequences of our choices and we often choose wrongly, resulting in evil and suffering in the world.

So far, so good. But if we push this argument to its conclusion, we can see that it, too, suffers from fatal flaws. First, if God is omnipotent, couldn't God have created human beings so that we always freely choose the good? Is there anything inherent in freedom itself that requires us sometimes to make the wrong choices? We clearly do make the wrong choices, and we do so quite frequently, but is that the inevitable result of freedom itself, or is it something of a "design flaw" in human nature? Further, an omnibenevolent God would want to eliminate even the possibility of evil results of our free choices, and this omnibenevolence, coupled with omnipotence, should have resulted in free human beings who always freely choose the good. But that's not what happens. If we counter these arguments by suggesting that God couldn't create genuinely free human beings who always freely choose the good, then we're implicitly denying God's omnipotence. On the other hand, if we suggest that God could create genuinely free human beings whom God subsequently can't control, then we're again implicitly denying God's omnipotence.

This is what Mackie calls the "paradox of omnipotence." However we frame the question, either way we answer it we end up denying God's omnipotence. The classic example is to ask if God can create a boulder so big that God can't move it. If we say yes, God can create a boulder so big that God can't move it, then there's something God can't do (namely, move the boulder). If we say no, God can't create a boulder so big that God can't move it, then there's something God can't do (namely, create a boulder so big that God can't move it). To update this example with the help of *The Simpsons*, Homer Simpson asks his pious Christian neighbor, Ned Flanders, if Jesus could microwave a burrito so hot that Jesus couldn't eat it. Ned immediately recognizes the paradox and can't answer the question (his actual response is vintage Flanders: "Well, as melon-scratchers go, that's a honey-doodle!").[24] Some will counter that there are all sorts of things God can't do that don't compromise God's omnipotence, such as creating a square circle or water without oxygen or hydrogen. A free

---

24. https://www.youtube.com/watch?v=JhhXCuUG2pw

will that always freely chooses the good, they argue, should be included in these logical absurdities. But there is nothing *logically* absurd about always freely choosing the good (even if it's never happened in practice), unlike the obvious logical absurdities of a square circle or water without oxygen or hydrogen atoms. So that argument, too, falls flat.

We're left in a difficult position. It would seem that it is impossible to maintain all three of the original propositions: God is omnipotent, God is omnibenevolent, evil exists. Each solution proposed to maintain all three ultimately fails. The only way out, it would seem, is to modify or eliminate one of the propositions. We can say that God is powerful, but not all-powerful, or that God is good, but not all-good, or we can say that God is not at all powerful or not at all good, or we can say that evil doesn't really exist. In the aftermath of the twentieth century it's exceedingly difficult to suggest seriously that evil doesn't exist (although some theologians and philosophers, beginning with Augustine, do take this approach by defining evil as a lack of the good, a *privatio boni*), so it would seem that we're left with modifying or rejecting either omnipotence or omnibenevolence. And there are many examples of both approaches in the history of the Christian tradition and even in the Bible itself. The "omnis" (omnipotence, omnibenevolence, omniscience, omnipresence, etc.) are not themselves biblical terms or concepts, but rather were borrowed from Greek and Roman philosophy and incorporated into the Christian theological tradition. There is biblical precedent for questioning God's absolute goodness while maintaining God's absolute power (we can read the Book of Job in this way), and there is also biblical precedent for questioning God's absolute power while maintaining God's absolute goodness (Philippians 2 is a classic example). How we approach this question has a lot to do with what formulation most adequately expresses the content of our ultimate concern, which is what all theological doctrines are meant to do.

Faith, Doubt, and Doctrine

The relationship between doctrines and faith, as Mackie's critique reminds us, is a helpful reminder of the difference between belief and faith and between methodological doubt and existential doubt. The academic discipline of theology is, at its core, the rational reflection on and critical analysis of the faith of the church, especially its symbols and doctrines.

These doctrines function somewhat like beliefs, as they are finite attempts to express, systematize, and make sense of what Christians mean when they do theology: talk (*logos*) about God (*theos*). Where those doctrines no longer make sense, either in terms of internal cohesion or in terms of lived experience, they must be amended or sometimes even discarded as no longer having anything meaningful to say about God, humanity, or the world.

Just as Descartes used methodological doubt to question what he thought he knew about the world, theologians use methodological doubt to submit doctrines and beliefs to critical scrutiny to determine what is true about what Christians have thought and continue to think about God. For theologians, existential doubt is often the catalyst for this methodological inquiry into the truth of doctrines. Job is a particularly instructive example of this process, as his existential doubts about the meaning of his life and the character of God prompted him to rethink and refine his understanding of God, the world, and human experience. Job's doctrine of God underwent profound and even cataclysmic changes over the course of the book, as he discovered that his earlier beliefs about God were incapable of making sense of his experience of profound, unjustified suffering. His friends, on the other hand, continued to force their preconceptions about God onto Job's experience, despite the obvious fact that their doctrines of God were woefully inadequate to the task. While God remained Job's ultimate concern (in other words, he remained faithful to God throughout the book), what he believed about God (his doctrine of God) was radically altered by the end of the story.

Mackie's essay follows a similar pattern. He begins with some assumptions about God operative in most Christian communities and proceeds to submit those assumptions to unflinching critical analysis, showing how these beliefs suffer from internal contradictions and often fail to make sense of our own experience. As a result, one or more of those propositions must be altered or perhaps even discarded for the sake of logical consistency and fidelity to the Christian tradition and its convictions about God, humanity, and the world. And while Mackie himself was an atheist, we need not necessarily commit to atheism to take Mackie's challenges seriously, provided we understand the relationship between belief and faith as we've been discussing both concepts.

The problem of evil and suffering highlights the important and necessary role existential doubt plays in faith, and Mackie's essay reminds us of the contributions methodological doubt can make towards clarifying what we think and say about God, humanity, and the world. Each of the main figures we've encountered in this chapter—René Descartes, Job, Ivan Karamazov, and J. L. Mackie—embraced doubt as a powerful tool for discovering truth and meaning. Likewise, each of these figures approached their questions and commitments with a tool every bit as powerful and indispensable as doubt, and this tool will be the focus of our next chapter on reason.

Chapter 3

Reason

REASON IS ONE OF those concepts that is exceptionally tricky to define. We all know the word and we all assume that we know exactly what it means, but when we're pressed to give a precise definition we will often struggle to put it into clear language. Oftentimes we find ourselves using the word or some variation of it in the definition, which is always a telltale sign that we don't really know what we're talking about. "Reason," "rational," "reasonable," "rationality": these are words that we read, hear, and use all the time, but when we need a clear definition of exactly what we mean, we sometimes find that their precise meaning is rather hard to nail down.

Reason sometimes gets a bad rap these days, connected as it is with facts and evidence and research and careful, critical thinking. We often prefer to follow our gut, our hunches, our instincts, our desires, our preconceived notions and biases and prejudices and ideologies, rather than submit our assumptions to careful scrutiny and sustained investigation to follow the evidence wherever it might lead us. But without reason we would be adrift in a sea of shifting opinions, unable to determine what is true and false, unable to rely on the facts and evidence to guide us toward the truth. Reason plays such a central role in what it means to be human that it is even contained (ever so subtly) in the name of our species: *Homo sapiens* ("wise human"). Without reason, we would be unable to make sense of the world around us, to solve problems, to generate ideas, to think deeply, to be creative, to develop language, to form communities, to think and act morally and ethically, to wonder, to make meaning, to be fully human. Everything that we are as human beings depends on our ability to use our reason!

Two Types of Reason

It should come as no surprise by now that, like faith and doubt, reason is a more complex concept than it first appears. Tillich distinguishes between two types of reason: what he calls "technical" or "instrumental" reason and what he sometimes calls "ontological" reason,[1] but for the sake of consistency I'm going to call this second type "existential" reason. "Technical" reason is the type of reason most people mean when they use the word: it is reason as logic, as cognition, as problem-solving, as the tool we use to sift through the evidence to determine the facts, to understand relationships of cause and effect, and to make sense of finite reality. "Existential" reason, on the other hand, is our capacity for freedom, for creativity, for language, for art, for morality, for culture, for wonder and awe, for self-transcendence, for making meaning in our lives; it is what makes us fully human. Technical reason is reason as it relates to the finite world, and as such it is closely allied with methodological doubt and belief. Existential reason, on the other hand, is reason as it relates to the infinite realm, and as such it is closely allied with existential doubt and faith. Technical reason is reason "in the sense of scientific method, logical strictness, and technical calculation." Existential reason is reason "in the sense of the source of meaning, of structure, of norms and principles." Technical reason "gives the tools for recognizing and controlling reality," while existential reason "is identical with the humanity of man [sic] in contrast to all other beings. It is the basis of language, of freedom, of creativity. It is involved in the search for knowledge, the experience of art, the actualization of moral commands; it makes a centered personal life and participation in a community possible."[2] To put it simply, technical reason determines what is true and false; existential reason determines what is meaningful.

Technical reason is one of the gifts that makes us unique as a species, as no other creature that we know of has such a profound capacity for logical, instrumental thought. Although there are many examples of other animals using technical reason, the human animal has used technical reason to achieve all of the wonders of human civilization in a way that no other species can match. Technical reason has given us the ability to control fire, to invent the wheel, to create mathematics and science, to map our world, to explore outer space, to develop the internal combustion

1. Tillich, *Systematic Theology*, vol. 1.
2. Tillich, *Dynamics of Faith*, 75.

engine and the internet and the smart phone: the "tech" in "technical reason" corresponds to our human knack for developing increasingly more sophisticated "technology" (both rooted in the Greek word *techne*, which means "craft," referring to the capacity to make things and to do specific tasks). Technical reason marshals all the available evidence, sifts through it, weighs the options, and determines the facts of the matter in its never-ending quest for knowledge. Technical reason also gives us the capacity to take everything we've learned about finite reality and to apply it to our mastery of the world around us (what we might call its "technological" application). Technical reason is our best way of dealing with finite reality when determining what to believe as we seek to settle our methodological doubts. Every time we solve a problem, every time we determine the best way to accomplish a task, every time we invent a better way of doing something, every time we learn something new about the world around us, we are using technical reason.

Descartes' Rationalism

One champion of the power and promise of technical reason was René Descartes, whom we met in the previous chapter. For many centuries before Descartes, everything around us was assumed to possess some sort of innate reason, some innate purpose, some goal toward which it was striving. Understanding the world meant aligning oneself with the patterns and trajectories that pushed us closer to the goal toward which all existence was tending. The Greek word philosophers and theologians often use to describe this purpose is *telos*, which means "goal," "end," "aim," "completion," or "perfection." When ancient and medieval philosophers and theologians used the word in this sense, all things could be said to have "reason," because all things were assumed to have their own *telos* and are therefore headed somewhere, have some aim or goal, some divinely determined end.

But as we saw in the last chapter, Descartes threw all of that into radical doubt, going so far as to doubt the very existence of God, the external world, and even himself. In other words, he questioned whether there was any infallible, inscrutable "mind" directing us and everything around us toward some predetermined goal. He doubted *everything*, and what he discovered as a result of that radical methodological doubt was that the only thing that could not be doubted was his existence as a thinking thing, as a rational agent. Even when he doubted his own existence, he must still exist in order to doubt. With this one move Descartes revolutionized philosophy and science, installing the concept of the "rational subject" at the center of the modern project. The thinking, reasoning individual subject was now the center of the universe, an agile mind sifting through the evidence of the senses and thinking its own pure thoughts to determine what is true and false about the self, the world, and God.

Canadian philosopher Charles Taylor, in his book *A Secular Age*, describes the transition from pre-modern to modern thinking about the self by pointing out a crucial shift in how people thought about the relationship between themselves and the world around them. Before the modern period (initiated in large part by thinkers such as Descartes), people thought of themselves as "porous selves," as open to influences from the world around, above, or beyond them, as absorbing information and influences from natural and supernatural sources, which they then incorporated into a holistic worldview, so that they felt themselves to be in tune and even in a sense enmeshed with everything around them, as part of the larger whole of reality. After Descartes, people thought of themselves as "buffered selves," as somehow isolated, removed, and cut off from the world around them, standing aloof and observing the world from afar, "objectively" learning its patterns and secrets in order to name and understand and ultimately control reality from an epistemic distance. After Descartes, human beings discovered a newfound pride of place at the center of the universe, occupying a privileged position "outside" the whole from which to know and understand reality as a collection of distinct, independent objects.

As we saw in the last chapter, Descartes precipitates this shift by calling everything he thought he knew into question using methodological doubt. He questions the evidence of his senses, he questions the existence of a good and loving God, he questions the reality of the physical world, and, finally, he questions his own existence. Once he's managed to question the existence of everything around and beyond him, he's left with one incontrovertible truth: he alone *must* exist to ask any question at all. He alone exists to ask questions and to determine what is true and what is false. He has invented the modern subject.

Descartes rejects the evidence of his senses as the sure and certain foundation of his beliefs because he has observed that his senses can and do deceive him all the time. If he wants to discover sure and certain knowledge, then he knows he can't trust his senses to provide it. So he turns inward, to his own rational faculties, and he therefore marks an important shift from Empiricism to Rationalism. He uses an example of wax to illustrate his argument. He imagines sitting by a fire holding a piece of beeswax. He observes it carefully and makes a note of everything he can know about this piece of wax through his senses. It is solid, cool to the touch, a pale yellow color, and it smells and tastes faintly of honey. All of his senses are telling him that this is obviously a piece of beeswax. But then he puts the wax in a dish and moves it closer to the fire. As the wax warms, it starts to lose its shape as it melts and becomes a liquid. It is now hot to the touch, colorless, and it no longer smells or tastes of anything. Every sensory property of the wax has changed, and yet he knows that it is still wax.

How does he know it's still wax, if not from his sense perception? Descartes concludes that he knows this through his powers of reasoning alone. Using his reason, he knows that wax has different properties when it is in different states. His senses have given him the raw data, but it's his mind, his powers of reasoning, that allows him to draw conclusions about what this substance really is. Despite the changes to all of its observable physical properties, he knows it is still the same beeswax. If he relied on his senses alone he would have to conclude that these are two different substances, but because he has the ability to reason he knows that it is really the same substance in two different states. For Descartes, this is a compelling argument in favor of technical reason as the arbiter of truth and knowledge, and this is why Descartes prefers Rationalism to Empiricism.

But he doesn't stop there. In the first meditation he resolved to put everything into doubt, including even the existence of a good and perfect God, presuming instead that God could be an evil genius intent on deceiving him about the existence of the world and even his own existence. In the third meditation, Descartes returns to this question because without knowing that he is not being deceived, he can't hope to know anything at all about the world around him, even if it really exists. So Descartes sets himself the task of proving the existence of a good and perfect God, using technical reason alone.

He goes about this in a few different ways. First, he notices that he has this idea (what he calls a "clear and distinct perception") of a good and perfect God already in his mind before he's ever thought too much about it. Where does that idea come from? Is it an "adventitious" idea, something we receive through our sense perception, like the physical characteristics of the wax he studied in the second meditation? Is it a "fictitious" idea, something we make up out of thin air using our powers of imagination, like a unicorn or a hippogriff?[3] Or is it an "innate" idea, something implanted in our minds from birth?

Descartes quickly realizes that the idea of God can't be an adventitious idea because we don't have any sense perceptions of God like we have of the things all around us. The idea of God also can't be a fictitious idea because we are finite, limited creatures and God is infinite and perfect, so our making up the idea of God would be like making a copy that was clearer than the original, and that doesn't make sense to Descartes. If we were the creators of all reality, surely we would have created ourselves to be perfect and infinite, but clearly we are neither perfect nor infinite. And the very fact that we recognize our imperfections and limits could only be possible if we already had some idea of perfection implanted in us, in comparison to which we recognize our lack of perfection. This means that because we finite beings have the idea of perfection in our minds, it could only have been placed there by an infinite being (God). Descartes describes this idea of God in our minds as being something like the stamp a potter puts on the bottom of their pots, saying to anyone who sees it, "I made this." The idea of God in our minds, and, by extension, our rational minds themselves, are for Descartes powerful proof of the existence of a good, perfect, infinite God.

But Descartes takes another angle on the question to provide additional rational proof of God's existence. He wonders where he himself came from and he immediately thinks of his parents. But where did his parents come from? They had parents too. And what about them? They also had parents. We can extend this line of argument to any object in the finite world. Everything around us is the effect of a prior cause, which is itself the effect of a prior cause, which is itself also the effect of a prior cause, and so on and so forth, *ad infinitum*. But this line has to stop somewhere; otherwise the human race and everything else in the world would be infinite, but that's obviously not the case. Somewhere back the line there had to be a "first cause," and that first cause must be God. But what

3. While it might come as quite a shock to fans of the *Harry Potter* series, J. K. Rowling did not invent the hippogriff; it's there in Descartes' *Meditations,* over 350 years before Hagrid introduced Harry, Hermione, Ron, et al. to Buckbeak! And to complicate matters even further, Descartes in turn was drawing on a long history of hippogriffs, reaching all the way back to the classical Latin writer Virgil in the first century BCE. As it turns out, there really is nothing new under the sun, not even hippogriffs.

caused God? According to Descartes, God must have caused Godself. God is the cause of God, the "first cause." Everything that exists needs a cause, and that includes God because God exists, but if God is perfect, then only a perfect being could cause God, and since God alone is perfect, God must be the cause of God, the one and only "self-caused cause."

At first glance this sounds perfectly reasonable, at least to Descartes, but when we take a closer look it doesn't really make much sense at all. How can something be its own cause? That's like you being your own mother and father! But for Descartes, technical reason requires him to say that God is the cause of God because everything that exists has to have a cause, including God, and because God is God, God must be the cause of God. Several centuries before Descartes, in the Middle Ages, there were a lot of theological arguments about this question, but no one ever suggested that God caused Godself, because that doesn't make sense, and if God is perfect Truth, then the idea of God certainly can't be nonsense! The great medieval theologian Thomas Aquinas preferred to say that God was the "uncaused first cause," that God doesn't have a cause: God simply *is*, by necessity, eternally, without beginning or end. But for Descartes that argument doesn't pass muster because technical reason demands that *everything* has a cause, and that includes God. The field has changed hands: now it's Reason that judges everything, including God.

I don't want to get too bogged down in the details of Descartes' arguments here, but for the record I'll say that I think his arguments fail miserably *as proofs*, precisely because there can be no proofs when we're dealing with the infinite reality. Technical reason is our best tool for dealing with finite reality, but technical reason is punching far above its weight class when dealing with infinite reality. I side with Blaise Pascal, another French philosopher from a few decades after Descartes, who walked around France with a piece of parchment sewn into the lining of his coat that read, "God of Abraham, God of Isaac, God of Jacob, not of philosophers and scholars."[4] Pascal knew that even the best philosopher could only "prove" a woefully inadequate caricature of God, not the living God of the Bible and the Christian tradition. Once we're dealing with the ground of being, the Alpha and Omega of all that was, is, and shall be, the irreducible mystery at the heart of all existence, we're way past the limits of technical reason. Or, to put it another way, as Hamlet chided

---

4. See Pascal, *Pensées*, 266.

Horatio, there are more things in heaven and earth than are dreamt of in our philosophy.

Having said that, I'm much more interested in highlighting what Descartes is doing in these arguments and why, rather than getting tangled up in the minutiae of his arguments and their conclusions. In the *Meditations* Descartes is utterly uninterested in any of the traditional ways of thinking about or relating to God. It's true that philosophers long before Descartes pondered arguments for God's existence, but they always did so with the assumption that the reality of God was so obvious and so real that it didn't require logical proofs to accept. Perhaps the most famous of the medieval "arguments for God's existence" (and I put that in quotes on purpose!) is Anselm's ontological argument from his *Proslogion*, in which he argues that God is that than which nothing greater can be conceived. This argument is always included in textbooks on medieval philosophy and on the philosophy of religion, but we make a serious mistake if we ignore *how* Anselm made this argument. He includes these reflections on the reality of God's existence within the context of a prayer addressed to God. He is not making a philosophical argument to persuade a nonbeliever to believe in God so much as he is attempting to flesh out, as best he knows how, the sheer obviousness of God's reality in his life and in the life of his monastic community. Anselm wasn't interested in trying to convince a skeptic to believe that God really exists; he was much more interested in providing his fellow monks a fuller and richer appreciation for the bountiful presence of God in their lives, in their prayer, and in their work. Anselm begins from the assumption that God is more obviously real than everything else we can possibly conceive: so plentifully, bountifully real that our task is simply to describe that reality in terms that might make some glimmer of sense to our finite human minds.

Descartes, however, has a fundamentally different purpose in mind in the third meditation. He is not at all interested in prayer, liturgy, or devotion. Not once in the entire third meditation does he ever refer to scripture or tradition, the two primary sources of Roman Catholic doctrine. He cites no biblical texts, no theologians, no popes, no authorities whatsoever. He relies entirely on his own powers of reasoning to prove anything and everything, even God. This had never really been attempted before in the history of Western thought, and it marked a profound sea change in the Western intellectual tradition. For Descartes, the individual subject stands at the center of the universe and determines the truth of all things based on technical reason alone. Reason has become judge and jury, and everything—even God—must pass Reason's tests before it can be determined beyond a shadow of a doubt to be true.

John Caputo, a popular contemporary philosopher of religion, also notices what Descartes is up to in the third meditation, and his thoughts on Descartes' approach are worth quoting at some length:

> Notice what has happened here. God, the subject matter of theology par excellence, has come under the principles of reason, which are the jurisdiction of philosophy, rather than reason coming under God, the subject matter of theology. God has to stand in line like everyone else; what's fair is fair. Both finite and infinite beings must pass in review under reason's scrutiny. God, in effect, gets in line, gets shrunk down, is cut to fit the principles of reason, and theology now becomes a "particular discipline" . . . monitored by the higher principles of philosophy, which keeps watch over all knowledge and all science generally. But from a theological point of view, no matter how high you heap your praise of God, if that praise is based upon measuring God by the tests written and administered by reason, you are debasing God, even if God comes out first in his [sic] class by your standards. In theology, where God is first, last, and always, God is the one who sets the standards, not the one who is measured by them, even if God is up to the test. What theologians ultimately worry about when it comes to the philosophers is that they have a tin ear for religion and theology, that they do not understand its distinctive discourse and form of life, so that even when they are offering arguments on behalf of God, the philosophers are still getting it wrong.[5]

It's not terribly difficult to grasp the earth-shattering importance of Descartes' move here, even if he ended up going too far by applying technical reason to the infinite realm where it can rightly have very little to say. Suddenly, human beings were the center of the universe, and around our new center we discovered objects and patterns and processes to be understood and eventually mastered and controlled for our own ends. The entire world was opened up for our discovery, analysis, manipulation, and even exploitation. We began to subject nature to scientific experimentation, we studied human beings, human history, and human institutions to determine patterns and trajectories in order to understand, to control, and to direct them toward our own ends. Human beings became the final measure and standard for judging reality, and as a result

---

5. Caputo, *Philosophy and Theology*, 27–28.

we sought to bend reality to our own will and needs. It's worth noting that Descartes is writing in the midst of a scientific revolution, in the heat of the Age of European Exploration and not long before the Industrial Revolution, all rooted in the power of human reason.

The Limits of Technical Reason

And what a world we created with this newfound power of technical reason! We harnessed the power of fire, water, air, electricity, and the atom, we named the species all around us with precision that Adam himself would envy, we created efficient machines and assembly lines to produce work-saving devices like laundry machines and vacuum cleaners and chainsaws and electric drills and automobiles and airplanes and computers and smartphones, we developed medicines to cure diseases that once decimated populations, we refined agriculture to grow enough food to feed the entire world, we put human beings on the moon, and once we let that genie out of the bottle we never looked back. So much of our contemporary world can be traced back to Descartes' insistence that technical reason can tame and master the world, and very few of us would want to go back to a world where those conveniences didn't exist. And yet, we've also used technical reason to create nuclear weapons, spy drones, antibiotic-resistant viruses, pollution, climate change, and so many other threats to the wellbeing of the planet and ourselves. Technology, and technical reason, is always a double-edged sword. None of this occurred to Descartes, of course, because he was the pioneer, the first to suggest a new way forward, and we can perhaps cut Descartes a little slack for his overweening pride in the newfound powers of technical reason. We can cut him some slack because we recognize the power and potential of technical reason to give us a clearer sense of finite reality and to propel us forward in our quest to understand nature and to make our lives demonstrably safer, healthier, and longer than our forebears could ever dream possible. None of us would prefer to live in the thirteenth century instead of the twenty-first century, because, for example, none of us would want to die of the plague thanks to a total ignorance of basic hygiene, sanitation, and epidemiology. We value the advances we've achieved thanks to technical reason because it has made our lives quantifiably better in so many ways.

Technical reason has inarguably done wonders for our understanding of ourselves and our world. Without technical reason we would still be huddling in caves, eking out a miserable existence totally dependent on the whims of nature to keep us alive. So even if Descartes had a tendency to overestimate the proper scope of technical reason, it remains the key to our contemporary digital, globalized, technological society. We wouldn't be the creatures that we are today without technical reason. And yet we would be well-served to take a step back and reflect on just what we've unleashed with this limitless confidence in technical reason. Have we become more humane, more loving, more just? Have we managed to address the deepest longings of the human spirit through technical reason? Have we solved the riddles of death, despair, and meaninglessness, questions that have plagued humankind from the first moments we could ask these questions? We don't seem to be any closer to answering these questions today than we were hundreds or even thousands of years ago (for a quick reminder, flip back to the last chapter and reconsider the Book of Job). But perhaps we ask too much of our capacity for technical reason. Perhaps we need to return again to the fundamental distinction between technical reason and existential reason, to understand what tool we ought to use to address the questions our existence raises in our collective consciousness. Existential reason takes us down the path of meaning and value, but it can't answer questions of concrete concerns like how to feed a planet of more than seven billion people or how to keep the climate from warming to a level that is incapable of supporting human life. Those are questions for technical reason, and technical reason is an indispensable tool for solving the concrete, immediate problems we confront every day as the human race.

Yet technical reason is under attack these days because sometimes its findings conflict with what we deeply, dearly *want* to be true. Sometimes we feel the need to choose between our heart and our head, between what we want to be true and what the evidence clearly shows us is actually true. We might have a vested interest in affirming some facts and denying others, or we might have been taught for our entire lives that something is true when it turns out that it isn't, or we might reject the clear evidence in front of us because the evidence conflicts with our firmly-established worldview. In earlier chapters we discussed topics such as the origins of the universe, evolution, and climate change, all of which are hotly debated topics in our contemporary society. But if we allow technical reason to be our guide in these matters, we must accept that these are, in fact, settled questions. The origin of the universe is understood by cosmologists in most of its details, even if some of the details continue to elude them (it's also worth pointing out that Georges Lemaître, the first scientist to suggest the Big Bang Theory as a plausible description of the origin of the universe, was a Jesuit monk and priest). The evolution of the human species from earlier hominid species is well-established. Climate change is an incontrovertible fact and we see its effects all around us all the time, with increasing frequency and urgency.

The debate in these cases is not between two competing perspectives relying on technical reason, but between one perspective using technical reason and one perspective using emotion, or ideology, or cynical manipulation of public opinion. Facts are facts, and technical reason is the tool we ought to use to make sense of those facts in order to establish true beliefs. Emotion or ideology or opinion have no standing in this case, because facts rooted in finite reality have clear standards of proof, rooted in methodological doubt and technical reason. What we *want* to be true doesn't (or at least it shouldn't) enter into the discussion, however much we might wish otherwise.

Technical reason relies on evidence, rigorous examination and experimentation, deduction and induction, and clear-headed marshalling of the facts of the matter to determine what is true and what is false. There is overwhelming evidence that the universe is billions of years old. There is overwhelming evidence that life on Earth evolved over millions of years and that modern humans emerged from a long and winding road of evolutionary stops and starts leading to you and me. There is overwhelming evidence that the climate is warming and that human activity (use of fossil fuels, destruction of forests, unsustainable consumption patterns, etc.) is largely to blame. These are settled facts, determined by methodological doubt and technical reason. Beyond the "bigger picture," we see that technical reason plays a vital role in our day-to-day lives as well. For example, technical reason determined that we need to cook that chicken to a temperature of approximately 165 degrees Fahrenheit to avoid the possibility of getting sick. Technical reason determined that we must vaccinate our children to avoid devastating communicable diseases. Technical reason made it possible for me to write this book on a laptop and for you to read it across a number of platforms. Technical reason figured out the key to controlled combustion that allowed many of you to get to school or work by automobile, bus, train, or airplane. Technical reason allowed our ancestors to figure out how to build permanent structures using materials such as clay and stone and lumber and concrete and steel, without which we all would be sleeping outside tonight. Every luxury and convenience we enjoy as modern human beings can be traced to our use of technical reason.

And yet, we seem to be infinitely capable of abusing this gift. Technical reason has also allowed us to develop weapons so powerful that they can destroy civilization in a matter of minutes. Technical reason has given us the ability to exploit and abuse our natural home. Technical reason has been misused and abused to divide human beings into races and classes and ethnicities and genders and sexualities to determine who is "fully human" and who is not. Technical reason has given us the power to wage war, to abuse nature, to oppress and dehumanize fellow human beings, to assume that our rational abilities give us the status of conquerors and lords of the universe. Technical reason, on its own, is value-neutral; it is a double-edged sword. It can be used for good or it can be wielded for evil, and even the most cursory glance at human history reminds us that we are more than capable of using technical reason for good and for ill.

It is vitally important to remember that technical reason never operates in a vacuum. It is a tool used by flesh-and-blood human beings, each with our own history, culture, language, worldview, biases, assumptions, and agendas. While the capacity for technical reason is universal among human beings, exactly *what* is deemed "rational" is often dependent on the specific culture within which technical reason is employed. For centuries it was assumed that only males could be fully rational, while females suffered from mental deficiencies, either because, as Aristotle thought, women were underdeveloped men, or because, as other ancient Greeks thought, women tended to suffer from "hysteria" (literally "wandering womb"). For centuries it was assumed that only white males of European descent could be fully rational participants in and beneficiaries of political and economic life, while women and people of color were assumed to be inherently deficient, irrational, congenitally susceptible to emotion and superstition, incapable of being fully human. And we could make a very long list indeed of beliefs and behaviors that were once presumed to be eminently rational that now we regard as deeply flawed, incorrect, or even offensive. I'll let Caputo speak for those of us who want to be careful not to absolutize technical reason, who want to be sure that we remain cautious of assuming that our own perspective is always the norm, who want us to be suspicious of turning finite "reason" into hubristic "Reason":

> Because the Enlightenment had too narrow an idea of what "reason" means and too chauvinistic an idea of where it is to be found, for the longest time it placed the crown of reason on white male European heads, whose duty it was, it said with its eyes cast heavenward, to spread Euro-white maledom around the globe. . . . To this day, the indigenous peoples of the Western world, as well as women of all races, and non-Westerners of every stripe, endure and have endured enormous suffering to drive home the full length and breadth of the egalitarian forces that the Enlightenment set loose.[6]

We do very well to remember that reason, like all other human faculties, is a *human* faculty, which means that it is finite, limited, prone to misuse and abuse, inherently flawed. Human beings have an innate tendency to elevate whatever we personally happen to believe to the status of universal truth. We have a tendency to allow the victors to write the history, to allow the powerful to define the terms, to assume that whatever the privileged few believe and assert is universally valid. But we would do well to remember that technical reason, like every other human faculty, is inherently limited and contingent. This means that we must always add to our use of reason a healthy dose of humility, a willingness to acknowledge and accept that sometimes we are shortsighted, mistaken, and occasionally even catastrophically wrong. Without that acknowledgement of our finite human limitations, reason can all too easily become Reason, with its absolutist tendencies that brook no disagreement, that equate different perspectives with heresy or rebellion, that all too often respond to healthy disagreement with lethal force. Our capacity for technical reason is one of the most human things about us, but it is also one of the most dangerous tools we possess.[7]

Existential Reason

But technical reason is only one aspect of reason. The other aspect of reason is just as important for a life well-lived, even if it's often ignored in our contemporary world. And this other type of reason is often the best tool we have to keep our worst tendencies and baser instincts in check. This other type of reason is what I'll be calling "existential" reason. While

---

6. Caputo, *Philosophy and Theology*, 38.

7. To see more clearly how our human capacity for technical reason and technology is always a double-edged sword, see Freud, *Civilization and Its Discontents*.

technical reason deals solely with the finite world, existential reason deals with the infinite reality, with all that transcends our mundane, quotidian concerns. In *Dynamics of Faith*, Tillich stresses the idea that the human personality is an integrated whole, which means that anything that threatens to divide the human personality must be treated as a threat to human wellbeing. What he means here is that we ought to develop patterns of thought and modes of being that integrate each part of ourselves into a harmonious whole, so that we are capable of responding to and integrating anything that comes our way throughout our journey through life without splitting our personality into warring factions.

While technical reason is our main tool for making sense of the finite world, existential reason operates on a different plane. Existential reason is the human capacity for transcendence, for wonder, for creativity, for freedom, for complex language, for art, for morality, and for so much more. So much of what makes us distinctively human is rooted in our capacity for existential reason. The "spark" that animates humanity, the sense of "something more," the deep and abiding desire to make our lives meaningful, the endless drive to create, the yearning for justice, the awestruck wonder we experience when we step back from our daily lives and reflect with sheer amazement on the beauty and improbability of our even being alive: we can do all of these things thanks to existential reason.

Perhaps most importantly for our reflections in this book, existential reason is that capacity in us to be grasped by and to respond to the infinite reality that is relentlessly seeking us out and luring us forward throughout our lives. The medieval theologians, going all the way back to Augustine, liked to define reason as the human being's *capax dei*, the "capacity for God." Reason in this mode is the intersection, the crossroads, where the finite and the infinite meet in the human being. We are capable of faith because we possess existential reason, and it is this capacity that makes us most fully human because it is also our capacity for creating art, music, and literature, for developing complex languages and symbol systems, for reflecting on the past and anticipating the future, for debating what is right and what is wrong, for desiring the good, the true, and the beautiful, for delighting in discovering the secrets of the world all around us through scientific investigation, for establishing religious traditions with their scriptures, rituals, practices, and worldviews, and, through it all, for making meaning in our lives; in short, existential reason is our capacity to be ultimately concerned.

Just like we saw with faith and belief and with existential doubt and methodological doubt, existential reason and technical reason deal with two different levels of reality. Technical reason gives us the tools to understand, manipulate, and control finite reality, while existential reason is the capacity for relating to the infinite reality that gives us meaning and value. And because the human being is a centered personality, there can be no inherent conflict between our faculties; there is only conflict where there is a misunderstanding or misuse of one or more of the parts. This means that these two types of reason—technical reason and existential reason—can't conflict with one another, and neither can conflict with faith, if we properly understand faith as ultimate concern in the infinite reality.

If faith is misunderstood as believing in something finite with little or no evidence, or, even worse, believing in something finite when there is very strong evidence *not* to believe it, then obviously faith and reason (especially technical reason) will be in conflict. But if we understand faith as the state of being ultimately concerned, as an existential commitment of our entire being to the infinite, unconditional, ultimate reality, and if we understand existential reason as the uniquely human capacity for transcendence, for freedom and creativity, for having a sense and awareness of the infinite, then faith and reason can't possibly contradict one another or be in conflict with one another. They are absolutely essential for one another and cannot be separated. As Tillich puts it, "If faith were the opposite of reason, it would tend to dehumanize man [sic]. . . . A faith which destroys reason destroys itself and the humanity of man. For only a being who has the structure of reason is able to be ultimately concerned."[8]

So how are faith and reason related? According to Tillich, "[existential] reason is the precondition of faith; faith is the act in which reason reaches ecstatically beyond itself."[9] What Tillich means here is that existential reason is what makes faith possible, and faith is our reaching beyond ourselves toward the infinite reality that transcends the finite realm we inhabit. "Ecstatic" literally means "standing outside of," so in faith we "stand outside of" our finitude and reach for the infinite. Because we have existential reason, we are able to recognize our finitude, which also somewhat paradoxically means that we are able to transcend our own

---

8. Tillich, *Dynamics of Faith*, 87.
9. Tillich, *Dynamics of Faith*, 87.

finite limitations, to take a step back and realize that there's something "more" than the finite reality that is most familiar to us ("transcend" literally means "to climb across"). This something "more" is the ultimate, infinite reality, which we describe using symbols drawn from finite reality. Because each of us is a rational creature and therefore has a sense of this ultimate, infinite reality, each of us has faith, even though we use different symbols to talk about it: some call it God, some call it YHWH, some call it Allah, some call it Brahman, some call it Ek Onkar, some call it the Dao, some call it Sunyata or Nirvana, some call it the Good, some call it Justice, some call it Truth, some call it Love, and some use other images or symbols for this ultimate reality, but each of us is ultimately concerned with whatever it is that gives our lives meaning and purpose, whatever symbols we use to name it.

If we pay attention to what really matters to us, what really has the capacity to give our lives meaning and value and depth and fulfillment, we'll recognize what Tillich means by the relationship between faith as ultimate concern and existential reason as our capacity for transcendence and meaning and creativity and imagination. A helpful way to think about what this means is to think of existential reason as what Genesis 1 calls the "image of God" in the human being: existential reason is that point of contact between our own finite nature and the infinite, ultimate reality, that awareness we have of "something more," which is what makes it possible for us to have faith in the first place. As Tillich puts it, "Reason is the presupposition of faith, and faith is the fulfillment of reason. . . . There is no conflict between the nature of faith and the nature of reason; they are within each other."[10] This is why human beings are the only creatures who have faith, because human beings are the only creatures (that we currently know of) who have the capacity for transcendence, who have freedom and creativity and imagination, who ask questions of meaning, and who seek to "stand outside of" and "climb across" their finitude to connect with the infinite.

So from this it's clear that faith and existential reason are not only compatible but are absolutely essential for one another, just as faith and existential doubt are absolutely essential for one another (and now, hopefully, the title of the book finally makes sense!). But faith is also compatible with technical reason, again because the different components of our personality cannot be in permanent conflict. Here, too, everything

---

10. Tillich, *Dynamics of Faith*, 88.

depends on properly understanding faith as ultimate concern and not as belief in something finite with little or no evidence or as belief in something finite when there is actually very good evidence against it. The key is to remember that faith deals only with the infinite and belief deals only with the finite. Once we remember that, we shouldn't have any problems.

Because the recent history of Christianity has been so frequently marred by conflicts between religion and science or religion and historical scholarship, Tillich spends quite some time discussing the relationship between faith and technical reason, especially between faith and scientific knowledge and between faith and historical knowledge. We use technical reason to acquire scientific and historical knowledge about finite reality (beliefs) and it's not a coincidence that these tend to be the battlegrounds for perceived conflicts between faith and reason. Above all, in this context it's especially important to remember that faith is not belief in something finite with little or no evidence, nor is it simply assent to certain propositions about finite reality; this is belief, not faith. When faith becomes nothing more than acceptance of certain propositions about finite reality (such as Noah really putting two of every animal on the ark or Jesus really walking on water), it is no longer faith. Beliefs—dealing with the finite—are established using technical reason and have to do with facts that we learn from science and history; faith—dealing with the infinite—is built on the foundation of existential reason and has to do with symbols and myths that we learn from religion but also from literature and music and art. As long as we maintain this distinction between faith and belief, there shouldn't be any conflict between faith and reason in either its technical or existential mode.

Faith and Science: Two Spheres of Reason

This is especially the case in many of the supposed conflicts between science and faith, such as those concerning the origin of the universe or the evolution of species. Because faith is not belief in or acceptance of certain propositions about finite reality (such as the origin of the universe or of the human species), there needn't be any conflict whatsoever between faith and scientific knowledge. This is because science deals only with finite reality and faith deals only with infinite reality. They are two different dimensions, and conflict only arises when either science or faith oversteps its bounds and infringes on the other's "turf." To put this another way, if you have a question about what might have happened at the very beginning of our universe in the Big Bang, you should ask a physicist, not a theologian or a pastor. But if you have a question about what it means to live after the Big Bang in a universe that is understood symbolically as creation, as a good gift of God, you should ask a theologian or a pastor, not a physicist. This is because science deals with concrete facts and religion deals with symbolic narratives, which are two unique but equally useful and indeed necessary approaches to truth.

An even simpler way of saying this (maybe even an oversimplification, but we'll risk it) is to say that science asks "how" questions while religion asks "why" questions. Science investigates finite reality—mechanisms, causes and effects, empirical evidence—and offers preliminary conclusions based on rigorous testing with the help of methodological doubt and technical reason. Religion is concerned with questions of meaning and value and it responds to these questions using existential doubt and existential reason. Science and religion can learn from one another, but they can't conflict with one another when they both stay within their proper spheres. The evolutionary theorist Stephen Jay Gould described religion and science as "non-overlapping magisteria," or "NOMA."[11] Tillich says something quite similar when he argues that "science has no right and no power to interfere with faith and faith has no power to interfere with science. One dimension of meaning is not able to interfere with another dimension. If this is understood, the previous conflicts between faith and science appear in a quite different light."[12]

Faith and belief occupy their own spheres and have their own "turf," so that no conflict should arise as long as we recognize where those boundaries are and we don't confuse one for the other. We live in a world forged by modern science, philosophy, and historical understanding, *and also* religion, literature, art, and music. We swim in these complementary waters all the time, usually without even realizing it. To borrow from Genesis 1 once again, if God is the creator of the entire universe and everything in it, and if God declared everything God created to be "very good," then, so Tillich's argument goes, that must mean that our

---

11. Gould, "Nonoverlapping Magisteria."

12. Tillich, *Dynamics of Faith*, 94. It's worth mentioning that when Tillich wrote *Dynamics of Faith* in the 1950s, he assumed that the conflicts between some Christian groups and scientists over topics such as evolution were a thing of the past (notice that he refers to *previous* conflicts in this passage). As we know all too well, Tillich was certainly wrong about that!

use of reason was intended by God for discerning truth wherever and however we might discern it. Thomas Jefferson once counseled a friend to "fix Reason firmly in her seat, and call to her tribunal every fact, every opinion. Question with boldness even the existence of a God; because, if there be one, he [sic] must more approve the homage of reason than of blindfolded fear."[13] Or as Galileo insisted in response to the Roman Catholic Church's efforts to silence him, "I do not feel obliged to believe that the same God who has endowed us with senses, reason, and intellect has intended to forgo their use and by some other means to give us knowledge which we can attain by them."[14] What he means is that if God gave us a brain, then we should use it! And he suffered greatly for this conviction. Galileo had observed the heavens with telescopes he himself invented and he determined, based on those observations using technical reason, that Nicolaus Copernicus was right when he proposed that the Earth revolved around the sun. But the scientific and theological orthodoxy of his day insisted that the Earth was the center of the universe and that the sun revolved around the Earth. Was Galileo to ignore the results of his careful experiments? Of course not. He insisted that what he observed was true, despite the protests of his ecclesiastical adversaries, because he had the evidence on his side. And we know now that Galileo was right.

Pushing Galileo's insights even further, we can ask a deeper question: if, as all theistic religious traditions have always claimed, God is the ultimate source of all truth, then is it possible for one truth to contradict another truth, whether that truth is scientific, historical, philosophical, or religious? It all depends on what dimension we're dealing with and what tools we're using to reach that truth. As long as we recognize the proper boundaries of each search for truth, we don't have to worry about conflicts. But if we forget those boundaries or try to erase them, we end up with big problems. Tillich agrees:

> [Faith as the state of ultimate concern] liberates the faithful from a burden they cannot carry after the demands of scholarly honesty have shaped their conscience. If such honesty were in a necessary conflict with what has been called the "obedience of faith," God would be seen as split in himself [sic], as having demonic traits; and the concern about it would not be ultimate

---

13. Jefferson "Letter to Peter Carr, August 10th 1787," 399.
14. Galileo, "Letter to Madame Christina of Lorraine," 183.

concern, but the conflict of two limited concerns. Such faith, in the last analysis, is idolatrous.[15]

To put this more simply, what Tillich is saying here (and he stands in a long line of Christian theologians stretching all the way back to Augustine in the fifth century) is that if we think there's a conflict between faith and what we know by reason, then we're not understanding faith or reason (or both) correctly. We don't have to check our brains at the church door! To use an extreme example, if we think that faith requires us to believe that there's no such thing as gravity, even though technical reason gives us overwhelming evidence that gravity really does exist, so that we want to prove our faith by jumping out of high buildings and trust that we'll float gently down to the ground and not hurtle helplessly to our death, then we're misunderstanding faith. This would be confusing faith with belief, and a bad belief at that, because this is a belief that contradicts the overwhelming evidence for the reliability of gravity. Or to use a potentially more controversial contemporary example, if we suppose that faith means taking Genesis 1 and 2 literally and rejecting the overwhelming evidence we have for the Big Bang and for evolution, then we're misunderstanding faith as belief and confusing symbolic religious narratives with scientific facts, rather than understanding faith as ultimate concern and existential commitment to the infinite, ultimate reality, which must be expressed symbolically rather than literally. Faith is the commitment and trust of our entire personality, but in this example of misunderstanding we would also be required to reject our reason, which is an essential part of what makes us human.

This applies just as much to those cases where the best scientific research seems to support our faith as when it seems to contradict our faith. For a long time it was believed that the Earth was stationary and the sun and the moon and the stars and planets revolved around the Earth. That happened to line up exactly with the scientific assumptions of the Bible, so many Christians felt justified in pointing to the best science of the day to claim support for their faith. But that is a category mistake, because faith has nothing to do with scientific conclusions about finite reality. For a very long time the best science of the day *did* line up with and seemed to support specific religious beliefs, but then the science changed and suddenly those same Christians were forced to make a choice: accept the

---

15. Tillich, *Dynamics of Faith*, 102.

new data and conclusions provided by science, or reject them because they supposedly conflicted with their faith.[16]

In this misunderstanding of faith we would have to reject part of ourselves (namely our technical reason) to be ultimately concerned, and God would simultaneously demand and refuse our whole self. Clearly this can't work. This is what Tillich means when he says that a faith that destroys reason ends up destroying faith itself. Faith as ultimate concern works harmoniously with existential reason and existential doubt, just as belief works harmoniously with technical reason and methodological doubt. It's only when we confuse these categories that we end up splitting ourselves into conflicting parts. A good example of this confusion is a quote attributed to William Jennings Bryan, the star witness for the prosecution in the famous Scopes Monkey Trial of 1925,[17] in which he shares a common view that highlights the dangers of confusing faith with blindly believing clearly irrational and impossible statements of fact. Bryan allegedly said, "If the Bible had said that Jonah swallowed the whale, I would have believed it simply because the Bible said it." Whether or not Bryan ever actually said this, it reveals a common temptation to take leave of one's rational faculties when approaching questions of faith and religious commitment. But if we understand faith properly, there's no need to resort to clearly false beliefs such as a human being swallowing a whale, or a whale swallowing a human being and spitting him up on shore three days later for that matter (Jonah 1:17, 2:10), in order to claim a strong faith. Understanding the distinction between faith and belief and between existential reason and technical reason allows us to keep our brains firmly inside our heads wherever we go, even through the church doors. If we recognize the distinction between faith and belief and maintain their proper boundaries, we affirm the unity of our personality and the harmony of all three of our most human faculties: faith, doubt, and reason.

16. For more on the significance of these "paradigm shifts" in the history of science, see the classic work of Thomas Kuhn, *The Structure of Scientific Revolutions*.

17. For a detailed historical analysis of this famous trial and its implications for understanding the relationship between faith and science, see Larson, *Summer for the Gods*. Fast-forward to the early 1980s and another famous trial focusing on the relationship between faith and science: *McLean v Arkansas Board of Education*, featuring one of Tillich's star students, Langdon Gilkey, as a witness for the ACLU. Gilkey argued that teaching creationism as science in Arkansas public schools violated the Constitutional separation of church and state. For Gilkey's own account of the trial and his deeply Tillichian commitments, see Gilkey, *Creationism on Trial*.

Faith, Reason, and Transcendence

As we can see, it is vitally important that we understand the relationships between the various faculties we possess as human beings. We have a sophisticated "toolbox" full of finely-tuned instruments that help us navigate our way through our lives. Methodological doubt and technical reason allow us to make sense of the finite world around us, to have an accurate understanding of reality, to know what to believe and why. But we have a capacity to set our sights higher than the world around us. We have the ability to wonder, to dream, to aspire, to ask questions we can never hope to answer. Even though we are finite creatures inhabiting a finite world, we sense that something more is going on, something within or beyond ourselves and the world we experience with our senses, something that gives life its flavor, its intensity, its deeper meaning. We yearn for this "something more," we want to possess it and be possessed by it, we crave depth and breadth and zest. We're not content just to exist: we want to really *live* our lives with a sense of purpose and meaning. For most of us, we soon realize that our day-to-day existence isn't enough to give us that deeper meaning and fulfillment. We find that if we only attend to immediate concerns, we never seem to get anywhere. Our lives begin to feel flat, dull, and ultimately pointless. It's only when we raise our sights higher, or when we plunge ourselves ever deeper into the world, that we begin to get an inkling of that "something more" that's stirring within the daily concerns and cares we all share.

For Tillich, this "something more" is the infinite reality that transcends the finite reality we inhabit every day. The infinite reality is always beyond our reach and beyond our possession, but we can't turn away from it; we never stop reaching for it, because we know deep down that therein lies the key to the meaning of our lives. And we feel, somehow, that this "bigger" reality, this "something more," this hint of the infinite, is already reaching out to us before we ever try to reach out to it. We feel grasped, possessed, claimed by this "something more" in a way that is difficult to describe. We experience it only in fleeting moments, in snatches and gasps, in serendipitous occasions or random encounters. But when we do experience it, we feel that we're finally fully alive, that life has meaning and purpose and dignity, that things are getting really *real*. In the Christian tradition the word for this experience is "grace." But more often than not, we're searching for this "something more" rather than possessing it. We're restless because we want to own that "something more" as a possession, but it's constantly eluding our grasp.

This feeling is nothing new. In the closing years of the fourth century, Augustine wrote in his *Confessions* (generally considered the first autobiography ever written), "You [God] have made us for yourself, and our heart is restless until it rests in you."[18] He knew all about the restlessness of the human spirit, the ceaseless striving for meaning and purpose, the never-ending quest for something more. Augustine tried to satisfy those desires with sex, career, and fame, but he never felt satisfied until he realized that finite things can never satisfy our deepest longings. He only found peace and fulfillment and meaning when he climbed across ("transcended") the daily concerns and struggles to pursue a more lasting peace. Eventually he recognized the insistent, persistent pleading of the infinite reality in his life: "Late have I loved you, beauty so old and so new: late have I loved you. And see, you were within and I was in the external world and sought you there."[19] All the while, God was nearer to Augustine than Augustine was to himself. God was always there, relentlessly searching for him. The ever-present knocking on the door of his very being was always there, but he refused to acknowledge it, until he finally let down his guard and accepted that God was already there, waiting for Augustine to acknowledge God's presence, a presence even more obvious than Augustine's awareness of his own self.

This capacity we have for asking existential questions, questions about the meaning and purpose of our lives, is existential reason. This capacity for asking these deeper questions also compels us to write, to paint, to compose, to build, to reflect, to seek wisdom, to love, to pursue justice, to wonder, to be brought up short before the profound mystery and beauty of the world and of our lives. Our hearts are indeed restless, so we throw ourselves into the perennial human quest for meaning, responding to the nudging, whispering presence of that "something more" that is always just beyond our reach but is at the same time always closer to us than we are to ourselves.[20]

Many cultures throughout history have told stories about heroes who leave their home to experience the world in all its magnificent beauty and threatening danger. The hero often has a quest, a task to be

---

18. Augustine, *Confessions*, 3.
19. Augustine, *Confessions*, 201.
20. For more on this "whispering presence," see Caputo, *The Insistence of God*.

completed that will reveal to them the deepest secrets of their lives and of the world we all inhabit. The hero sets off on their journey not knowing where it will lead, but they throw themselves completely into their task, trusting that they will finally attain something of great value: they will receive their own deeper, fuller humanity as a gift, as a treasure to be shared with others. Joseph Campbell, in his book *The Hero with a Thousand Faces*, traces this archetypal pattern through dozens of myths from around the world, which he describes collectively as a "monomyth" (read Campbell's book and then watch the original *Star Wars* trilogy or *The Lord of the Rings* series again to see exactly how this works!). Each of us, in our own way, is a "hero" like the heroes of these ancient tales. We each have our own quest for meaning and significance. We each have a burning desire to discover the purpose and the meaning of our lives. Our individual stories might never be recorded or passed down from generation to generation, like the heroes of old, but each of us in our own way does heroic work, lives heroic lives, persistently seeking the meaning of it all. More than anything else, we want our lives to *matter*.

If we're lucky, like Augustine, we'll eventually realize that what we've been seeking all along is the infinite reality, what Augustine learned to call "God," the reality that makes sense of our lives and everything we experience all around us. But oftentimes we come up short and we can't say for certain that there actually is anything out there to discover that will help all of this make sense. Sometimes when we take a step back from our lives to reflect on them, all we discover is more questions. Or sometimes we take that step back and we suddenly realize that we tend to take many things with far more seriousness than they rightfully deserve. What we're dealing with in these moments is the sneaking suspicion that life is absurd, that there is no inherent, obvious deeper meaning or lasting significance to our lives. We have on average eighty years on this planet, if we're lucky, and then we're gone. A new generation takes our place, destined to ask the same questions without getting any closer to the answers than all the generations before us. We're left to wonder, finally, if there is any objective, inherent meaning of life out there to discover, or if the point is to create some meaning for our lives that works for us here and now and to accept that this is the best we can do.

The Absurdity of Life

The American philosopher Thomas Nagel, perhaps most famous among undergraduate philosophy students for writing an essay called "What Is It Like to Be a Bat?" wrote another essay called "The Absurd," in which he raises precisely the questions we're pondering here. Nagel agrees that the ceaseless quest for meaning is one of the most human things about us, one of the capacities that makes us unique among the animals (at least as far as we know). What makes this quintessentially human quest for meaning possible is our capacity for self-transcendence, the ability we have to take a step back and ponder our own existence and ask about its meaning: in other words, our capacity for existential reason.

But what do we find when we take that step back and ask what our lives really mean? What we find might surprise us: in the end, we aren't really sure how to answer that question, at least if we're honest with ourselves. Each of us takes our lives with utmost seriousness, and yet we can't really explain why we do that. If someone asks us enough questions about why we live our lives the way we do and why we've made the choices that we've made, we'll eventually discover ourselves at a dead end, unable to say much more than, "Well, because!" And yet—and here's the beautiful thing about us—that doesn't stop us from taking our lives so seriously! The fact that we can't explain exactly *why* we search for meaning doesn't keep us from pursuing our lives *as if* they have meaning and purpose. If we're religious, we might ground the meaning of our lives in a deity, such as God. We might conclude that the meaning of our lives is somehow given to us by God, the source and goal of our existence. But even here, if we push this line of questioning far enough, we discover that we can't really know for certain that the meaning we so desperately desire will be provided by God; when it comes right down to it, we must take this on faith.

Whether or not we couch our quest for meaning in religious language and ground the meaning of our lives in a deity, if we're honest with ourselves we have to admit that we don't really *know* that we're right. This void, this lack of a concrete answer to our deepest questions, unsettles us and knocks us off our pins. And we express that discomfort in a number of ways. When we think about the vast size of the universe and realize that we inhabit a tiny rock in a small solar system in a nondescript galaxy in one corner of the seemingly infinite universe, we start to feel rather insignificant, like nothing we do really matters. If we search online for images of Earth taken from NASA's Mars mission we'll notice that our entire planet—the site of the entirety of human history, all of our triumphs and defeats, our hopes and dreams, our successes and failures, billions upon billions of lives—appears as a tiny little dot of light way out there on the horizon of Mars. And Mars is one of our closest neighbors! If we draw back a little further, even in our own solar system, our human eyes won't even be able to pick out our planet Earth. And if we expand our scope beyond our solar system, which itself comprises only a tiny speck of the vastness of the whole universe, the entire Milky Way will be totally unrecognizable and undetectable amongst the myriad stars and planets of the myriad galaxies comprising our universe.

The same feeling of insignificance looms when we think in terms of time instead of space. For example, if we were to map the history of the universe from the Big Bang to the present onto a regulation 100-yard American football field, our species, *Homo sapiens*, wouldn't arrive on the scene until 1/8th of an inch from the goal line! 99 yards and 35 and 7/8th inches of that field would have no human presence whatsoever. Everything human beings have accomplished—all of our greatest cultural achievements, all of our grand experiments in democracy and self-governance, all of our works of art, all of our scientific discoveries, all of our most meaningful relationships, all of our religious institutions, all of our hopes and fears and dreams and successes and failures—can be shrunk down to 1/8th of an inch out of 100 yards. That realization should stop us dead in our tracks, reeling at the insignificance of it all in the grand scheme of things. The German philosopher Friedrich Nietzsche told a story that powerfully captures the dizzying scope of this realization:

> In some remote corner of the universe, poured out and glittering in innumerable solar systems, there once was a star on which clever animals invented knowledge. That was the highest and most mendacious minute of "world history" — yet only a minute. After nature had drawn a few breaths the star grew cold, and the clever animals had to die. One might invent such a fable and still not have illustrated sufficiently how wretched, how shadowy and flighty, how aimless and arbitrary, the human intellect appears in nature. There have been eternities when it did not exist; and when it is done for again, nothing will have happened.[21]

---

21. Nietzsche, "On Truth and Lie in an Extra-Moral Sense," 42.

Nietzsche puts his finger on the dreadful inkling we have that nothing we do finally matters, that the universe is ultimately indifferent to us and our desire to make meaning out of our lives.

And yet, for Nagel, these comparisons miss the point entirely. If we're so insignificant in terms of time and space, then that insignificance is also insignificant as far as we're concerned. As he puts it, if nothing we do right now will matter a million years from now, then the fact that nothing we do now will matter in a million years *also* doesn't matter, so we don't need to worry about it! And the vast size of the universe also doesn't really matter, because it's not like our lives would have any more inherent and objective meaning if the Earth were the center of a much smaller universe. The fact that the universe is incomprehensibly big and incomprehensibly old doesn't change the fact that we can't nail down exactly what our lives mean and why, and that wouldn't change if the universe were only a few thousand years old and a few thousand miles across. So clearly the enormity of space and time isn't the *cause* of our sense that life is absurd; it's merely an analogy or an image we use to express our sense that maybe nothing has any inherent meaning. So we haven't really put our finger on the root cause of our feeling of absurdity just yet.

When we take a closer look at our lives, we realize that so much of what we do doesn't seem to have any grander purpose, any heroic impulse, any noble goal: we simply live our lives because that's what we do. We get up in the morning, we shower and brush our teeth, we eat breakfast and have some coffee or tea, we head off to school or work, we do our jobs, we might meet someone for a drink or dinner, we spend some downtime in the evening going for a walk or playing with our pet or spending time with our families or catching up on a show on Netflix, we go to bed, and we get up the next morning to do it all over again. Every once in a while we take a vacation that gives us the freedom to change the routine and pursue some peak experiences, and we can look forward perhaps to a few extraordinary moments where life seems to burst with meaning (graduating, finding the perfect job, getting married, having children, checking off an item on our bucket list), but the vast majority of our lives are spent on this treadmill of routine and mundane obligations. But we do it anyway, because what else are we going to do? We might have a moment when we fantasize about chucking it all and sailing around the world, or going off the grid to live in a hut deep in the mountains, but that feeling usually passes and we go back to the grind.

And that's perfectly fine! Just because we can't explain why we do every little thing at every moment of our lives doesn't mean that we should stop living our lives just the way we do.

What it does mean, according to Nagel, is that we might have to adjust our attitude and tweak our way of thinking about our lives. Nagel, apparently having a thing for musing philosophically about what animals might be thinking, asks in this essay on the absurd what it might be like to be a mouse. A mouse lives its life trying to find food, a safe place to sleep, and a mate to pass its genes on to the next generation of mice. This is the sum total of a mouse's life. Is the mouse's life absurd? No, not according to Nagel. And why is a mouse's life not absurd? Because, as far as we know, a mouse does not possess the gift of existential reason and is therefore incapable of self-transcendence. As far as we know, a mouse never stops to think about its life, where it's headed and what it all means. A mouse just does its mousy thing and exists from moment to moment, doing whatever it is a mouse does. But if a mouse *could* wonder about its own life and its deeper meaning, then a mouse's life would become absurd, because the mouse would be unable to come up with a definitive answer to that deepest, most significant question of all: what does my life *mean*?

So does that mean that the mouse is better off than we are? Sometimes we might think so, but we would be wrong. No, the mouse doesn't have to worry about what its life means, what purpose its mousy life is serving, where it's all headed. But the mouse also has very little reason to strive for anything deeper in its life, no reason to commit itself to noble ideals, no capacity to risk everything for love or justice or meaning. We humans have that capacity, even if we can't ultimately explain where it comes from or where it's headed. We have the capacity to step back from our lives and ask what they really mean. We have the capacity to pursue noble work, to give ourselves completely to another person, to throw ourselves into the world for the sake of justice, to commit ourselves without reservation to the ultimate reality, and to ponder with great profundity what it all means. Even if we can't ultimately answer those questions or know for certain if what we've committed ourselves to is worth it in the end, we do it anyway because that's what human beings do. We plow through the profound existential doubt we experience—asking, with Hamlet, "To be or not to be?"—because that's what it means to be human. We know deep-down that we don't need answers to those questions to live a meaningful life.

It was fashionable in the decades just after World War II to observe the human quest for meaning and end up in a deep despair, so much so that some intellectuals even counseled suicide as the only justifiable response to a meaningless world. Others didn't go quite so far, but they still ended up painting a picture of humanity that looked rather grim and hopeless. Albert Camus, a French-Algerian philosopher and novelist who wrote about absurdity and despair, disagreed that the only noble response to absurdity was suicide. Instead, Camus suggested that the proper human response to meaninglessness is scorn, a defiant shaking of our fist in the face of a universe that refuses to make sense to us.

In one of his most famous essays, "The Myth of Sisyphus," Camus tells the story of the mythical Greek king Sisyphus, who outsmarted the gods and tricked them into allowing him to escape death. The gods eventually got wise to Sisyphus's trickery and as punishment Sisyphus was condemned to roll a boulder to the top of a hill, only to have it roll back down to the bottom again, for all of eternity. Camus reflects on this task and its meaninglessness, and he insists that, even in his condemnation to an eternity of performing a meaningless task, Sisyphus has agency, a real choice. He doesn't have a choice about whether or not to submit to the task of rolling the boulder up the hill, but he does have a choice in how he feels about that task, in whether or not he makes meaning out of it. He can accept it as a punishment, or he can choose defiance. He can roll that boulder up the hill, watch it roll back down again, and set his shoulder to the stone again and again, shaking his fist at the gods who condemned him while vowing never to be defeated. Camus ends his essay with praise of Sisyphus, the erstwhile king condemned to an eternity of supposedly meaningless drudgery: "This universe henceforth without a master seems to him neither sterile nor futile. Each atom of that stone, each mineral flake of that night-filled mountain, in itself forms a world. The struggle itself toward the heights is enough to fill a man's heart. One must imagine Sisyphus happy."[22]

But is this all we have to hope, that we will discover within ourselves the defiant audacity to shake our fist at a meaningless universe and endure our pointless labors with a smirk on our face until we die and fade into eternal nothingness? Nagel doesn't think so. In fact, Nagel thinks that our awareness of the absurdity of our lives is one of the most beautifully human things about us. We alone, as far as we know, are capable of

---

22. Camus, "The Myth of Sisyphus," 123.

taking that step back and wondering about the meaning of our lives. And we alone, as far as we know, are capable of discovering that when it comes right down to it, we can't really explain why we take things so seriously, why we incessantly search for meaning, why we desperately hope that everything about our lives and about the world around us will finally make sense. When we realize that these questions don't have concrete answers, we can resolve to shake our fists at the cold, indifferent universe, we can succumb to escapism and flee the quest for meaning altogether, or we can despair and resort to nihilism.

But there is a fourth option: we can embrace that mystery as one of the great gifts of being a living, loving, hoping, dreaming, meaning-making human being. We can appreciate our lives all the more because our lives seem to be so improbable, so lucky, so fundamentally, irreducibly gracious. The theists among us will ascribe the gift of our very existence to a loving Creator. Other religious people will have their own ways of naming the reality that gives us life. Secular people might focus on the sheer improbability of the seemingly random encounters that produced you and me. But all of us, regardless of our particular commitments, religious or otherwise, will eventually be struck with wonder and gratitude at the amazing gift of being here at all. How did we get here? Where are we going? We have no idea, but isn't it wonderful to be alive to ask those questions!

This doesn't mean that everything is always perfect. Far from it. There is profound injustice and suffering in the world. And Nagel's conclusion reminds us that the realization that we can't determine with any certainty what it all means should compel us all the more forcefully out into the world to ensure that every being has the opportunity to live a life of dignity because, even if we can't know exactly why we're here, we should do our best to make life as dignified and meaningful as possible for all beings because, at the very least, that's what we want for ourselves. We can't explain exactly why we feel that way, but something deep in our being urges us to care for our neighbors because they, just like you and me, are trying to make their way through this life as best they can. Our capacity for self-transcendence allows us to recognize and appreciate that every human being possesses this same capacity, which lies at the heart of the Golden Rule: we must treat others the same way we want to be treated. Only by stepping outside of my own life to think about its meaning and value can I begin to acknowledge and appreciate others as having that same capacity and that same yearning. Only by stepping outside of my own self-centered concerns can I begin to understand the deep and meaningful relations I have with every human being, with every living thing, with the entire world. Only then can I affirm, with Martin Luther King Jr. in his "Letter from Birmingham City Jail," that "we are all caught in an inescapable network of mutuality, tied in a single garment of destiny. . . . I can never be what I ought to be until you are what you ought to be,"[23] and vice versa. This insight is beautifully summarized in the South African philosophy of *Ubuntu*, popularized by Nelson Mandela and Desmond Tutu: "I am because we are."

And even if, after my most sincere and earnest commitments to peace and justice, I can't come up with a definitive, final, good-for-all-times-and-all-places answer to the question of the meaning of life, so what? That shouldn't stop me from searching anyway, because that's part and parcel of what it means to be human. Not having a definitive answer to that question certainly shouldn't stop me from doing everything I can to make sure that I and my fellow creatures have every chance to make our own lives meaningful and worthwhile. Nagel's suggested response to the inherent absurdity of life isn't nihilism and despair, nor is it idealistic rage and scorn. Instead, his rebuttal is lighthearted irony. We know that we take our lives absolutely seriously, and at the same time we know, deep-down, that there's no foolproof, definitive answer to the questions we so desperately want to be answered. This could be cause for despair, but there's no reason to react so drastically to something that ultimately isn't really a problem at all. Instead, we are free to respond with humor, with good cheer, and with wit, powerful tools in their own right and not something to be so cavalierly disregarded. Nagel uses a charming example to illustrate his point: absurdity, he says, is when someone is being knighted by the queen and, in that most solemn and dignified moment, their pants fall down. This isn't a cause for despair or attempted suicide; rather, it's a moment to laugh and appreciate just how weird, wild, and wonderful is the privilege of being alive. And maybe wear a better belt next time.

---

23. King, "Letter from Birmingham City Jail," 290.

Chapter 4

The Meaning of Life

As we saw in the last chapter, our existential reason—that capacity for self-transcendence, for taking a step back and reflecting on our own lives—is one of the most human things about us. When we take that step back we hope that we will discover some inherent meaning to our lives, something that makes all of our striving and effort worth it in the end. We want everything about our lives to make sense! And yet when we do take that step back, we often find that determining precisely what our lives ultimately mean can be rather more difficult than we might have presumed. And yet that doesn't stop us from searching; in fact, it makes the search even more urgent. It's a question as old as humanity itself, and the bread and butter of any intro to philosophy course: what is the meaning of life?

Every one of us has asked this question at some point in our lives, and if you ask it constantly, you just might be a philosopher! But we all ask this question at least occasionally, regardless of our station in life. For some of us it's an extremely urgent question. For others, it's an invitation to get "deep" once in a while. For still others, the question and the search for an answer becomes a way of life. The meaning of life is perhaps *the* question because all other questions are in some sense contained within it, and we human beings will pursue any path available to us to find the answer. We might begin our search with the assumption that there is an objective meaning of life waiting to be discovered, or we might assume that the meaning of life is more subjective than that, something we must finally create for ourselves. For some of us the meaning of life will be a constant anchor that keeps us grounded and focused as we make our way into the unknown future, while for others the meaning of life might shift and evolve as our lives unfold in unforeseen directions. But regardless of our assumptions and perspectives on these finer points, each of us will inevitably seek the meaning of life because it is a quintessentially human thing to do.

Montaigne's Essays on Experience

One fellow traveler on our path toward discovering the meaning of life was an early modern French aristocrat, statesman, military leader, and amateur philosopher, Michel de Montaigne. Montaigne lived in the sixteenth century in southern France where he was born into considerable privilege and enjoyed a life of leisure, punctuated by periods of military campaigning and engagement with politics and international affairs. He was well-traveled and a keen reader of the literature of ancient Greece and Rome. He dabbled in just about every area of human inquiry and creativity imaginable, as was befitting his station and his pedigree. He spent most of his life engaging with the ideas and movements of his time and place, one result of which was a series of short reflections that he called, in French, *Essais*, a title he took from the French verb, *essayer*: "to try out" or "to test." These were the very first essays ever written, so for everyone who ever loathed the thought of writing another essay for a high school or college course, now you know whom to blame!

In his *Essays*, Montaigne set out to analyze his life down to its most quotidian, even bizarre details, so that he could more fully know and understand himself and the world around him. He picked a topic and looked at it from several different angles and perspectives, without knowing where he would end up in his conclusions. He "tried out" (*essayer*) a number of approaches to a topic and drew from a rich history of ancient and medieval learning, contemporary customs and norms, and his own curiosity and incessant questioning of why things are the way they are. For example, he had learned through reports from recent European explorations of the Americas that there were entire groups of people who had never worn clothes, so he wrote an essay called "On the Custom of Wearing Clothes," in which he pondered the social custom of wearing clothes in some cultures and of not wearing clothes in other cultures. He wrote another essay called "On Cannibalism," in which he asked quite honestly and earnestly why some cultures believe it appropriate or beneficial to eat other human beings, while for his culture it was considered unthinkably barbaric. As far as possible, he sought to bracket off his own assumptions, prejudices, and biases to understand the world as fully as possible, on its own terms. Above all, through each of these essays he wanted to understand himself and his own angle on the world, so much so that he came up with a personal motto that he had inscribed on a medallion he can be seen wearing in his portraits: *Que sçay-je?* "What do I know?"

In his longest essay, Montaigne puts himself under the microscope, so to speak (the microscope hadn't been invented yet, of course), to know everything about himself it was possible to know. He titled this essay "On Experience" and he begins his reflections with a famous passage:

> There is no desire more natural than the desire for knowledge. We try every means that may lead us to it. When reason fails us, we make use of experience . . . which is a feebler and less worthy means. But truth is so great a thing that we ought not to despise any medium that will conduct us to it.[1]

This might sound so obvious to us today that it hardly bears mentioning, because of course we should rely on our own experiences and on the experiences of others to gain a better understanding of the world and our place in it. But when Montaigne wrote these lines, this was not at all an obvious statement; in fact, it was downright radical. Many of Montaigne's contemporaries thought he was a sloppy and undisciplined writer because he insisted on including anecdotes and autobiographical reflections rather than relying solely on the wisdom of the classical authors and pure, abstract reasoning to make his points. The notion of investigating and reflecting on our own unique experiences of the world, our own "life stories," as a means to truth and understanding was, until Montaigne, often overlooked in favor of abstract reasoning and metaphysical speculation, which we see so clearly in the work of Descartes. Montaigne agreed that reason was the surest and most reliable path to knowledge, but he also suggested that sometimes reason has little to say about a topic, and when that happens we must rely on other means, including our own experience of the world.

Montaigne firmly believed that knowledge, understanding, and wisdom were the key to a life well-lived, and he used every means available to him to pursue these goals. He relied on the wisdom of classical authors and his own powers of reasoning, but he soon realized that these paths

---

1. Montaigne, *Essays*, 343–4.

often had little to reveal about his own unique, individual existence as a flesh-and-blood human being. So he took another approach. He reflected carefully and honestly on his past, on his habits, on his values, on his beliefs and opinions, on his preferences, on his assumptions and instincts and biases. He scrutinized what he ate, what he wore, what he felt in his body (contemporary readers can't help but chuckle at his fascination with his kidney stones!). He also obsessively analyzes his habits at the dinner table, what he likes to eat and drink and with whom and how he likes his food and drink to be prepared and served. He wonders why he likes to wear a hat in some situations but not in others, why he finds it most pleasurable to sleep at this precise temperature rather than others, why he likes wine from this particular grape more than other varietals. As he continues to reflect on these quotidian details of his daily life, he realizes that each of these habits and preferences is uniquely *his* and his alone, and yet each one of us has our own habits and preferences that are equally *ours*. Each of us likes good food and drink, each of us likes to sleep comfortably, each of us inhabits a body of flesh and blood that is at once remarkably fragile and remarkably resilient. In our shared humanity there is infinite diversity, and yet in our infinite diversity there is always the unity of our shared humanity.

By paying attention to the seemingly insignificant details of our habits and routines, we can learn much about what it means to be human. In what is one of the oddest yet most profound statements in the history of Western literature, at one point in his essay Montaigne suddenly proclaims, apropos of nothing in particular, "Both kings and philosophers defecate, and so do the ladies."[2] There is something profoundly wise about this random and slightly embarrassing realization: each of us, finally, is an animal, and we do what all animals do. We eat, we sleep, we defecate, we have sex, we die (not always in that order, of course, with the exception of dying, which always comes last). When we remember this simple fact of life, it can help us to view everything else with a certain ironic distance, even a sense of humor. The rich and the powerful, the so-called "masters of the universe"? They have the same bodily functions as you and me. The poor and the outcast and the forgotten? They have the same basic human needs and desires as everyone else. Our animal necessities are the great equalizer, even when we try to convince ourselves that

---

2. Montaigne, *Essays*, 368.

there really are distinctions of worthiness or value that divide us. But they don't, not really.

While we are without question animals, we also strive to be more than our physiology dictates. We seek knowledge, understanding and wisdom, goodness, beauty and truth. We want to live lives that really mean something. This, for Montaigne, is our noblest purpose as human beings, and he praises this quest in a particularly memorable passage:

> It is a sign of failing powers or of weariness when the mind is content. No generous spirit stays within itself; it constantly aspires and rises above its own strength. It leaps beyond its attainments. If it does not advance, and push forward, if it does not strengthen itself and struggle with itself, it is only half alive. Its pursuits have no bounds or rules; its food is wonder, search, and ambiguity.[3]

This restless yearning for more, this unquenchable desire for wisdom and meaning in face of the inevitable ambiguity of life, propels us forward into the future, never knowing exactly where we'll end up. This yearning is the catalyst for every desire, every goal we set for ourselves. It is the source of our planning, our pursuing, our reflecting, our dreaming. It is what makes it possible for us to have faith, doubt, and reason. It is the root of our impulse to seek out memorable and meaningful experiences, to discover new things about the world and about ourselves, to *live* rather than merely exist.

It is what drives us to create our "bucket list," the list of things we want to experience before we die. We might want to visit specific places, we might want to accomplish certain feats, we might want to check all the boxes that our society has defined as requirements for a life well-lived. But what we're really after here are experiences that make us feel that we've made the most of our limited time on Earth, that we didn't waste this one inconceivably glorious opportunity to be alive. Each person's bucket list will be different, and that's exactly the point. Each of us has our own understanding of what a life well-lived looks like, of what will give us meaning and purpose. And that is exactly as it should be.

A privileged few will succeed in checking off every item on their bucket list and die with no regrets or unfinished business. But the vast majority of us will have to make our peace with missed opportunities, lost chances, wrong turns, and unfulfilled desires. We might find ourselves

---

3. Montaigne, *Essays*, 348.

trapped in a life that precludes seeking out these peak experiences. Even if we are privileged to have the opportunity, we will sometimes make bad choices or fail to seize the moment (this is so common that almost everyone has heard the Latin aphorism *Carpe diem!* "Seize the day!"). Montaigne himself had several regrets, as most of us do. But for him, even those regrets and failures were teaching moments, opportunities to reflect on the sum total of his life laid bare, warts and all, for honest analysis. He realized that it was often the mistakes, the missed chances, that taught him more about himself than the successes. He also realized that it was only by living his life that he finally came to understand himself more deeply. It's one thing to know everything famous authors have said about what it means to live in the world, but that knowledge didn't become wisdom until Montaigne experienced those things for himself.

We intuitively know that this is true. For example, it's one thing to read all about a foreign country and know everything there is to know about its history, its politics, its language, its geography, its culture, its cuisine, and its people. But none of that compares to visiting that country for ourselves and experiencing it first-hand. It's rather like someone who has spent a lifetime reading books about playing the piano but has never sat down at the keyboard themselves. Reading all the books in the world won't make them a good pianist. Only by playing the piano themselves, by practicing for countless hours, can someone become a pianist. It's only by experiencing something for ourselves that we can fully understand and appreciate it for what it is and make it part of ourselves. For Montaigne, it's only by throwing ourselves completely into the world and embracing every experience that comes our way, good and bad, that we can hope to live a meaningful human life. Reading and learning and study are important and indeed necessary pursuits, but that alone will not give us meaning.

Living a fully human life, with all its ambiguity, its triumphs and defeats, its successes and its failures, its peaks and valleys, simultaneously humbles and ennobles us. Ever the realist, Montaigne closes his essay on experience with a reminder that, when all is said and done, we are all human beings, no more and no less:

> The [person] who knows how to enjoy [their] existence as [they] ought has attained to an absolute perfection, like that of the gods. We seek other conditions because we do not understand the proper use of our own, and go out of ourselves because we do not know what is within us. So it is no good our mounting

on stilts, for even on stilts we have to walk with our own legs; and upon the most exalted throne in the world it is still our own bottom that we sit on.[4]

We have noble goals and lofty aspirations, and this is of course a good and necessary thing. But we are still flawed and finite human beings making our way through the world as best we can. We should embrace anything that will assist us in living a meaningful life, and that includes both abstract learning and concrete experiences. Ignoring either of these resources robs us of essential opportunities for growth and depth. Relying solely on abstract "book learning" robs us of meaningful experiences that make life really worth living, while relying solely on "street smarts," on random experiences without disciplined reflection on their deeper meaning and value, threatens to plunge us into hedonism and meaninglessness from the other direction.[5] As Socrates said, "The unexamined life is not worth living,"[6] and as Søren Kierkegaard said, "Life must be understood backwards [but] it must be lived forwards."[7] In other words, we must discover that sweet spot where experience and reflection intersect to create the deeper meaning of our lives.

Faust's Existential Crisis

Montaigne thought he had discovered that sweet spot by combining his respect and appreciation for reason and classical learning with his own unique experiences of the world around him and disciplined reflection on his own habits and routines. A few centuries later and across the border into Germany, Johann Wolfgang von Goethe asked similar questions in his retelling of the legend of Doctor Faust. The Faust legend goes back to medieval Germany and is based on the story of a mysterious professor who sells his soul to the devil in exchange for wisdom and occult powers. The English playwright Christopher Marlowe wrote a play about him at the end of the sixteenth century,[8] but Faust really became famous when

---

4. Montaigne, *Essays*, 406.
5. See all of the so-called Social Media Influencers for all you need to know about the superficiality of this approach to living a meaningful life.
6. Plato, "Apology," 41.
7. Kierkegaard, *Papers and Journals*, 161.
8. Marlowe, *Doctor Faustus*.

Goethe wrote his own version of the legend, which he called *Faust: A Tragedy*.⁹

Set in sixteenth-century Germany, a time of tremendous social, political, economic, cultural, and religious upheaval thanks to the Lutheran Reformation that marked the end of the Middle Ages and the transition into the first stages of modernity, Goethe's *Faust* is the story of a professor in the midst of an existential crisis who is desperate to make some meaning out of his life however he can. Goethe worked on this play off and on for most of his life, and the play reflects Goethe's own role in the nineteenth-century German Romantic reaction to what he and his colleagues criticized as the arid and stifling Rationalism of the Enlightenment (represented in Germany by Kant, whom we met in the preface, and in France by Descartes, whom we met in the chapters on doubt and reason). It's difficult to overstate the significance of this play for German culture, but the best way to express it is to say that Goethe is for German speakers what Shakespeare is for English speakers: the pinnacle of that culture's literary tradition and a major source of its cultural self-understanding. German thinkers for centuries have cited Goethe the way English thinkers cite Shakespeare, as an enduring font of truth, wisdom, and cultural excellence.

Faust tells the story of Dr. Faust, a professor who has spent his entire life deep in thought, study, and rational reflection on the nature of humanity, God, and the universe. After a lifetime of study, Faust comes to a rather shocking conclusion: he's no closer to his goal of wisdom than when he first began:

> Well, that's Philosophy I've read,
> And Law and Medicine, and I fear
> Theology too, from A to Z;
> Hard studies all, that have cost me dear.
> And so I sit, poor silly man,
> No wiser now than when I began.
> They call me Professor and Doctor, forsooth,
> For misleading many an innocent youth
> These last ten years now, I suppose,
> Pulling them to and fro by the nose;

---

9. For a contemporary retelling of Goethe's version of the Faust legend (with LEGOs!), do yourself a favor and watch this video: https://www.youtube.com/watch?v=mIY6xO7A7Qw

> And I see that all our search for knowledge is in vain,
> And this burns my heart with bitter pain.
> I've more sense, to be sure, than the learned fools,
> The masters and pastors, the scribes from the schools;
> No scruples to plague me, no irksome doubt,
> No hell-fire or devil to worry about—
> Yet I take no pleasure in anything now;
> For I know I know nothing, I wonder how
> I can still keep up the pretense of teaching
> Or bettering mankind [sic] with my empty preaching.
> Can I even boast any worldly success?
> What fame or riches do I possess?
> No dog would put up with such an existence.[10]

Faust has spent a lifetime studying every aspect of human existence and knowledge from every conceivable angle, and he feels no closer to wisdom or meaning than when he first began his studies. All of this learning seems to leave him hollow and empty, without real purpose or joy. He sinks deeper and deeper into a profound depression until he finally decides the only solution is suicide. He takes down from his shelf a potion that will kill him quickly and painlessly, but as he raises the vial to his lips he is suddenly stopped by the sound of distant church bells and a choir singing an Easter hymn to the glory of new life. Faust has long since ceased being a Christian, but the nostalgia of this hymn, the longing for hope lodged deep in his soul unleashed by this reminder of the Easter story, pulls him back from the brink of suicide. He puts the vial back on its shelf and is soon interrupted by his assistant, Wagner.

Wagner is an earnest young student keen to make his mark in the academic world. He has no interest in experiencing the world on his own; he's content simply to read about others' experiences and to reflect from a safe academic distance on the lessons they have to teach. Faust can't stand Wagner, and he makes his displeasure known with every syllable of his interactions with his poor assistant. Nevertheless, Faust and Wagner take a walk together outside the town walls on a sunny Easter Sunday and they encounter an alien world of laughing, playing, joking, happy townspeople. Faust and Wagner aren't sure how to relate to them, as they're much more comfortable in their safe bubble of books and experiments.

---

10. Goethe, *Faust*, 15.

After a few awkward interactions with *hoi polloi* they decide to head back to Faust's study, but as they make their way home they notice that a black poodle is following them.

Once back in his study, Faust turns to the dark arts to make some meaning of his malaise. He thinks perhaps magic and the occult can give him some insight into the meaning of life that philosophy and theology, law and medicine have failed to provide him. Suddenly he notices that the poodle is changing shape right before his eyes and before he knows it he is face to face with a devil named Mephistopheles. Mephistopheles addresses Faust as an old friend and fellow-traveler, offering him assistance on his quest for meaning and purpose . . . for a price. Mephistopheles accurately diagnoses Faust's despair as an existential crisis. Faust is experiencing profound despair because he can't discover the meaning or purpose of his life, more specifically because his life's work of learning and scholarship has failed to provide that meaning. Mephistopheles is all too happy to help Faust discover what his life has been missing, so he promises Faust that he will do everything in his power to help Faust experience everything there is to experience about the world and the human condition. But if Faust ever experiences a moment so perfect, so pure, that he wishes it would never end, then Faust forfeits his soul to Mephistopheles. The bet is rather simple: Faust wants to have every possible human experience in order to discover true happiness and meaning; Mephistopheles will "help" him and will win Faust's soul if Faust succeeds in discovering true and lasting meaning.

Faust's crisis is one we all recognize and relate to if we're honest with ourselves. We do everything society expects us to do, we make all the right decisions, we check all the required boxes, we pay our dues, and at the end of the day we sometimes still feel that our lives have no real meaning or purpose. Because we so desperately want our lives to make sense, to have some valor and dignity and intensity, when that intensity and meaning continue to elude us we often despair and maybe even suspect that life is playing a cruel joke on us. What we expected will give us meaning often turns out to be incapable of providing what we need, so we seek alternatives: in today's parlance, we set out to "find ourselves." We question the values passed on to us by our parents, we resist conforming to social norms and expectations, we insist on making our own way in the world. And all of this is good and healthy! But sometimes even that self-blazed path forward isn't enough to satisfy us, and we become increasingly desperate. At that point we will often turn to anything that promises answers. For Faust, those answers were offered by Mephistopheles.

But of course Mephistopheles is a devil, the very embodiment of mischief and chaos and nihilism, so he has no interest in staying true to his word to provide the true and lasting meaning Faust so desperately seeks. His goal is to lead Faust astray, to present him with nothing but bad options and horrible choices, to ruin everything he wants to do. Mephistopheles believes that human beings are petty, bitter, small-minded critters who will sell our souls for fleeting pleasure, but Faust proves to be a worthy adversary. Faust knows enough to appreciate the ambiguity of human existence and the elusive nature of meaning. Faust believes that he can use Mephistopheles to have the experiences of the world he is unable to have on his own, but he's also confident that he will never say to a specific single moment, "Stop and stay forever!"

So Faust and Mephistopheles set off on their adventures. More than anything else, Faust realizes that what he is missing in his life is genuine love, given and received. He has spent his entire life surrounded by moldy books and dusty scientific instruments, rarely having interacted with another living, breathing human being besides his students and his loathsome assistant, Wagner. Faust knows, deep in his being, that he must experience love in order to create genuine meaning in his life. So he tells Mephistopheles that he wants to fall in love, and Mephistopheles sets off to make that happen by bewitching Faust so that he will fall madly, hopelessly in love with the next woman he sees. Their victim is a teenaged peasant girl named Gretchen, a devout Christian and a morally upright young woman. Mephistopheles arranges things so that Faust and Gretchen will cross paths (perhaps the original "meet-cute"), and, predictably, Faust falls madly in love with Gretchen, even though he knows virtually nothing about her. Gretchen, to her credit, is suspicious of this stranger and his even stranger friend, but she eventually succumbs to their seductions and sets off down the path to her own destruction. Long story short: Gretchen and Faust have an illicit affair, Gretchen's mother and brother are both tragically killed, and Gretchen ends up pregnant with Faust's child. She drowns the baby to avoid the shame of being an unwed mother and finds herself in prison awaiting execution for infanticide. (And you thought soap operas and reality TV were modern inventions!)

Along the way, Mephistopheles has other experiences in store for Faust in addition to his lusting after poor Gretchen. Perhaps most importantly, Mephistopheles wants Faust to experience Walpurgisnacht. Walpurgisnacht is the German version of Halloween and it takes place on the night of April 30th and May 1st, with demons and goblins and witches having free rein for that one night to revel in the darkness and depravity of our worst nightmares. Mephistopheles takes Faust to the Harz Mountains to experience this congress of evil spirits and, predictably enough, it scares the bejesus out of Faust. He quickly realizes that it's a very bad idea indeed to make a deal with the devil, but by this point it's far too late. Faust is thoroughly horrified by what he's seen and done, so much so that he tries to ditch Mephistopheles in order to rescue Gretchen from her certain doom. In the end, Faust fails to save Gretchen, but in the last lines of the first part of the play, as Gretchen is being executed, a voice from heaven reveals that pure, innocent Gretchen is redeemed, while we must wait for closure on Faust's increasingly tragic story.

What do we learn from the story of poor Faust and his deal with the devil? Besides being a monument of German literature and a timeless story of human striving and tragic failure, there is much to learn from *Faust* about our innate desire for meaning and purpose. More than anything else, Faust wants to break through his existential crisis to discover the deeper meaning of his life. In the prologue to the play, in a scene intentionally modeled on the prologue to the Book of Job, we are privy to a conversation between God and Mephistopheles, in which Mephistopheles shares his thoughts on the human condition:

> The little earth-god still persists in his old ways,
> Ridiculous as ever, as in his first days.
> He'd have improved if you'd not given
> Him a mere glimmer of the light of heaven;
> He calls it Reason, and it only has increased
> His power to be beastlier than a beast.
> He is—if I may say so, sir—
> A little like the long-legged grasshopper,
> Which hops and flies, and sings its silly songs
> And flies, and drops straight back to grass where it belongs.[11]

For Mephistopheles, human beings are pitiable creatures gifted with just enough insight to fly ever-so-briefly above the crushing concerns of our daily drudgery, to ask important questions and to think grand thoughts,

---

11. Goethe, *Faust*, 10.

but without the capacity to discover the answers. We are condemned to ask these questions without hope of receiving an answer, and, more often than not, we will use these limited powers of reason to do more harm than good. That is Mephistopheles's dim view of human nature. God, unsurprisingly, has a different perspective. God asks Mephistopheles if he knows God's servant, Faust (with clear echoes of God's conversation with the Satan in the prologue to Job). God insists that Faust is a worthy adversary to Mephistopheles, because Faust understands that the glory of human nature is to strive without ceasing, to keep leaping above the grass like the long-legged grasshopper, to seek meaning for all the days of our lives, even if we fail. As God says to Mephistopheles, "Man [sic] errs, till he has ceased to strive."[12]

And what is it, finally, that Faust strives to understand? He wants to discover meaning and purpose, he wants to know that his life has value, he wants to live a life that matters. As we come to see in the play, what Faust wants more than anything is to give and receive love, and that makes perfect sense because most of us would agree that a life without love is a life without meaning.

What Is Love?

Faust makes his deal with the devil because he thinks that anything is worth the chance at genuine love, even to the point of forfeiting his own soul. But what is love?[13] And does Faust actually find love, or does he find himself trapped in lust? To answer this question, we need to understand that "love" often means different things in different cultures. In our own twenty-first-century US-American culture, love has powerful connotations of emotion, sentimentality, and sometimes little more than saccharine greeting card platitudes. We "love" just about anything and anyone around us: speaking strictly for myself, I can honestly say that I have declared my love for everything from a delicious bowl of Vietnamese pho to the Butler men's basketball team, to the ridges and valleys of central Pennsylvania, to the organ works of Johann Sebastian Bach, to an intensely hoppy imperial IPA, to my mother, to my dog Pepper, to my wife Kate, to God. In our culture, "love" covers so many different things

---

12. Goethe, *Faust*, 11.

13. You knew this was coming: https://www.youtube.com/watch?v=HwVh8pmOot4

that it has virtually lost all meaning. But what do we really mean when we say we *love* something?

The ancient Greeks were often much more precise in their language than we are in English, and it turns out that they had three distinct words for what we mean in English by the word "love": *philia, eros,* and *agape. Philia* refers to friendship and companionship, reciprocal relationships of mutual respect and delight with fellow human beings as equals. This is the word at the root of Philadelphia, the "city of brotherly love." *Eros* refers to our creative capacities, the reunion of the separated, and physical, sexual love, the latter of which is captured in the English word "erotic." *Agape* is the Greek word used in the New Testament to translate "love," which in older translations is rendered as "charity." For example, "Love your neighbor as yourself," "Love your enemies," "For God so loved the world," "God is love," "Faith, hope, and love abide, these three; and the greatest of these is love," etc. *Agape* love is unconditional, other-focused, self-sacrificial love in pursuit of justice and the wellbeing of the neighbor and the world.

It should come as no surprise that we human beings need to give and receive all three types of love in order to live a meaningful, dignified life. We need friendship and social bonding with our fellow human beings. We need creative, constructive outlets for our deepest human longings and desires and we need the reconciliation and reunification with those from whom we are separated and estranged. We need physical touch and sexual union with another human being. We need justice and wellbeing for our neighbors and ourselves. Each type of love defines us as human beings, and without giving and receiving all three types of love we are diminished and deprived of the full range of human meaning and dignity.

Faust wants to give and receive love, as he rightly understands that a life without love is a life without meaning. But Mephistopheles has no intentions of allowing Faust any genuine experiences of real love in any of its modes as outlined above. Instead, Mephistopheles creates opportunities for lust: the superficial, ultimately meaningless use of another human being as an object. Faust thinks he loves Gretchen, but he knows nothing about Gretchen as a three-dimensional human being. He sees her from a distance and thinks he loves her, but love at first sight is not genuine love. At most, we can lust at first sight. Faust never moves past this first step. He lusts after Gretchen and he is willing to do anything it takes to possess her as an object. But he never considers her own desires and longings, never gets to know her as a person, never asks for her own thoughts on the relationship he insists on consummating all on his own. Faust lusts after an idealized image of Gretchen, but he never loves Gretchen herself.

In our own lives, what do we really *love*, and what do we lust after or just "like" a whole lot? If love requires genuine appreciation and acceptance of another, and not just our own warm fuzzy feelings about them, if it means desiring the wholeness and wellbeing of another for their own sake and not just our own, what, finally, do we really love? If the meaning of our lives is determined in large part by what we love, then what we genuinely love will show us what we value without reservation or condition. Tillich described idolatry as elevating finite realities to a level of ultimacy, and this same definition applies just as well to what we love. Do I love authentically and selflessly, transcending my own selfish desires and fully willing the wellbeing of the beloved for their own sake? Or do I love only who or what already loves me back, only who or what I can control, for my own satisfaction? According to the New Testament, the only love worth having is a love that will lay everything down for the beloved. This authentic love seeks the genuine welfare of the beloved, regardless of the cost. As Jesus tells his disciples in the Gospel of John, "This is my commandment, that you love one another as I have loved you. No one has greater love than this, to lay down one's life for one's friends" (John 15:12–13). And this is possible because, as the First Epistle of John puts it, "perfect love casts out fear" (1 John 4:18). This is the love (*agape*) that builds a just and flourishing community. This is the love that transcends boundaries and breaks down walls. This is the love that conquers death itself.[14]

Faust was unable to experience this love because he was trapped in lust. He never regarded Gretchen as anything more than an object, as a conquest. He never considered Gretchen as a subject, with her own hopes and dreams and desires and integrity as a human being. Where do we find ourselves following Faust's path? In what ways do we use and abuse others for our own sense of worth or value? What do we love inordinately, and what do we love that is not really worthy of the weight of love? What or whom do we really, passionately, authentically love? If we can answer that question, we will be well on our way to determining the meaning of our lives, because a life without giving and receiving genuine love is a sad, wasted, pitiable life.

---

14. Tillich gave a series of lectures on just this topic, published as *Love, Power, and Justice*.

The philosopher Eugene Long, in an essay on the problem of evil, said that "love apart from vulnerability makes little sense."[15] Genuine love is risky. Genuine love will inevitably hurt us. Genuine love forces us beyond the safe enclosures we've constructed for our lives, out into that scary, unfathomable arena of genuine meaning. If I love you, I must be willing to put everything on the line for you, come what may, even if it means the loss of everything else I hold dear. If I love you, I must be willing to lay down my life for you, to sacrifice everything for your wellbeing. But it doesn't end there. Jesus says, "Love your neighbor *as yourself.*" In order genuinely to love you, I must also genuinely love myself. I must acknowledge and accept myself as worthy of love and dignity. I must know and appreciate and love myself before I can know and appreciate and love another. These are two sides of the same coin: love of neighbor and love of self. We can't have one without the other.

The meaning of life, it turns out, has everything to do with love. What do I love with my whole heart, my whole mind, my whole strength (Deut 6:5; Matt 22:37; Luke 10:27)? What do I love without reservation or condition or exception? We'll find that what we love unconditionally is what we take to be ultimately meaningful and significant: our ultimate concern. We will find that committing our heart and soul and strength to another comes with significant vulnerability and insecurity, otherwise known as existential doubt. We will find that loving another without reservation is only possible thanks to existential reason, when we take that crucial step back from our lives and ask what really matters, what it all means. We will find that genuine love is only possible when we understand and embrace the deeper meaning of faith, doubt, and reason.

And yet, we rarely attain this state of perfect love. We rarely reach the heights of genuine *agape*. We yearn for it, and yet it only appears in fleeting moments. And that's entirely understandable, given our inherent limitations as finite creatures. So much of our lives is spent in search of this genuine, lasting love, and that's as it should be. But so often we encounter obstacles in our quest for genuine, lasting love. More often than not, we confront the specter of fear.

---

15. Long, "Suffering and Transcendence," 146.

What Are We so Afraid of?

Mephistopheles does everything in his power to distract Faust from nobler pursuits and to keep him wallowing in superficial, selfish, meaningless desires, especially his lustful obsession with Gretchen. In one of the more bizarre scenes of the play, already mentioned above, Mephistopheles takes Faust to a witches' Sabbath deep in the Harz Mountains of central Germany on Walpurgisnacht. All manner of gruesome, uncanny, frightening, evil beings are in attendance, the stuff of our worst nightmares all gathered together in one place. Faust is both confused and terrified, as we all would be! We can use this scene as a springboard to a consideration of the darker sides of our consciousness and our subconscious and ask directly one of the questions we would rather not think about: what is my greatest fear?

When people are asked what they fear, they will typically respond with certain phobias. Some of us are afraid of snakes, or spiders, or bats. Some of us are afraid of the dark, or of thunderstorms, or of heights. Some of us are afraid of flying, or of water, or of enclosed or open spaces. Most of these phobias are so common that they have specific names, such as arachnophobia (spiders), acrophobia (heights), agoraphobia (open spaces), claustrophobia (enclosed spaces), or my personal favorites, coulrophobia (fear of clowns) and triskaidekaphobia (fear of the number thirteen).[16] We often recognize that these phobias are irrational and that there is nothing inherently dangerous about any of these quite normal things, but their being irrational doesn't make the fear any less real for those who suffer from these phobias. But when we push things a little further and dig beneath the surface of these specific phobias, we might discover what it is that we're *really* afraid of.

Fear, as Mephistopheles understood all too well, has a tendency on occasion to so dominate our consciousness that we become paralyzed and can think of nothing else. It consumes us to the point where we will do anything to avoid it. It distracts us from committing fully and unreservedly to relationships, to having new experiences, to taking risks and leaps into the unknown. If the fear is strong enough, it can even keep us from creating meaning in our lives. All we know and experience is the gnawing, suffocating fear.

---

16. Many more phobias are hilariously listed in a scene from *A Charlie Brown Christmas*, including Charlie Brown's own deepest fear, pantophobia (a fear of everything): https://www.youtube.com/watch?v=NkCgrVocLow

Phobias, by their nature, are directed at specific objects (e.g. spiders, heights, the dark, clowns), but these phobias often mask a deeper, more existential fear that has no object or direct cause. When we dig beneath the surface of our phobias and our fears, we often discover that what we're really dealing with is something we might better call anxiety or dread. Unlike phobias, anxiety and dread don't have specific objects we can name as the source of our fears. Instead, anxiety and dread transcend specific causes and point toward something deeper, more fundamental, in the human experience that dredges up these feelings that we would rather not name out loud. When we take a closer look at each of these phobias, we will discover that they share certain things in common. For example, many of these phobias reveal a fear of losing control, of being in a situation where we are at the mercy of forces beyond our power. And if we push even further, we will discover that each of these phobias simultaneously masks and manifests our deeply human fear of dying, the threat of nonbeing.[17] But why is it that we are so afraid of death and dying? Each of us knows that we will someday die, although we'd prefer that day to be far off in the future. Is it the process of dying itself that upsets us, or is it the thought of actually being dead, of ceasing to be? And why should that be something to fear?

Death Comes for Us All

Thomas Nagel, from whom we heard in the previous chapter on the absurdity of existence, wrote another essay on death[18] in which he asks a surprising, deceptively simple question: is it a bad thing to die? I suspect most of us would respond without thinking too much about it that, yes, of course it's a bad thing to die! What kind of a question is that? But when we think more carefully about what that question really means, we will discover layers upon layers of important revelations about what we value, what we love, what we fear, and what we hope.

Nagel explores the deeply unsettling concepts of death and dying that lurk in the deepest recesses of our minds. What is it, finally, that so unsettles and frightens us about dying and being dead? Is it the actual process of dying that bothers us so much? If so, we needn't worry, because

---

17. For more on fear, anxiety, the threat of nonbeing, and the courage to live meaningfully all the same, see Tillich, *The Courage to Be*.

18. Nagel, "Death."

dying itself is only a momentary process, and once it's finished we won't exist anymore to be bothered by it. Do we fear the experience of actually ceasing to be, of being dead and gone?[19] Again, we needn't worry too much about that, because when we're dead we will no longer be conscious, so we will have no idea or awareness that we're no longer alive. We have a tendency to think of death, of actually being dead, as a sort of eternal state of being, as a conscious awareness that our lives are over. But if we're truly dead and gone then we are no longer conscious because we no longer exist, so there will be no "me" there to know that I'm dead.

Do we mourn the fact that there will be thousands, millions, perhaps billions of future years of which we will be deprived because we will be dead and gone, unable to experience those years for ourselves? Perhaps, but very few of us bemoan the billions of years that passed before we were born. On the face of it there is no difference: we didn't exist for billions of years before we were born, and we won't exist for billions of years after we die. But nevertheless we do recognize a difference between the time before we were born and the time after we will die.

By the same token, we don't mourn the years of our lives, cumulatively speaking, that we spend in the unconsciousness of sleep. We are "dead to the world" when we sleep, but we don't mourn as a tragedy the living we miss when we're asleep (although we might experience a touch of FOMO, or "fear of missing out"), because we know that we will awaken and get back to the business of living. And then there's the famous urban legend about Walt Disney, who allegedly instructed that his body be cryogenically frozen after he died so that he could be reanimated once technology had sufficiently advanced to make such a thing possible. Supposing for the moment that this legend is true (it isn't) and that Mr. Disney will eventually walk among us again in some distant future, would we mourn the decades (or centuries) Disney spent on ice? Probably not, because in this case he will still have more life ahead of him. Those intervening years don't count as a tragedy because for him it would be as if awakening from a very long and deep sleep. So the fact of unconsciousness isn't what we fear about being dead, either. Clearly something else is going on here.

It turns out that when we contemplate our own death, it's not dying and it's not even being dead that we fear. Rather, we really fear being deprived of more life. This is an important realization, because it reminds

19. As in so many other things, the lads of Monty Python provide witty clarity on this profound existential question: https://www.dailymotion.com/video/x2hwqnp

us how much we value life in general and especially our own being alive. We value life as a good in and of itself, so we will obviously curse the end of our life as a profound evil. If it is a good thing to be alive, then we will want that good to continue indefinitely, and we consider the fact that this is not the way things work as a profound shock and a damnable evil. We really do know that we have a limited lifespan and we really do know that we will die at some point in the future, but these facts typically remain for us little more than hypothetical abstractions. For most of us it never feels like the "right time" to die. We always want more time, more life, more experiences of the glory of being a living, breathing human being. Even as we get older, we never assume that there is a big red circle around a particular date on our calendar marked "Today I Will Die!!!" Instead, we live our lives as we always have, until one day it's suddenly all over and we're gone, much to our own surprise.

As human beings we have the gift and the curse of knowing that we will die. We alone, as far as we know, are unique in the animal kingdom in being conscious of our own inevitable end. I dearly love my dog Pepper, and I'm convinced that she's an exceptionally smart poodle, but I'm positive that she has no idea that she will one day die. This existential awareness of her own mortality has likely never occurred to her. But it has occurred to me many, many times. And surely it's occurred to you, too. And so it is with every human being. We alone are blessed and cursed with the knowledge that we are mortal, that we are finite, that we will die. And therein lies so much of the magic and the mystery and the pathos of being human.

What does it mean for us, to know that we will die? What does it mean to be fully aware of our own mortality, to know that we have a limited number of years on this Earth, that the clock is always ticking? For Nagel, this is a singular gift. If we're honest with ourselves, we will admit that it's a far better thing for us to know that we will die than to be blissfully unaware of that one inevitable fact. For if we didn't know that we will die, would we ever try to really live? If we had no idea that our time is limited, would we bother to make the most of our time, to experience as much as we can of this wild and wonderful world? Would we ever do the hard work of making meaning out of our lives if we assume they will go on forever?

There is a profound truth connecting our knowledge of our own mortality with our deeply human quest for meaning. It is precisely because we know that we will die that we make every conceivable effort to live a life of meaning and purpose while we're alive. Otherwise we would be locked for our whole lives in the caricature of the blissfully unaware teenager, convinced that we are immortal and totally unconcerned with the realities of danger, aging, and death. If we thought we would live forever, why would we put any effort into living meaningful lives? If we had an eternity stretching out before us, would we ever bother to get an education, to fall in love, to raise a family, to work for justice, to volunteer on the weekends, to coach that youth soccer team, to rescue pets from shelters, to take a cooking class, to compost and recycle, to travel, to celebrate milestones, to try to eat well, to bike to work instead of driving, to hug our loved ones tight? If everything lasted forever, what would anything really mean?[20]

In the words of that illustrious contemporary philosopher, country musician Tim McGraw, what would it mean to live like we were dying?[21] What would it mean to take seriously, with every breath we take, the reality of our inevitable end? Would we live differently if every choice were made in full awareness of the contingency, the ephemerality of our very existence? I suspect we would live quite differently if we took with absolute seriousness the possibility that every moment were potentially our last moment on Earth. That awareness of the sheer graciousness of every moment of our existence would radically transform the way we live each and every day. We wouldn't take anything for granted and we wouldn't put off into the distant future the things that really matter to us: we would get right down to the business of really *living*.

But, of course, this isn't how life actually works. We know, at least conceptually, that we are going to die, and yet we do a rather remarkable job of conveniently ignoring this one incontrovertible fact. It turns out that embracing this reality is often too much for us to bear, so we ignore, deflect, and repress. And that might actually be a healthy thing to do. When I teach this essay of Nagel's on death, I ask my students if they would want to know the precise date they will die. The vast majority of them, without hesitation, answer "no." There is profound wisdom in this instinctual response. We don't want to know when we will die because that would put a big, bold, underlined "period" at the end of the sentence

---

20. Kurt Vonnegut (born and raised in Indianapolis) wrote a marvelous short story called "Tomorrow and Tomorrow and Tomorrow" about the dystopian future awaiting humanity if we finally manage to conquer death.

21. For more, see his magnum opus on the topic: https://www.youtube.com/watch?v=_9TShlMkQnc

of our life. We vastly prefer our lives to stretch out into the potentially infinite future, without a predetermined end. We want life, and we want more of it. Knowing exactly when we will die would cause us to fixate obsessively on that box on the calendar, circled frantically in bright red ink, barreling toward us like a freight train. It would color everything we think and do and believe and hope and dream, from our first day to our last day. It would write the end of our story before we ever got started.

This is an instructive and enlightening thought experiment. We don't want to know when we will die because we think of life as a story that we write ourselves, or, to be more accurate, that we write in collaboration with a legion of companions and fellow travelers along our journey toward an unknown destination.[22] The uncertainty and unknowability of our end is precisely what gives life its zest and its intensity. We might die tomorrow, or we might die decades from now: we just can't know either way. For some of us, those ellipses stretching out between the present moment and the end of our journey provide a motivation to live life to the fullest, as clichéd as that sounds. For others, the ellipses keep us from taking anything too terribly seriously at any given moment. For others, the ellipses mock us, keeping the final answer hidden from us until it's too late to change course. When we realize with absolute seriousness that the entirety of our lives is contained in that hyphen between our birth date and death date on our tombstone, suddenly everything comes urgently into startling and often unsettling perspective.

For many people, the inevitable end of our lives is a thought too terrible to contemplate, so we create alternate endings for our lives. How we think about the afterlife—what happens after we die—is perhaps as important in our quest for meaning as how we think about death and dying. Tillich, in a sermon on the concept of eternity,[23] mentions that many Christians insist that this life that we're living now is variously a "practice run" or the "final exam" for eternal life, which we tend to conceive as an infinite extension of the lives we enjoy living right now. We imagine a perfect, magical place beyond time and space where we will live happily ever after, reunited with every pet and friend and loved one we've ever lost, where we will exist in perfected human form for all eternity, world without end, amen.

---

22. For a unique twist on this insight, watch the film *Stranger than Fiction*.
23. Tillich, "The Eternal Now."

But Tillich isn't so sure that this is a helpful way to think about our mortality, precisely because this view discourages us from accepting that we are really *mortal* creatures. If we believe that we will live forever in a glorified version of our current lives, then we might be tempted not to take our finitude seriously and we might be unwilling finally to admit that this life is the only life we know we have. We can defer all sorts of things to the "next" life, so that we don't necessarily have to take anything happening here and now with any genuine seriousness or urgency.

This can certainly be comforting, but it can also sometimes be turned to nefarious ends. For example, slaveholders in the antebellum United States frequently told their slaves that they should suffer their current situation gladly because everything will turn out for the best in the sweet by and by, that their heavenly rewards will more than make up for the brutal treatment they experienced in this life. That might sound pretty good on the surface, but it also provides significant cover for those who want to mistreat and oppress their fellow human beings here and now.

What would it mean for us to take seriously our own mortality? What would it mean for us to acknowledge and accept and even celebrate the limited years we have to be alive? In the thought world of the Hebrew Bible there was no conception of an afterlife of eternal bliss. The assumption was that once we die, that's it: we're dead and buried and gone, "gathered to our ancestors" who have already died and been buried in this same ground. This explains the obsession so many of the patriarchs and matriarchs had with having lots and lots of babies! The only way to live on after death was to have many descendants, "as numerous as the stars of heaven and as the sand that is on the seashore," as God promises Father Abraham and Mother Sarah (Gen 21:17).

If we assume that our "real" home is in heaven after we die, what might we neglect to pursue while we're alive here and now? Might it be that it is this very awareness of our mortality that compels us to create meaning and significance in our lives? If we knew without doubt that we would live forever, would we ever bother seeking meaning and purpose in our lives here and now? Would we commit ourselves to leaving the world a better place than we found it? Would we seek out meaningful and memorable experiences? Would we make the effort to better ourselves through education and culture? Would we value with the same intensity the blessings of family and friends? Would we bother doing our part to push the moral arc of the universe a bit closer to justice? It's impossible to answer these questions with any finality because there have been plenty of people doing all of these things and more with different understandings of the afterlife, but Tillich's point in his sermon on eternity is worth bearing in mind all the same: what does it mean, finally, to accept that I am a mortal, finite creature?

Some people are perfectly content to emblazon their lives with the metaphorical (or literal) hashtag #YOLO, "You Only Live Once." Living our lives under this sign can produce surprising results, from taking that leap out of an airplane on a skydiving adventure to working tirelessly to cure cancer or end homelessness, and everything in between. If we knew we only have one life to live, we might devote more energy to making the most of this gift of life, not just for ourselves, but for everyone and everything around us. We might notice that in the gospels Jesus spends a lot more time urging his disciples to create justice and peace and the beloved community here and now and a lot less time describing the afterlife. We might notice that we only have one planet Earth, and we are trashing it to the point of uninhabitability, faster than it can recover. We might notice that millions of people are pleading for a meaningful existence here and now, and that we have the means to provide a decent life for all, if only we marshal our resources and our political will to make it happen.

It is certainly possible to do the work of justice and peace in pursuit of the beloved community here and now while at the same time hoping expectantly for the world to come. These two ideas are not mutually exclusive, and there is a long history in the Christian tradition of holding these two hopes together. As Martin Luther King Jr., put it in his last speech, the night before he was assassinated:

> It's alright [sic] to talk about "long white robes over yonder," in all of its symbolism. But ultimately people want some suits and dresses and shoes to wear down here. It's alright to talk about "streets flowing with milk and honey," but God has commanded us to be concerned about the slums down here, and his [sic] children who can't eat three square meals a day. It's alright to talk about the new Jerusalem, but one day, God's preacher must talk about the [new] New York, the new Atlanta, the new Philadelphia, the new Los Angeles, the new Memphis, Tennessee. This is what we have to do.[24]

---

24. King, "I See the Promised Land," 282.

It's only when we assume that these hopes are mutually exclusive that we find ourselves headed down the wrong path. It's only when we assume that our calling to a heavenly home means that we are permitted to neglect and reject our earthly home that we fundamentally miss the point. At the same time, the hope and expectation of the "New Jerusalem," the heavenly city where there is no more suffering or weeping (Rev 21:1–5), can be a powerful motivation for doing the hard work of peace-building and justice-making here and now.

The ways we think about and prepare for death will profoundly influence the way we attempt to create meaning in our lives. How we define that meaning will depend in large part on what we think life is all about and it will also depend on what we think happens after we die. Through it all, regardless of our hunches about what comes next, each of us wants to live a meaningful life; we want our lives to matter. Two books in the Hebrew Bible address these questions in radically different ways, and they're worth delving into in some more detail. Both of these books are contained in the section of the Hebrew Bible commonly called "Wisdom Literature," which includes Job, the Psalms, Proverbs, Ecclesiastes, and the Song of Songs. These books do not recount the history of Israel, nor do they offer commandments or instructions for religious and political life. Instead, these books raise fundamental questions of human existence and invite us to reflect more deeply on what it means to be a human being seeking meaning and purpose in our lives.

Two books within the Old Testament genre of Wisdom Literature stand out as particularly useful and instructive examples of what it means to reflect on the meaning and purpose of life, from quite different perspectives and with quite different conclusions. Although both are included in the same section of the Old Testament, it is difficult to find two books more seemingly diametrically opposed than the Song of Songs and Ecclesiastes. One is an exuberant hymn to love and sex and the glories of being alive, and the other is a world-wise and sometimes cynical reflection on the realities of living in a world that rarely lives up to our optimistic expectations. And yet both are revered as sacred scripture by billions of people (even if they aren't read all that often). In these two books we can discover a surprising range of human experience and signposts on our shared quest for the meaning of life.

The Song of Songs and the Power of Love

The Song of Songs is a book unlike any other in the Bible. For example, the Song of Songs shares with the Old Testament Book of Esther the distinction of being the only two books of the Bible that never mention God! The Song of Songs is, despite centuries of attempts to convince us otherwise, a straightforward example of ancient erotic poetry. This book of the Bible tells the tale of two young lovers, enraptured at the very thought of the other, pining and yearning and aching for the embrace of their beloved. There is nothing explicitly "religious" about this book of the Bible; instead, the book is a dialogue between two lovers who describe in explicit and longing detail the contours of the beloved's body, the delight of fleeting embraces, the soul-crushing ache of being apart, and the burning desire for the beloved that consumes the pair all the days of their life.

The dialogue is shared between the two lovers with occasional remarks by a group of friends who delight in sharing the couple's love and passion for one another. The couple speak rapturously about the physical features of their beloved, comparing their bodies to gazelles and sheep and stags, cedar trees and pomegranates and apples, wine and olives and heaps of wheat, lilies and roses and cinnamon. These earthy, unashamedly sexual descriptions of the beloved evoke intense sensory experiences of the beauty of the Earth and its creatures, inviting us to involve all of our senses in the experience of love and the quest for meaning. Each partner describes in intimate detail the ecstasy of their embrace and the pain of being separated, as we can see in this passage:

> As an apple tree among the trees of the wood,
> so is my beloved among young men.
> With great delight I sat in his shadow,
> and his fruit was sweet to my taste.
> He brought me to the banqueting house,
> and his intention towards me was love.
> Sustain me with raisins,
> refresh me with apples;
> for I am faint with love.
> O that his left hand were under my head,
> and that his right hand embraced me!
> I adjure you, O daughters of Jerusalem,
> by the gazelles or the wild does:

> do not stir up or awaken love
> until it is ready! . . .
>
> My beloved speaks and says to me:
> "Arise, my love, my fair one,
> and come away;
> for now the winter is past,
> the rain is over and gone.
> The flowers appear on the earth;
> the time of singing has come,
> and the voice of the turtle-dove
> is heard in our land.
> The fig tree puts forth its figs,
> and the vines are in blossom;
> they give forth fragrance.
> Arise, my love, my fair one,
> and come away. . ."
>
> My beloved is mine and I am his;
> he pastures his flock among the lilies.
> Until the day breathes
> and the shadows flee,
> turn, my beloved, be like a gazelle
> or a young stag on the cleft mountains. (Song 2:3–7; 10–13; 16–17)

This striking passage is told from the woman's perspective, a hymn to the vigor and physical attractiveness of her beloved and to her own sexual desires for him. The woman is an equal partner in this relationship; as we can see in the last stanza of her song, she is not the man's property, nor is she without her own desires and agency. This is in striking contrast to many other biblical descriptions of sex and marriage, where the woman is often treated as the property of her husband or father, without any genuine agency and autonomy of her own.

The man, too, speaks of his partner as an equal, even going so far as to call her his "sister," and he evokes the same sensory experiences of delight and joy at the very thought of embracing his beloved:

> You have ravished my heart, my sister, my bride,
> you have ravished my heart with a glance of your eyes,
> with one jewel of your necklace.
> How sweet is your love, my sister, my bride!
> How much better is your love than wine,
> and the fragrance of your oils than any spice!
> Your lips distil nectar, my bride;
> honey and milk are under your tongue;
> the scent of your garments is like the scent of Lebanon.
>
> A garden locked is my sister, my bride,
> a garden locked, a fountain sealed.
> Your channel is an orchard of pomegranates
> with all choicest fruits,
> henna with nard,
> nard and saffron, calamus and cinnamon,
> with all trees of frankincense,
> myrrh and aloes,
> with all chief spices—
> a garden fountain, a well of living water,
> and flowing streams from Lebanon. (Song 4:9–15)

What is especially curious about this book of the Bible is that it never mentions God, nor does it mention anything that we might recognize as "religion." It is an entire book of the Bible devoted to sexual love and the ecstasy of romantic relationships. There is no hint of judgment, shame, or puritanical disdain for the body or for human sexuality. There is nothing but stanza after stanza of explicit joy and rapturous celebration of two people's intense sexual love for one another.

Needless to say, many commentators throughout the centuries have balked at this book of erotic poetry and have attempted various interpretive moves to make it mean anything but what it clearly means. Rabbinical commentators often took it as an analogy for God's love of Israel, while Christian commentators often interpreted it as an allegory of Christ's love of the church, anything but erotic poetry and a celebration of sexual love for its own sake! There is certainly merit to these allegorical interpretations of the Song, but the plain-sense meaning of the Song of Songs is clear: human sexuality, human embodiment in the flesh, human delight in the natural world all around us, all are good and beautiful gifts to be enjoyed and celebrated for their own sake, simply because they are lovely and life-affirming pleasures.

Quite often throughout its history the Christian tradition has taken an ambiguous stance towards the physical world, seeing it as fallen, corrupt, and sometimes even evil, while at the same time also acknowledging it as a good gift of the Creator who saw that it was "very good" (Gen 1).[25] Often in these interpretations, the assumption is that our true home is not on this Earth but in the world to come. According to this view, we ought to make our way through this world as pilgrims destined for some other place, so we best not get too attached to anything while we're here. Sexual relationships in particular were often denigrated as necessary evils for the sake of perpetuating the human race, but certainly not something to be enjoyed and valued for their own sake. As a result, far too often Christians have neglected to embrace the full range of the human experience, rejecting sexuality and denigrating our material, physical embodiment as somehow inferior to "higher," spiritual pursuits. Romantic love, particularly sexual love, has often been vilified as profane and fallen, as something to be kept in check, as something fundamentally at odds with faith and piety.

But the Song of Songs shows us another way to think about romantic and sexual love in the context of religion and spirituality. Here is a book of erotic poetry contained in the Bible, an unashamed and extravagant hymn to the glories of sensual, physical love and companionship between two equal partners. The Song of Songs seems to suggest, despite centuries of commentary to the contrary, that it is good and right to embrace our sexuality, our physical embodiment as finite creatures, and therein to discover meaning and purpose in our lives. As the final chapter of the Song of Songs adjures us:

> Set me as a seal upon your heart,
> as a seal upon your arm;
> for love is strong as death,
> passion fierce as the grave.
> Its flashes are flashes of fire,
> a raging flame.

---

25. For more on this ambiguity and its lasting effects, both good and bad, see Merchant, *The Death of Nature*.

> Many waters cannot quench love,
> neither can floods drown it.
> If one offered for love
> all the wealth of one's house,
> it would be utterly scorned. (Song 8:6–7)

For the author of the Song of Songs, the meaning of life is quite simple: it is to be found in the authentic giving and receiving of genuine, mutual, physical love and in celebrating the goodness of creation in all its dizzying and delightful diversity and splendor.

Ecclesiastes: Vanity of Vanities! All Is Vanity

While the Song of Songs provides a rather straightforward response to the question of the meaning of life, another example of Wisdom Literature invites readers to engage in decidedly more ambiguous reflections on the meaning and purpose of human life. Ecclesiastes provides a more worldwise and sometimes ironic or even cynical reflection on the meaning of life. Anyone plugged into Western popular culture has heard passages from Ecclesiastes before, even if they have no idea that these are biblical texts. "Vanity of vanities; all is vanity," "For everything there is a season," "A living dog is better than a dead lion," and "Eat, drink, and be merry": all of these time-honored aphorisms are originally found in Ecclesiastes.

Ecclesiastes purports to be the musings of a king of Israel (traditionally but mistakenly identified as King Solomon), also known as *Qoheleth* in Hebrew, which literally means "the Gatherer" but is often translated as "the Teacher" or "the Preacher." The explicit theme of this book is the quest for the meaning of life, but it does address questions of religion, morality, politics, relationships, and many other themes as well. What is particularly significant about Ecclesiastes is the realization that, even though it is contained within the genre of Wisdom Literature, the book itself is profoundly skeptical—thanks to its healthy acknowledgment of existential doubt—of the very notion of wisdom as something finite human beings are capable of achieving.

The main theme of Ecclesiastes is that all human efforts are inherently vain and futile because every human being will inevitably die. Thanks to our existential reason we create ever-more complex and highminded ideas, institutions, and philosophical or theological approaches to human life, but every single one of us, without fail, will die before we achieve our goal of ultimate wisdom and purpose. We create grand concepts and noble principles, we form complex political organizations and enter into sophisticated economic arrangements, we pledge ourselves to venerable ideals and sacred religious commitments, and it all inevitably ends in death. "Vanity of vanities; all is vanity!" is the Teacher's ceaseless refrain. You might think you have an inside track on the real meaning of it all, and you might believe that you've discovered the Secret, the Truth with a capital "T," but you, too, will die, and it will all disappear like dew in the midday sun.

The Teacher delights in pricking holes in the smug self-satisfaction of those who assume they have everything figured out. To anyone who claims to have discovered the Secret—the final, ultimate meaning of it all—he has the same response, again and again throughout the book: "Vanity of vanities; all is vanity," or "This too is vanity, and a chasing after wind." Another way of translating that first phrase is "Futility of futilities; all is futile." In other words, none of what we take so seriously *really* matters because none of its lasts forever. We're just cerebral animals making our way through life the best way we know how, but none of us really knows what we're doing, and we certainly don't know what the point of it all is, at least not if we're brutally honest with ourselves, because we know, deep-down, that our lives are but a fleeting breath and the world will keep on spinning after we're gone:

> Vanity of vanities, says the Teacher,
> vanity of vanities! All is vanity.
> What do people gain from all the toil
> at which they toil under the sun?
> A generation goes, and a generation comes,
> but the earth remains forever. . . .
>
> I, the Teacher, when king over Israel in Jerusalem, applied my mind to seek and to search out by wisdom all that is done under heaven; it is an unhappy business that God has given to human beings to be busy with. I saw all the deeds that are done under the sun; and see, all is vanity and a chasing after wind. (Eccl 1:2–4; 12–14)

The Teacher acknowledges the earnest effort we human beings put into making sense of our lives in the pursuit of wisdom, meaning, and purpose, but he concludes, almost with a sense of grim resignation, that none of it really matters because it is ultimately "a chasing after wind."

Being well-versed in the Wisdom tradition, the Teacher reflects on the several stages of a life lived in pursuit of wisdom to see where, if anywhere, genuine meaning is to be found. For most of us, we first raise this question of the meaning of our lives during our teenage years, when we are beginning to stake out our own independent path in life. We determine our own likes and dislikes, we make friendships, we seek out new and rewarding experiences, and we begin to plan for our futures. "All is vanity and a chasing after wind," says the Teacher. Once we head out into the world on our own, we begin to take more responsibility for our lives. We get an education, we make more lasting friendships, we might seek romantic relationships, and we eventually embark on a professional career. "All is vanity and a chasing after wind." As we get older, we realize what is really important. We cultivate deeper and more authentic friendships, we might get married and start a family, we commit ourselves to just and righteous causes, we engage in politics, we set up retirement accounts and create household budgets, we avail ourselves of cultural opportunities and meaningful experiences of the world. "All is vanity and a chasing after wind." We slowly, even grudgingly realize that the Teacher is correct, that all of this is so much vanity and futility, that none of this is ultimately satisfying. But this thought, too, is vanity and a chasing after wind. At every step of the way, when we think to ourselves that now we're *really* living life and discovering its deeper meaning, the Teacher is there to remind us that this, too, is vanity and a chasing after wind. Who do we think we are, to discover the Secret? The secret is that there is no Secret!

> Then I said to myself, "What happens to the fool will happen to me also; why then have I been so very wise?" And I said to myself that this also is vanity. For there is no enduring remembrance of the wise or of fools, seeing that in the days to come all will have been long forgotten. How can the wise die just like fools? So I hated life, because what is done under the sun was grievous to me; for all is vanity and a chasing after wind.
>
> I hated all my toil in which I had toiled under the sun, seeing that I must leave it to those who come after me—and who knows whether they will be wise or foolish? Yet they will be master of all for which I toiled and used my wisdom under the sun. This also is vanity. So I turned and gave my heart up to despair concerning all the toil of my labors under the sun, because sometimes one who has toiled with wisdom and knowledge and skill must leave all to be enjoyed by another who did not toil for it. This also is vanity and a great evil. What do mortals get from

all the toil and strain with which they toil under the sun? For all their days are full of pain, and their work is a vexation; even at night their minds do not rest. This also is vanity. (Eccl 2:15–23)

If it's not clear by now, the main theme of the Teacher's words is that everything is vanity, everything is futile, and nothing we do really, ultimately matters in the end. But if that's the case, then the fact that nothing really matters also doesn't matter, so we should just calm down, relax, and enjoy the ride! (There are obvious parallels here between the Teacher and Nagel's thoughts on the absurdity of life we discussed in the last chapter.) The Teacher doesn't leave us in despair, though, because for the Teacher the vanity and futility of all of our striving should liberate us from the expectation that we're supposed to have everything figured out. It's precisely our insistence on taking everything we do so very seriously that weighs us down and causes us to despair. But once we take the leap and give up that insistence, life can be so much sweeter:

> For everything there is a season, and a time for every matter under heaven:
>
> a time to be born, and a time to die;
>
> a time to plant, and a time to pluck up what is planted;
>
> a time to kill, and a time to heal;
>
> a time to break down, and a time to build up;
>
> a time to weep, and a time to laugh;
>
> a time to mourn, and a time to dance;
>
> a time to throw away stones, and a time to gather stones together;
>
> a time to embrace, and a time to refrain from embracing;
>
> a time to seek, and a time to lose;
>
> a time to keep, and a time to throw away;
>
> a time to tear, and a time to sew;
>
> a time to keep silence, and a time to speak;
>
> a time to love, and a time to hate;
>
> a time for war, and a time for peace.[26]
>
> What gain have the workers from their toil? I have seen the business that God has given to everyone to be busy with. God has made everything suitable for its time; moreover, [God] has put a sense of past and future into their minds, yet they cannot find

---

26. You might be more familiar with this passage as a song: https://www.youtube.com/watch?v=W4ga_M5Zdn4

out what God has done from the beginning to the end. I know that there is nothing better for them than to be happy and enjoy themselves as long as they live; moreover, it is God's gift that all should eat and drink and take pleasure in all their toil. I know that whatever God does endures forever; nothing can be added to it, nor anything taken from it; God has done this, so that all should stand in awe before God. That which is, already has been; that which is to be, already is; and God seeks out what has gone by. (Eccl 3:1–15)

This memorable passage is a reminder that life is so much bigger and grander than we can possibly fathom and that none of us is finally in control of the life we live. We make our choices as best we can and then life happens. We try to do our best and we roll with the punches as they come. We always already find ourselves here, already alive, before we've ever consented to the arrangement (the fancy Heideggerian German terms for this are *Geworfensein*: "being-thrown," or *Geworfenheit*: "thrownness"[27]). So much of our lives is already determined for us before we've had any say in the matter, and the sooner we come to terms with our contingency, the fact that we already find ourselves "thrown" into the world before we can even agree to the terms, the better. But at the same time, we really do have significant agency over our lives and the direction they take. We have commitments, values, desires, hopes and dreams. We want to live lives that mean something, and we want to leave the world a better place than we found it. That is part of what it means to be human, to have this deep and burning desire to do something that matters.

The Teacher isn't telling us to give up; he simply reminds us that all of this will inevitably come to an end because we are all finite creatures, with a limited capacity to make sense of it all. This can be a cause for despair, or, as the Teacher urges, this can be a cause for joy. Our lives, just as we live them, are an indescribable gift, utterly undeserved and ultimately incomprehensible, so we should make the most out of this wonderful opportunity to be alive. But we should never get too big for our britches and think that we can somehow solve the ultimate mysteries, because those mysteries will always elude our grasp.

---

27. See Heidegger, *Being and Time*.

Living under a Question Mark

The vanity and futility of everything under the sun can be cause for despair, or it can be a call to action. We can take the nihilistic route and forswear making any effort at all, but what sort of life would that be? What a waste of the one life we know we've been given! Instead, we can acknowledge that all is ultimately vanity and futility and we can steer into the skid, leaping into the unknown and making everything we do really matter as much as it possibly can, here and now. We can cultivate wisdom, we can pursue peace and justice, we can seek the truth, we can find somebody to love,[28] we can enjoy the good gifts of a loving and gracious God, we can love the fate (*amor fati*[29]) we've been given as finite human beings by embracing our finitude and living a fully human life, with all its questions and ambiguities and joys and sorrows and frustrations and triumphs.

Finally, we can leap into the unknown in genuine faith, trusting that there is an ultimate reality always beyond our grasp and comprehension that will provide us the ultimate fulfillment that we are incapable of producing on our own. Because really, what else can we do? As the Holocaust survivor Elie Wiesel put it in his novel, *The Town beyond the Wall*, "It isn't easy to live always under a question mark. But who says that the essential question has an answer? The essence of [humanity] is to be a question, and the essence of the question is to be without answer."[30]

And this is another clue to the meaning of life. We will always live under a question mark, because the nature of humanity is to be a question, and the nature of the question is to be without answer. That is a beautiful thing, in the end, because that existential doubt, born of existential reason, propels us faithfully forward on our quest for the answer, and that is what gives life so much of its urgency, its intensity, its sweetness, and its reward. For Christians, there is an earnest hope that God has the answers to the questions we raise, but it is the nature of faith to trust rather than to know with absolute certainty that we will ever discover

---

28. Grace Slick and Jefferson Airplane understood this and created one of the classic rock and roll tracks of the 1960s: https://www.youtube.com/watch?v=cBYv2wr9c00

29. As Nietzsche wrote in *Ecce Homo*, "My formula for greatness in a human being is *amor fati*: that one wants nothing to be different, not forward, not backward, not in all eternity. Not merely bear what is necessary, still less conceal it—all idealism is mendacity in the face of what is necessary—but love it." *Basic Writings of Nietzsche*, 714.

30. Wiesel, *The Town beyond the Wall*, 176.

the answers to these most burning questions. On this side of eternity, at least, we are left with the questions, with the persistent existential doubt, and the meaning of life lies in living into those questions and doubts with everything we've got, in seeking out meaningful experiences along the way, in forging deep and lasting relationships to provide companionship and sustenance and consolation on the journey, and to trust that nothing we do is lost to eternity: that it was, in the end, good that we were here to experience this wonderful, tragic, incomprehensible, beautiful world.

Conclusion
Faith, Doubt, and Reason

THE MEDIEVAL THEOLOGIAN, MONK, and archbishop Anselm of Canterbury famously described the task of theology as *fides quaerens intellectum* ("faith seeking understanding"). The commitment, or the leap, or the ultimate concern always comes first, in response to being grasped by the ultimate, infinite reality (what Christians call "God"); the life of faith, then, consists in making sense, with the aid of doubt and reason, of just what it means to have faith and in living ever more deeply into that relationship between our own finite being and the infinite reality to which we pledge ourselves in trusting hope. Centuries earlier, in the *Confessions*, Augustine reflected on his circuitous and sometimes tortured path toward his ultimate realization that the God he had so desperately sought his whole life was there all along, nudging him and luring him into a genuine relationship with God. For Augustine, that path took him to many different places—geographical, intellectual, and spiritual—but it all began with a question, and this persistent question turns out to be the most basic question of all: as Augustine put it, "I have become a question to myself."[1] Each of our journeys begins with a question, and we can never hope to find our way toward our destination until we realize that we're lost. We have, each of us, become a question to ourselves, and it is our life's work to engage that question in search of an answer.

---

1. Augustine, *Confessions*, 216.

What Do We Love When We Love God?

Another way Augustine framed this most fundamental question of his existence was to pose it in terms of his relationship with God: "But when I love you [my God], what do I love?"[2] In this question beats the heart of what faith, doubt, reason, and the meaning of life are all about. We can break it down into even smaller, more basic questions. Who am I? What do I love? Who are "you"? Who or what is "God"? And in what sense is this God *my* God? What does all of this mean for my life? Notice that the questions here are irreducibly relational. I can't love you until I know you, and I can't love you unless I love myself. I can't love myself until I know myself, and I can't know myself until I know the source and goal of my being. I can't know and love God until I know and love myself.

John Caputo, in his book *On Religion* (which, he confesses, is really a book about love), asks these same questions and he comes to a rather startling conclusion about the nature of Augustine's question: when it comes right down to it, is love another name we use for God, or is God another name we use for love? Which is the predicate of the other? Or is the meaning and the passion to be found in the not-deciding, in the letting-play of this fluidity between love and God, God and love? Another way to ask this question is to ask what gives my life its "salt": its flavor, intensity, and sustenance.[3] What do we love in a way that is "worth its salt?" What do we love unconditionally, without reservation, with a fierce and passionate love? Whatever it is we love in this way, that is really our God. Or, as Luther put it, it is the faith and trust of the heart that make both God and idol. We love all sorts of things in our life, but there is always something that we love above all else, something we love totally and unconditionally, something we love with a love that never dies. In Tillich's language, this is our ultimate concern, our faith. Our faith can be genuine or it can be idolatrous, but we can never be without it.

When we love an infinite reality passionately and unconditionally—when we love "God"—we love without proof that our love is well-placed. We love without guarantee of reciprocity or reward. This love, with which we commit ourselves totally and completely, without reservation or condition, to a reality that will always exceed our understanding, opens itself

---

2. Augustine, *Confessions*, 183.

3. In the ancient world salt was such a vital staple that each Roman soldier was paid a *salarium*, which was money the soldier needed to buy his ration of salt (*sal* in Latin). It survives in our word "salary."

to profound insecurity, suffering, and loss. This love drives us beyond ourselves, beyond our own fears and desires, into the infinite reality, the ground of our being, that loves us and accepts us before we even begin our quest. Our faith is always a response to a prior sense or intuition or realization, or maybe just a hope or a hunch, that there is more to our lives than we ever thought possible, that more is going on in, with, and under the world than we ever dared hope, that at the bottom of it all is a deep and abiding loving presence. We will experience fleeting glimpses of this loving presence, but we can never own it as a possession. In fact, we can never be absolutely sure that it's really real. But we leap into that unknown with trusting confidence (Latin for "with faith"!), accepting the risk of loving without condition and without measure. In Tillich's language, this is the self-transcendence born of existential reason that accepts the uncertainty and risk of existential doubt with liberating courage.

As human beings we alone, as far as we currently know, have the unique capacity to take a step back from our lives and wonder what they really mean. We have the capacity to commit ourselves totally and unconditionally to an ultimate reality from which we expect ultimate fulfillment, but because we are finite creatures we can never be certain that what we take with ultimate seriousness is really there to catch us when we leap. For most of our daily lives we don't consciously think about these things (unless we're professional theologians or philosophers!); most of us simply live our lives the best we can and take one day at a time. We fill our lives with work and play, family and friends, meetings and vacations, civic obligations and hobbies, appointments and routines. None of these concerns is inherently bad or unworthy of our attention, as they are all good and noble pursuits. But when this is the sum total of our lives, we soon discover that we are spending our lives skating on the surface of life rather than plumbing the depths of what really, ultimately matters.

The Surface and the Depths

In the 1940s Tillich preached a sermon titled "The Depth of Existence" that encapsulates so much of what this book is about. In this sermon he reflects on the metaphor or the symbol of *depth* as an important clue or revelation of the existential, spiritual heart of our lives as human beings, and he contrasts this depth with the surface where we spend most of our lives. All of those daily concerns mentioned above occur on the surface of our lives, rarely providing us with any deeper meaning than checking another item off our to-do lists. So often we confuse having a busy life with living a meaningful life, and perhaps that's no coincidence. We feel more comfortable on the surface of things because we feel that we can control what happens on the surface. For the most part, we determine our schedules. We have some control over how we engage with other people and carry out our daily routines. We have some say in how we spend our time and what we decide to do each day. But when we spend all of our time on the surface of our lives and assume that this is all there is to being alive, we miss so much of what gives life its salt, its passion, and its meaning.

Sometimes, though, the surface breaks open and reveals a depth to existence we didn't realize was there all along. Sometimes we can open up that rupture ourselves through reflection, meditation, study, or prayer. But more often than not, the surface breaks open when we least expect it or want it to. We experience a tragedy or we are confronted with our own mortality. Sometimes the daily grind loses its capacity to satisfy us and we ask what is missing in our lives to make them really mean something. When we gaze over the edge of the surface and peer into the abyss, it looks terrifying. As Nietzsche said, "If you look long into an abyss, the abyss also looks into you."[4] We will do anything to make this abyss go away and get back to our pleasant, comfortable, superficial lives. But there's the rub: the only way to genuine meaning is through those terrifying depths.

Tillich tells the story of two people, both going about their daily lives. One is a mechanic and the other is a promising student of philosophy. Each of them goes to work and completes their task every day, the mechanic by performing manual labor and the philosophy student by studying the questions and ideas and perspectives of the great thinkers of the past. We might assume that the philosophy student is closer to the meaning of life than the mechanic, but we would be wrong. Everything depends on the attitude and the perspective of each person. In Tillich's telling, the philosophy student is content to learn the ideas and insights of other great thinkers but never asks the questions for himself and never makes these ideas and insights a part of his own life and quest for meaning. The student assumes that knowing what other people have thought about meaning passes for his own meaning, but he never breaks through

---

4. Nietzsche, *Beyond Good and Evil*, 89.

the surface of things to experience the depths of life and its meaning for himself. The mechanic, on the other hand, does her job each day but suddenly steps back to reflect on the meaning of it all. She asks herself what it means that she spends her days doing manual labor and what that job contributes to her neighbors and to the world. She wonders about what really matters in her life and she resolves to do her work and live her life as conscientiously and meaningfully as she can. The mechanic, not the philosophy student, is on the way to depth and meaning because she has asked the really significant questions about her own life.[5]

These questions often cause a rupture in our lives, and for good reason: they are big questions! We sometimes call this experience an "existential crisis," like the crisis Faust had when he realized that he had spent his whole life learning what other people thought about life rather than genuinely and authentically living his own. When that rupture breaks the surface of our lives we often experience this as a catastrophe and a disaster. Here the etymology of these words is particularly instructive. The Greek root of "catastrophe" means "overturning," and the Latin root of "disaster" means "a bad star," referring to the ancient practice of navigating a ship by the stars. Both terms imply a loss of certainty, a feeling of abandonment, a sense of being set adrift without an anchor or a beacon to keep us on track, safe and secure. The surface was familiar and comfortable and easy, and now it's all blown to hell! Suddenly we're face-to-face with a yawning abyss with no discernible bottom and nothing to lead us to safety, and it's absolutely terrifying, just as Descartes discovered when he put everything he thought he knew into radical doubt and just as Job realized when everything he thought he knew about God and the world was suddenly shattered by the pain of undeserved suffering. Some of us will do anything we can to avoid the depths and get back to the familiar surface as quickly as possible. We would very much rather avoid gazing too long into the abyss.

But we are missing a powerful and indeed irreplaceable opportunity for meaning if we avoid the depths. The depths are frightening and traumatic, but there is no way to real meaning and joy without going through the depths. Job certainly came to realize this, as we saw in the chapter on doubt. The Psalms traditionally called the Lamentation Psalms teach this same lesson. The Hebrew Prophets all understood this as they reflected on

---

5. The philosophy student is a contemporary stand-in for Faust's assistant Wagner, who wanted nothing more than to understand what other thinkers have thought about the meaning of life, without ever asking that most important question for himself.

the impending destruction of Israel and Judah. Jesus himself understood this when he endured suffering and death on the cross. Martin Luther also understood this when he suggested that no one can truly become a theologian until they've suffered.[6] The Buddha understood this as well, so much so that the first of his Four Noble Truths is the simple realization that all life is suffering, and everything the Buddha taught was meant to help us make our way through the depths to discover true meaning and joy.[7] So many of the world's great religious thinkers come to the same conclusion: that it is only by going through the depths of suffering and despair that we become capable of making real meaning in our lives.

We US-Americans live in a culture that expends enormous amounts of energy doing everything we can to avoid the depths of existence at all costs. We as a culture are terrified of death and dying, so we deny the reality and the finality of death. We as a culture avoid asking difficult and potentially life-altering questions because we are far more comfortable skating along the surface of our bourgeois consumerist lives. We've become experts at presenting idealized versions of ourselves on social media and we equate likes and retweets with validation and meaning, without ever letting anyone see who we really are. We fear vulnerability and pain and loss, so we pretend that we can somehow avoid these inevitable parts of life. We cling to the surface for dear life because we are terrified of what lies beneath. As Tillich puts it in his sermon,

> Most of our life continues on the surface. We are enslaved by the routine of our daily lives, in work and pleasure, in business and recreation. We are conquered by innumerable hazards, both good and evil. We are more driven than driving. We do not stop to look at the height above us, or to the depth below us. We are always moving forward, although usually in a circle, which finally brings us back to the place from which we first moved. We are in constant motion and never stop to plunge into the depth. We talk and talk and never listen to the voices speaking to our depth and from our depth. We accept ourselves as we appear to ourselves, and do not care what we really are. Like hit-and-run drivers, we injure our souls by the speed with which we move on the surface; and then we rush away, leaving our bleeding souls alone. We miss, therefore, our depth and our true life. And it is only when the picture that we have of ourselves breaks down completely, only when we find ourselves acting

6. Luther, "The Heidelberg Disputation."
7. "The Buddha's First Sermon: Setting the Wheel of the Dharma in Motion."

against all the expectations we had derived from that picture, and only when an earthquake shakes and disrupts the surface of our self-knowledge, that we are willing to look into a deeper level of our being.[8]

We are fed a constant stream of distractions and advertising and self-help nostrums encouraging us to remain on the surface, there to find true meaning and joy. But the most we can hope to receive from the surface is fleeting comfort and happiness. True meaning and joy are not to be found on the surface; they are to be found in the depths of existence. Artists and poets and musicians and writers and philosophers and theologians and activists for centuries have encouraged us to dig beneath the surface to get a glimpse of the depths, of the profound things that really matter. They take it upon themselves to shatter the illusions of a calm, still surface. In our own times, abstract art, atonal music, minimalist poetry, avant-garde theater, postmodern theory, the LGBTQIA+ Movement, Black Lives Matter, and the #MeToo Movement all perform the prophetic task of uncovering the depths churning beneath our safe and easy surface. More often than not the masses find these works and movements unconventional, unsettling, inscrutable, or even offensive. Perhaps that is simply an aesthetic judgment, but more often than not it is an unconscious, existential resistance to peering beneath the surface and into the depths exposed by these prophetic voices.

We often avoid dealing with the deep things of life by assuming or insisting that they are too sophisticated, too complex, too difficult for ordinary people. But this is a self-serving dodge and a cowardly cop-out. The depths are not too sophisticated or too difficult for anyone to grasp; in fact, the depths are quite simple and straightforward. The problem isn't that they are too sophisticated or difficult; rather, the problem is that they are too unsettling or painful for us to deal with, so we excuse ourselves from the important and necessary work of plumbing the depths of our lives by insisting that it is all too complicated or sophisticated for us. It is far easier, and far safer, to remain on the surface, blissful in our self-imposed ignorance. As Tillich puts it in his sermon,

> The mark of real depth is its simplicity. If you should say, "This is too profound for me; I cannot grasp it," you are self-deceptive. For you ought to know that nothing of real importance is too profound for anyone. It is not because it is too profound, but

---

8. Tillich, "The Depth of Existence," 55–56.

rather because it is too uncomfortable, that you shy away from the truth. Let us not confuse the sophisticated things with the deep things of life. The sophisticated things do not concern us ultimately and it does not matter whether we understand them or not. But the deep things must concern us always, because it matters infinitely whether we are grasped by them or not.[9]

If we allow ourselves to be grasped by these deep things, if we seek our meaning and our purpose and our value not on the surface, but in the depths of our existence, we are well on our way to genuine faith. Faith means having an ultimate concern, committing ourselves totally to an infinite, ultimate reality that has the capacity to provide us with genuine meaning and fulfillment. In the Christian tradition this reality is identified with the symbol of "God." But if that symbol has too much baggage, has too many negative connotations, don't use it; find something else to express your ultimate concern, your experience of the depths of existence. Tillich again:

> The name of this infinite and inexhaustible depth and ground of all being is *God*. That depth is what the word *God* means. And if that word has not much meaning for you, translate it, and speak of the depths of your life, of the source of your being, of your ultimate concern, of what you take seriously without any reservation. Perhaps, in order to do so, you must forget everything traditional that you have learned about God, perhaps even that word itself. For if you know that God means depth, you know much about Him [*sic*]. You cannot then call yourself an atheist or unbeliever. For you cannot think or say: Life has no depth! Life itself is shallow. Being itself is surface only. If you could say this in complete seriousness, you would be an atheist; but otherwise you are not. He [*sic*] who knows about depth knows about God.[10]

Genuine faith is our total commitment to the infinite, ultimate reality (whatever we might call it), as opposed to idolatrous faith, which is total commitment to a finite reality that can never support the weight and intensity of our ultimate concern and can therefore never provide the ultimate meaning and fulfillment of our lives. Finite realities skim along the surface of our lives while infinite reality is encountered in the depths. Finite realities are fleeting and transient, which means they will

9. Tillich, "The Depth of Existence," 60.
10. Tillich, "The Depth of Existence," 57.

inevitably disappear and disappoint us, but the ultimate, infinite reality is eternal and is thus fully capable of supporting our commitment while always remaining beyond our grasp and comprehension. This is why genuine faith requires existential doubt as a permanent, necessary element, because we will never be certain that the object of our faith will deliver ultimate fulfillment and meaning. But we take the leap anyway, trusting that this ultimate reality will sustain us and support us in the end.

Idolatrous faith is content to live on the surface of our lives, engaging with what is fleeting and temporary and ultimately doesn't matter. Living this way is arguably easier and simpler, but it is ultimately unfulfilling and will inevitably disappoint us. Genuine faith breaks through the surface of our lives and plunges us into the depths, where things are much more uncertain, ambiguous, and even unsettling. Genuine faith leaps into the unknown with courage and trust, hoping that something is there to catch us despite the uncertainty that this is so. When we break through the surface and make our way into the depths it is only natural that we will experience a good deal of doubt, because nothing in the depths is clear, or certain, or secure.[11] Suffering, death, and despair are real threats to our wellbeing. But in many cases such suffering and despair function as refining fires, burning away the idolatrous elements of our faith to reveal the genuine, risky faith at the center of our being. The German Lutheran theologian Rudolf Bultmann, a contemporary of Tillich's, has this to say about genuine, risky faith:

> Those who want to have faith in God as their God must know that they hold nothing in hand in which they can believe; that they are, as it were, poised mid-air and can demand no proof of the truth of the word that has been spoken to them. For the ground and the object of faith are identical. Only the one who abandons all security can find security, only the one who—to speak with Luther—is prepared to enter into the inner darkness.[12]

When all else is gone, when everything we've constructed to support us is taken away, when we have nothing left but pure trust and hope, we

---

11. Anne Lamott expresses this well when she writes that "the opposite of faith is not doubt, but certainty. Certainty is missing the point entirely. Faith includes noticing the mess, the emptiness and discomfort, and letting it be there until some light returns." *Plan B*, 256–7.

12. My translation of a passage from Bultmann's 1952 essay "Zum Problem der Entmythologisierung," translated into English as "On the Problem of Demythologizing."

will discover what really matters. When we're distracted by the superficial things in life it can be easy to assume that these fleeting superficial pleasures are the sum total of our existence, but the ruptures in the surface remind us that this is an illusion. The depths remind us of our need for something far beyond our own capacities to give us meaning, something that eludes our best efforts to understand and control. According to Tillich, it is only in and through the depths where we will find true meaning and joy:

> Eternal joy is the end of the ways of God. . . . But eternal joy is not to be reached by living on the surface. It is rather attained by breaking through the surface, by penetrating the deep things of ourselves, of our world, and of God. The moment in which we reach the last depth of our lives is the moment in which we can experience the joy that has eternity within it, the hope that cannot be destroyed, and the truth on which life and death are built. For in the depth is truth; and in the depth is hope; and in the depth is joy.[13]

In this quest to plumb the depths of our existence, in our hope of discovering meaning and purpose, we come to appreciate more fully the role of faith, doubt, and reason in our lives. As human beings with the gift of existential reason we have the capacity to step back from our lives and ask what they really mean, which is the capacity for ultimate concern, or faith. Being grasped by an infinite reality that transcends our finite concerns, we respond with total commitment to something beyond finite reality to support us and to provide that meaning. But this commitment requires leaping into an abyss, into the inscrutable depths where we can never be certain there is anything there to catch us as we leap. The question of the meaning of our lives will remain unanswered as long as we live, as it is our blessing and our curse to be able to ask the question but to be unable to determine the final answer. We take the leap anyway, trusting that there is a deeper meaning to be made out of the trajectories of our lives. But we recognize at the same time that we are leaping into the darkness, and we question whether this faith is enough to sustain us and to give us the meaning we so earnestly desire.

So much of our lives is consumed with superficial efforts. We live as finite beings in a finite world, so naturally we will spend most of our time engaging finite reality with finite concerns. We want food and

---

13. Tillich, "The Depth of Existence," 63.

shelter and companionship, we want meaningful work and relationships, we want comfort and pleasure and happiness. And all of these are good and important things that should be available to all, without exception. But when we dig deeper we realize that there is more going on in our lives. We have deeper concerns, deeper questions, and deeper desires. We yearn for real and lasting meaning and joy. Superficial things will never provide that lasting meaning and joy, so we take a leap into the infinite reality, whatever we happen to call it, trusting that this leap will provide ultimate meaning and fulfillment.

Faith, Doubt, and Reason

This suggests that faith, doubt, and reason are universal human faculties, the tools we use to make sense of our lives and to give them meaning and purpose. Faith is far more than religious commitment or identity, although many people express their faith in specific religious symbols within specific religious communities. Faith is the total commitment of our entire being to whatever it is we take with absolute seriousness and from which we expect ultimate meaning and fulfillment. When the object of our ultimate concern is finite, we have an idolatrous faith that will inevitably end in existential disappointment, with no hope of meaning and fulfillment. But when the object of our ultimate concern is infinite (whether we call it "God" or something else, using religious or secular language), we have a genuine faith. We have the capacity for genuine faith in the infinite, ultimate reality because we have the gift of existential reason, the capacity for self-transcendence and for freedom, creativity, wisdom, and meaning. Though we ourselves are finite creatures, we discover that we are grasped by something more, something beyond the vicissitudes of our daily lives and the finite world around us. Our faith is a response to this infinite reality that grasps us and lures us beyond our immediate concerns and into the depths of our lives.

But because we are finite creatures, we can never hope to understand just what it is we're committing ourselves to in trusting faith, so there will always be questions about the object of our faith and its capacity to give us meaning and fulfillment. This uncertainty is expressed as existential doubt, which is a permanent and necessary element of genuine faith, and it is indeed a confirmation that our faith is genuine. Although this doubt can sometimes be unsettling or uncomfortable, it is something we must accept with courage as it is a consequence of the risk of faith. These three faculties—faith, doubt, and reason—therefore need each other to be what each of them ought to be. They support one another like the three legs of a tripod; without one of the legs, the tripod collapses.

If, as Tillich has suggested, faith is an act of the total personality and therefore includes all of our human faculties, then a healthy, genuine faith will not produce conflict within ourselves. If we find that there are contradictions between our faith and what we know through reason to be true about ourselves or about the world around us, or if we find that our faith compels us to ignore the doubts or questions that will inevitably arise in the course of our lives, then we should not dismiss these warning signs that something is going wrong. We must embrace the doubts and questions that will inevitably arise as indications that we're on the right track, and if we assume that we must choose between our faith and what we know by reason, we must submit our faith and our use of reason to critical scrutiny to be sure that both are remaining within their proper "spheres."

So much of the conflict that we experience in our quest for meaning can be traced to our tendency to idolatry, to our habit of elevating finite realities to the level of ultimacy. Part of this tendency is rooted in a failure to distinguish clearly between the finite and the infinite realms. If there is strong evidence for or against a particular proposition, then we are dealing with beliefs, not with faith. If we can definitively answer our questions and settle our doubts, we are dealing with beliefs, not with faith. If we can logically determine the factual truth of the matter, we are dealing with beliefs, not with faith. And if there is no evidence to support our truth claim, or if there is strong evidence against it, and we nevertheless insist on its factual truth despite its being illogical or irrational, then we are still not dealing with faith, but with bad beliefs. Elevating anything finite to the level of ultimacy and expecting it to provide us with ultimate meaning and fulfillment will inevitably lead to disaster, to despair, to the breakdown of our lives. The quest for genuine faith requires a constant awareness that, as John Calvin reminds us, the human mind is a "factory of idols." And this is so because we are deeply uncomfortable with ambiguity, uncertainty, and a lack of clear answers. We are far more comfortable clinging to easy answers and false security than taking the leap into the unknown depths, but until we take that leap we will never know true meaning and joy.

The life of faith must include honest self-awareness and self-criticism, tasks that can often be inconvenient and even distressing. But the effort is worth it because genuine faith is the only way to genuine meaning and joy. Healthy faith, doubt, and reason contribute to the deeper meaning of our lives because these are three of the faculties that make us fully human. When we cultivate a deeper appreciation of the meaning and scope of faith, doubt, and reason, we are liberated to throw ourselves completely into our lives without fear, to live and to love and to experience all we can of this weird, wild, wonderful world. These three faculties encourage us to seek out new experiences, to love our neighbors and our world, to embrace our mortality without fear, to pursue justice and peace, to embrace the big questions, to wonder at the incredible mystery of it all, and to live in humble gratitude for the improbable gift of being alive. Genuine faith has the capacity to keep us grounded while also propelling us with confidence into an unknown future, to provide meaning and purpose and value, to open our eyes and our minds and our hearts to what is really important in our lives. Genuine faith will embrace the big questions as opportunities to reflect deeply on matters of profound significance for us and for the world. Genuine faith will give us the lens we need to make sense of our experiences of the world, of our loves and our desires, even of our inevitable end, without fear. Faith, doubt, and reason open for us the way to deep and lasting joy.

The Liberal Arts

The pursuit of meaning and purpose with the aid of faith, doubt, and reason never happens in a vacuum because we always pursue meaning in the context of our actual lives, with all of the ups and downs, triumphs and failures, good times and bad. We have many concerns, and it is good and right that we live our daily lives with full awareness of the many concerns that shape and guide our lives. But we also want something more, something that transcends our daily lives and concerns. We seek truth, beauty, and goodness. We want to live lives that really matter to us and to others, and we want reassurance that we didn't waste this one beautiful life. We want an ultimate touchstone for the lives we lead here and now as best we can. And it turns out that we have at our disposal ancient and venerable traditions to guide us in our quest: in the academic world we call this approach to life and wisdom the liberal arts.

The liberal arts have their roots in ancient Greece and Rome, where a broad and deep education was assumed to be necessary for the cultivation of a free (*liber* in Latin) citizen who would then participate meaningfully and responsibly in public life. With the founding of the great medieval European universities, the liberal arts eventually took more specific shape and were divided into the *trivium* (grammar, logic, and rhetoric) and the *quadrivium* (arithmetic, geometry, astronomy, and music theory). A student who gained proficiency in the basic themes of these disciplines was awarded the degree Bachelor of Arts, while a student who mastered all of these subjects was awarded the degree Master of Arts. These disciplines were also considered necessary preparation for advanced study for terminal degrees in law, medicine, or theology, at which point one would be a doctor (literally a teacher).

In today's higher education landscape, the liberal arts comprise disciplines that are more purely academic as opposed to technical or professional degree programs such as pharmacy, business, or education, just to name a few. Universities always contain a College of Liberal Arts and Sciences (the specific name varies by institution), and in the United States there are also hundreds of smaller, private colleges whose entire curriculum is devoted to the liberal arts (these are known as liberal arts colleges). Today when we refer to the liberal arts we often mean subjects like literature, languages, history, philosophy, religion, anthropology, classics, biology, chemistry, physics, astronomy, environmental studies, psychology, sociology, economics, gender studies, area studies, art history, and music, subjects that are not primarily intended to train students for specific professions but to give them a "well-rounded" education in preparation for informed citizenship and the lifelong cultivation of wisdom. To put it another way, the liberal arts are often pursued for their own sake, simply for the love of learning and the joy of discovery and growth as a human being with a commitment to live justly and responsibly in community with our neighbors and with the natural world.

The liberal arts sometimes get a bad rap these days because they are often seen as impractical or difficult to translate directly into a career path (how many times have you heard the bad joke about an English or Philosophy major flipping burgers at a fast food restaurant after graduation?). But this denigration of the liberal arts is a singular failure of vision and imagination, as in our culture we've grown accustomed to thinking of education as little more than job training. While it's good and necessary to have gainful employment and a living wage, there is also something noble and beautiful about learning for its own sake, about delving deeply into the riches of the human experience, about asking challenging questions and engaging new and surprising ideas, about falling in love with thinking deeply and passionately about whatever it is that we take with absolute seriousness, with whatever gives our lives depth and breadth and zest and meaning.

The liberal arts invite us to shed our presumptions and check our biases for the sake of genuinely understanding and appreciating sometimes radically different perspectives. The liberal arts encourage us to drink deeply from the well of human experience and wisdom, to see the world from many different angles, to value and celebrate the incredible diversity of the human quest for wisdom and meaning. The liberal arts train us to see beauty all around us, to discover the common ties that bind all of us together, to delight in difference and uniqueness, to appreciate the vast treasures of human civilizations, to be inspired by the search for understanding and meaning, to put our learning into practice in pursuit of truth, wisdom, progress, and justice. Faith, doubt, and reason are indispensable tools in this pursuit, regardless of the particular discipline or field where we find ourselves most at home. The liberal arts compel us to set our sights higher, above and beyond immediate, quotidian concerns in search of something more, something *meaningful*. The best tools we have at our disposal to reach for these transcendent goals are faith, doubt, and reason, and therefore these quintessentially human faculties are the foundation of any quest for a life well-lived in pursuit of wisdom and meaning.

The liberal arts are so often maligned these days because we have become conditioned to think in the short term, thinking only of our jobs and our bank accounts and the next few pages of our calendar. But life has a way of intervening and disrupting those finite concerns, and if we're not prepared for these moments we can find ourselves lost and adrift, unable to make sense of what we're experiencing here and now. Faith, doubt, and reason push us beyond these immediate concerns to consider the deeper meaning of our lives, and they help us navigate those pregnant moments, those experiences of the peaks and the valleys of human life, in a way that invigorates rather than overwhelms us. The liberal arts are the best resources we have at our disposal to guide us on this journey toward depth and meaning in our lives, with all their unpredictability and mystery, beauty and joy.

John Caputo, in his book *Philosophy and Theology*, writes eloquently and passionately about the power of the liberal arts to evoke this sense of wonder and awe at the sheer improbability and mystery of our being here at all, of our being privileged to be able to ask and seek the answers to the deepest questions that inevitably arise in the course of our lives. He speaks here of philosophy and theology within the context of the liberal arts, and we can extrapolate from his reflection the abiding significance of faith, doubt, and reason as the keys to unlocking the deeper meaning of our lives:

> Philosophy and theology are for wounded souls. Indeed those of us who take up the study of any of the humanities, of language and literature, history and art, philosophy and theology, or any of the natural sciences, have been pierced to the heart by something precious, beautiful, deep, and enigmatic that leaves us reeling. We know that the doctors are not telling us everything, that the wound will not heal, that we are not going to recover. We have suffered a blow that has destroyed our equilibrium; we have been shaken by a provocation, by something that has left us breathless, pursued by questions that we cannot still. We have been visited by some affliction that results in tremors . . . but also has this other oddity about it—this disorder induces an affection for our affliction, so that the patients have no wish to be healed, to close this wound over, to arrest these tremors. For we live and breathe in the tremulousness of our lives, exposed to the questionability of things, made vulnerable to love's wounds, visited in the night by questions of elemental power, shaken to the core by voices that will not be stilled.[14]

Being struck by the beauty of the turning leaves in autumn, watching a child delighting in discovering something new about themselves and their world, being devastated by the news of a loved one's illness, finding ourselves weak in the knees at the intensity of a partner's love, feeling the goosebumps at the swell of a powerful musical performance, savoring a particularly poignant turn of phrase in a poem or novel, relishing the satisfaction of solving a difficult puzzle, being inspired by a new discovery about the natural world, treasuring an experience of a different culture, achieving a victory in the pursuit of justice, glimpsing ever so briefly the power of the transcendent in a religious ritual, coming face to face with our own mortality and the unspeakable beauty of being alive

---

14. Caputo, *Philosophy and Theology*, 71.

at all: all of these deeply human experiences, and many more like them, are enriched and enhanced by our capacity for faith, doubt, and reason. We rely on these faculties to stake out what is true, good, beautiful, and meaningful in our lives and in the world all around us, and the liberal arts provide the context and resources for making sense of these wonderfully human experiences, without which our lives would be woefully diminished. God bless the liberal arts and keep them safe. Long may they live and flourish to enrich us all.

Epilogue

WHAT IS IT, FINALLY, that gives your life meaning and purpose? What is it that you take with absolute seriousness, without reservation? When you take a step back from your life and reflect on the bigger picture, what do you notice? What questions arise as you ponder what it means to be human? Where have we come from, and where are we headed? What, ultimately, will make all of this worth it? These are the questions that keep us up at night, that knock us off our pins, that whisper in the deep, dark recesses of our minds. These are the questions that cannot be stilled because these are the most human of questions, the questions that remind us that we are beautifully, tragically finite human creatures. These are the questions that give life its salt. As we saw earlier, Elie Wiesel wrote in his novel *The Town beyond the Wall*, "It isn't easy to live always under a question mark. But who says that the essential question has an answer? The essence of [humanity] is to be a question, and the essence of the question is to be without answer."

Here in a nutshell is the significance of faith, doubt, and reason. What do we take with absolute seriousness? What leaps into the unknown are we prepared—or maybe unprepared—to take? What questions insist and persist at the edges of our certainty? What sense do we make of our lives as we take a step back to reflect on what it all means? Are we comfortable accepting that these questions might not have answers that we can ever understand, or that they might not have answers at all? Can we make our peace with always living under a question mark? Can we finally discover truth, beauty, and goodness in the questions themselves, in the relentless, endless quest for the meaning, purpose, and significance of our lives?

As we've come to the end of our reflections, I want to leave us with a word of profound wisdom from one of my own teachers, Louis

Hammann, with whom I studied religion as an undergraduate at Gettysburg College. At the end of each class, Lou would ask us if we were confused. For the first few weeks we would always insist that we weren't confused and that everything made sense. Lou would just shake his head and walk out of the classroom. One day, several weeks into our course, Lou asked if we were confused and one student finally blurted out, "Yes!" A smile stretched across Lou's face and he replied, "Good. Now I know you're paying attention. Because if you're not confused, you're not paying attention!" Suddenly everything shifted for all of us. The confusion we experienced as a result of digging deeply into these most profound questions of human meaning was not something to be avoided or ignored; it was something to be embraced, celebrated, and cherished. The confusion we were experiencing meant that we really understood the deeper point of what it was we were trying to figure out together, that the deepest, most significant questions of human existence are far beyond our capacity to understand, let alone answer.

Faith, doubt, and reason help us navigate the confusion we will inevitably experience as we plumb the depths of the human experience. It is a good thing to be confused, because it means we're paying attention to the profound insights and questions and provocations toward meaning and purpose that will inevitably elude our grasp, but it is precisely this confusion that reassures us that we are on the right track, that we are taking things seriously, that we have come to understand, appreciate, and maybe even celebrate the awesome wonder of the perennial human quest for meaning. In these moments of uncertainty we learn that the questions themselves have inherent and lasting value, that our uncertainty and instability is a gift, that our perpetual unknowing will compel us to spend the rest of our lives on the quest for meaning and fulfillment. We come to realize that the whole point is the questions, the uncertainty, the wonder.

The unanswered and unanswerable questions are indeed a precious gift to us. Without this gift of unanswerable questions, we would never rise above or dig below our daily concerns to reflect on what is ultimately meaningful and significant in our lives. May we always embrace these unanswerable questions. May we always be confused. And in the midst of that confusion—and perhaps even *because* we are so profoundly, richly, blessedly confused—may we leap confidently into the unknown, trusting that therein lies all the meaning and the passion.[1]

1. This final thought is paraphrasing the conclusion of John Caputo's *Philosophy and Theology*, upon which I couldn't possibly hope to improve.

Appendix 1

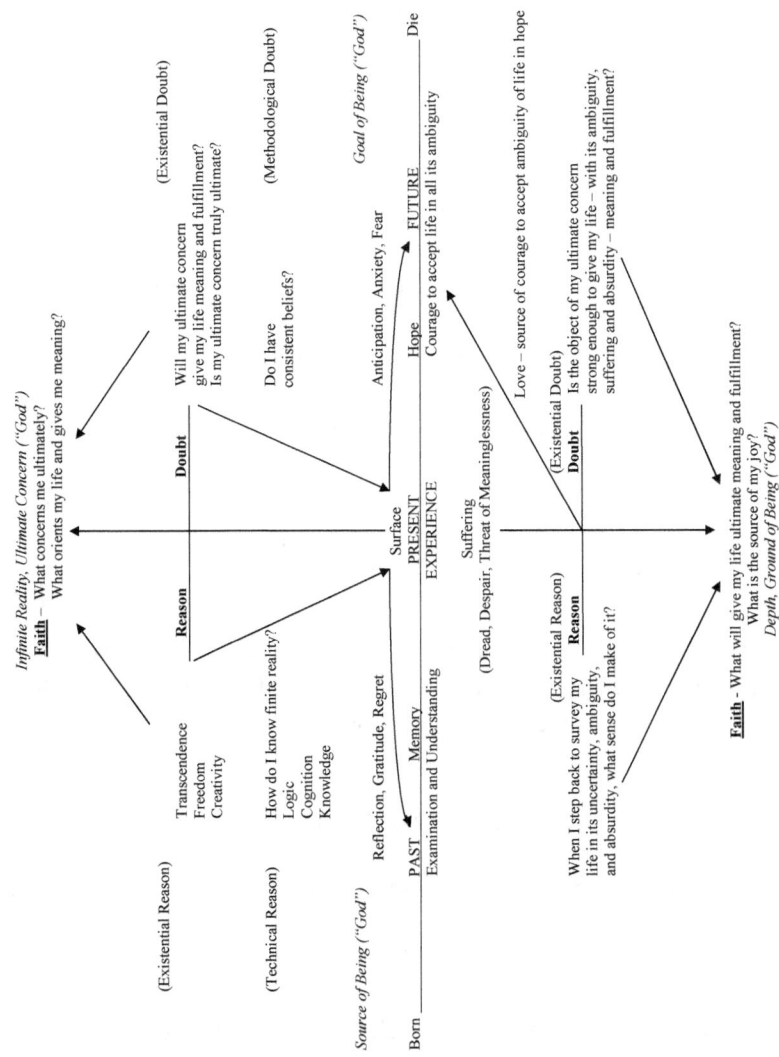

Appendix 2

Discussion Questions

Preface

What does Kant mean by "throwing off the yoke of immaturity"?

Why is it so often difficult to think for ourselves?

What are some questions you might be uncomfortable asking? Why?

Kant said that his was not an enlightened age, but it was an age of enlightenment. Would you say that we currently live in an enlightened age? Do we live in an age of enlightenment? Why or why not?

Socrates said that the unexamined life is not worth living. Do you agree or disagree with him? What does it mean to you to live an examined life? How do you go about examining your own life?

Chapter 1: Faith

How you would describe faith in your own words?

What concerns you ultimately?

Do you agree that everyone has faith, whether or not it's expressed through religious commitments?

What are some common idols in our contemporary culture? How might Tillich's analysis of idolatry help us to understand current social, cultural, economic, political, and religious issues?

What are some of your own idols? What is their attraction for you?

What are some powerful contemporary symbols? In what ways do they perform the different functions of a symbol as Tillich outlines them?

What symbol or symbols most clearly express your own ultimate concern?

What is the difference between reading a story literally and reading it as a myth? Why is that difference important?

What are additional examples of stories that some people take literally and others take as a myth?

Why is it important to understand the difference between faith and belief?

Do you agree with Clifford that what we believe is always a moral issue?

What are some popular beliefs that aren't supported by sufficient evidence? Why do people hold those beliefs anyway?

What does the Bible mean to you? How do you use the Bible?

Chapter 2: Doubt

What distinguishes the three types of doubt?

Why did Descartes want to "raze everything to the ground" and begin from scratch? Do you agree with him that this is sometimes necessary?

Do you agree or disagree with Descartes' famous claim that "I think, therefore I am"? What are its strengths and weaknesses?

Why are some people hesitant to embrace methodological doubt when deciding what to believe?

How does doubting make you feel? Are you comfortable doubting your faith? Why or why not?

What causes you to doubt your faith? How do you deal with it?

Do you agree with Job's friends that there are answers to all of our deepest questions, or do you agree with Job that we'll never know the answers to those deepest questions?

Why does God refuse to answer Job's questions? And why does Job accept that?

Does the epilogue to the Book of Job make sense in the context of the rest of the book? If so, what does it mean that Job was finally rewarded?

What are some explanations you have heard for the existence of evil and suffering? How persuasive do you find those explanations?

Can anger be an expression of faith? Why or why not?

Do you agree with Father Zosima and Alyosha that love is the best response to evil and suffering? Why or why not?

Is there a way to account for the existence of evil and suffering while also maintaining God's omnipotence and omnibenevolence? If not, are you more comfortable modifying God's omnipotence, God's omnibenevolence, or the reality of evil? Why?

In what ways has your thinking about God changed since you were a child? Do you embrace those changes or do they make you uncomfortable? Why?

Chapter 3: Reason

How would you define reason in your own words?

What role does reason play in your own life? Would you consider yourself a rational person?

Descartes thought that what we believe about God must be rational and provable by philosophy. Do you agree or disagree with him?

Do you think Descartes successfully proved God using technical reason? Why or why not?

Has our modern reliance on technical reason done more good or more harm, or both equally?

Why are some people so reluctant to accept incontrovertible facts? Are there any facts you personally have a difficult time accepting?

Why does Tillich think existential reason is the faculty that makes us uniquely human? Do you agree or disagree?

When you take a step back from your life and reflect on it, what questions arise for you?

Do you personally see a conflict between faith and science or between faith and historical scholarship? If so, where do you think they're incompatible?

Can you imagine a new discovery by scientists or historians that would cause you to have a crisis of faith? What might that discovery be?

Do you ever have a sneaking suspicion that life is absurd and ultimately meaningless? How does that suspicion make you feel? How do you respond to it?

Does the relative insignificance of human existence in the grand scheme of the universe make you feel anxious or liberated? Do you agree with

Camus that the best response is defiant scorn, or with Nagel that the best response is irony and gratitude? Or do you have a different response?

Chapter 4: The Meaning of Life

Do you recall the first time you wondered about the meaning of life? What was that experience like?

Why do human beings search for the meaning of life? Is it an important question or do you think it's a waste of time?

What was a particularly significant experience in your life, and what did you learn from it?

What is at the top of your "bucket list"? Why?

What makes you feel that you are really *living* instead of merely existing?

Have you ever had an existential crisis? If so, what caused it, and what, if anything, helped pull you out of it?

Can you ever imagine a moment in your life where you would feel absolutely satisfied, with no more goals or dreams?

How do you define love?

What or whom do you love unconditionally, and why?

What is your greatest fear?

Are you afraid of death?

Is it a gift or a curse that human beings are aware of our own mortality?

Would you want to live forever? How might you live differently if you knew you would never die?

Do you agree or disagree that sexual love can be sacred and spiritually enriching?

The Teacher in Ecclesiastes is a somewhat ambiguous character. Some think he's a pessimist, some think he's an optimist, and some think he's a realist. What do you think of his worldview?

"Vanity of vanities; all is vanity." What does this mean to you, and do you agree with the Teacher?

The Teacher concludes that if all is vanity, we might as well enjoy ourselves while we're alive by eating, drinking, loving, and taking pleasure in our labors. Do you agree with him?

Do you think there is an objective meaning of life out there to be discovered, or do you think each of us creates our own meaning?

What is the meaning of life, as you understand it now? Do you think you might someday change your answer to that question?

Conclusion: Faith, Doubt, and Reason

How does your faith compel you to dig deeper, to understand more about what you take with absolute seriousness? Do you embrace these questions or do you fear them?

How well do you really know yourself? What parts of yourself remain a mystery to you? Do you think others see you the same way you see yourself?

What in your own life keeps you on the surface? What experiences have you had that have plunged you into the depths?

Do you embrace the depths or do everything you can to avoid them? Why?

What language do you use to talk about the depths of your life? Do you agree that there is no real meaning without going through the depths and the darkness?

What is the difference between happiness and joy? What brings you happiness and what brings you joy?

How do faith, doubt, and reason contribute to your own sense of joy and meaning? Which of these three faculties is easiest for you to embrace and identify with, and why?

What "big questions" do you wrestle with, and why? Have you discovered an answer?

What would you like to learn more about, and why?

If money and time were no object, what you would do with the rest of your life, and why?

Do you agree with Elie Wiesel that it's the essence of humanity to be a question? How does that perspective make you feel?

What have you learned from this book? How will you apply the lessons you've learned here to your own life?

"Extra Credit"

This "extra credit" question invites you to think critically, comparatively, and creatively about the main themes of the book. A certain suspension of disbelief is required to answer this question, so just go with it!

Tillich, Kant, Clifford, Descartes, Dostoevsky, Mackie, Montaigne, Goethe, Nagel, and the authors of Job, Song of Songs, and Ecclesiastes are traveling on a trans-Atlantic cruise with every copy of everything they've ever written. The ship hits an iceberg and will sink. You have the resources, time, and strength to save only *one* of them and all their works for posterity. The others will be wiped from memory and it will be as if they, their work, and their ideas never existed. Whom do you save, and why?

Appendix 3

Brief Biographies

Augustine of Hippo (354–430)

ONE OF THE MOST important "fathers" of the early church, Augustine was born in North Africa (in present-day Algeria), on the edges of the Roman Empire. He was a rising star in rhetoric before he had a conversion experience and eventually became a bishop and theologian whose works made a profound impact on the development of Christian theology in the West. His most famous works are *Confessions* and *The City of God*, the latter of which he wrote in response to the sack of Rome by the Visigoths in 410. Twenty years later Augustine died as his own city of Hippo was being sacked by the Vandals.

John D. Caputo (b. 1940)

John Caputo is a prominent scholar of postmodern theology and philosophy of religion and is a leading American interpreter of religious aspects of the thought of the French poststructuralist philosopher Jacques Derrida. He has written dozens of books and essays on a wide range of topics, including several intended to introduce contemporary postmodern philosophy and theology to a general audience, including *Truth, What Would Jesus Deconstruct? On Religion,* and a memoir, *Hoping against Hope.*

William Clifford (1845–1879)

William Kingdon Clifford was an English mathematician and philosopher, professor of mathematics at University College London, and a member of the Royal Society. While most of his scholarly work was done in algebra and geometry, his essay, "The Ethics of Belief," is standard reading in theology and philosophy programs and this essay was famously attacked by William James in his lecture, "The Will to Believe." The story of the ship owner with which Clifford begins his essay is very likely based on a true story, as Clifford survived a shipwreck off the coast of Sicily as he was traveling to observe a solar eclipse. Clifford was famous for writing well into the night and rarely sleeping more than a few hours, habits that might have contributed to his early death from tuberculosis in his mid-30s.

René Descartes (1596–1650)

René Descartes is often called the Father of Modern Philosophy, thanks in large part to the profound impact of his books *Meditations on First Philosophy* and *Discourse on Method*, in which he wrote the phrase that has earned him lasting fame: "I think, therefore I am." Descartes was also a celebrated mathematician and scientist and is known for his work on optics as well as his invention of Cartesian coordinates, standard notation (adding a numeric superscript to indicate exponents), and using x, y, and z in algebraic equations. Although he was born in France, Descartes spent several decades in the Netherlands, including many years in the Dutch Army. He was hired as a tutor to the Queen of Sweden but gave her only a few lessons before dying of pneumonia.

Fyodor Dostoevsky (1821–1881)

Fyodor Dostoevsky was a giant of Russian literature and an important precursor of philosophical and religious Existentialism. After joining a subversive literary circle in St. Petersburg he was arrested and sentenced to death, but at the last minute he was spared and was instead sent to a Siberian labor camp for four years. He is regarded as one of the most insightful writers on human psychology, philosophy, and religion, and he is also known for his development of "polyphony" in his writing, in which he included a variety of narrative perspectives rather than one omniscient narrative voice. His most famous novels, besides *The Brothers Karamazov*, include *Crime and Punishment*, *The Idiot*, and *Notes from the Underground*. A devout Russian Orthodox Christian, Dostoevsky instructed that his tombstone be inscribed with a passage from the Gospel of John: "Very truly, I tell you, unless a grain of wheat falls into the earth and dies, it remains just a single grain; but if it dies, it bears much fruit" (12:24).

Johann Wolfgang von Goethe (1749–1832)

Johann Wolfgang von Goethe is to German language and culture what Shakespeare is to English language and culture. *Faust* is generally considered to be the crowning achievement of the German dramatic tradition, but Goethe was much more than a writer: he was a statesman, an educational reformer, a cultural and literary critic, and an amateur scientist. Goethe was perhaps the most influential figure in German culture over the course of the nineteenth century, beginning with the publication of his first novel, *The Sorrows of Young Werther*, in 1774 and his involvement in the *Sturm und Drang* literary movement. Due largely to Goethe's influence, the new German Republic formed after the German Empire's defeat in World War I chose Goethe's home city of Weimar as its capital. An international consortium of schools promoting German language and culture is named the Goethe Institut in his honor.

Immanuel Kant (1724–1804)

Immanuel Kant remains one of the most important and influential figures in modern philosophy, especially due to his trilogy on critical philosophy: *Critique of Pure Reason*, *Critique of Practical Reason*, and *Critique of the Power of Judgment*. He also wrote significant works on ethics (*Groundwork of the Metaphysics of Morals* and *Metaphysics of Morals*) and religion (*Religion within the Bounds of Mere Reason*). He is a standard figure in undergraduate ethics courses thanks to his work on deontology, or duty-based ethics, and for his categorical imperative. There are a number of stubborn legends about Kant's personal life that reveal something of Kant's personality, even though these legends have been thoroughly debunked. For example, it's often said that Kant was so punctual about his daily walks that his neighbors would set their clocks according to when Kant walked by their window. It's also commonly believed that, despite his claim to be a "citizen of the world" (a "cosmopolitan"), Kant himself never ventured more than five miles from his hometown of Königsberg, Prussia (present-day Kaliningrad, Russia). Kant did in fact venture further afield, but only just a little bit: he spent a few years as a tutor in a town about fifteen miles away from home.

John Leslie Mackie (1917–1981)

Australian philosopher J. L. Mackie wrote significant works on ethics, metaphysics, the philosophy of language, and the philosophy of religion, none more famous than "Evil and Omnipotence." In ethics he is known for his book *Ethics: Inventing Right and Wrong*, in which he offers a defense of moral skepticism, going so far as to argue that there are no objective values. He also wrote a defense of atheism, called *The Miracle of Theism*, which further develops his arguments from "Evil and Omnipotence." After serving in the British Army in World War II Mackie taught in New Zealand and Australia before moving to the United Kingdom, where he spent the rest of his life at Oxford. In his obituary his eulogist noted that Mackie was such a kind and gracious debater with a knack for expressing arguments and disagreements so genially that his opponents often mistook his criticisms as compliments!

Michel de Montaigne (1533–1592)

Michel de Montaigne was a French politician, soldier, diplomat, and writer, most famous for inventing the literary form of the essay. His parents raised him to be an intellectual, speaking only in Latin to him and insisting that the manor's servants and staff speak only Latin around him as well. He learned Greek at a young age and was sent off to boarding school and then to the court of King Charles IX. He participated in numerous military campaigns and served in the parliament of Bordeaux. He had an arranged marriage but in his writings he mentions virtually nothing at all about his wife. Montaigne's essays revolutionized modern literature and re-introduced autobiography into the Western canon. He is sometimes called "the first modern man."

Thomas Nagel (b. 1937)

American philosopher Thomas Nagel was born in Belgrade, Yugoslavia (now Serbia), to German Jewish refugees but moved to New York at age 2. He studied at Cornell, Oxford, and Harvard before obtaining teaching positions at the University of California, Berkeley, and Princeton, but he has spent most of his career at New York University. His work focuses on philosophy of mind, philosophy of science, and ethics. Among undergraduate philosophy students he is perhaps most famous for his essay, "What Is It Like to Be a Bat?" He has received numerous awards and prizes for his contributions to philosophy and is still active on the faculty at NYU.

Paul Tillich (1886-1965)

Paul Tillich was born in a small town in eastern Germany (now part of Poland), the son of a conservative Lutheran pastor. Tillich attended several universities, as was the custom in Germany, and was ordained a Lutheran pastor before serving as a chaplain on the front lines during World War I, a profoundly disorienting and traumatic experience. Upon returning from the war he learned that his wife had had a child with another man. After divorcing, Tillich embarked on his academic career in Germany and he soon attracted the attention of the Nazis thanks to a number of critical speeches. When the Nazis formally took power in 1933 Tillich was dismissed from his position and received an invitation to move to the United States to join the faculty of Union Theological Seminary in New York. Not long after arriving in the U.S. he delivered a series of radio addresses to his native Germany, continuing to warn them about the dangers of Hitler and the Nazis. After spending several years at Union he moved to Harvard and then spent the rest of his life at the University of Chicago Divinity School. Tillich referred to himself as a "theologian on the boundary" between the church and the world and he was a keen observer and critic of culture. In the U.S. he became something of a celebrity, even making the cover of *Time* magazine in 1959, not long after publishing *Dynamics of Faith*. His other popular work was *The Courage to Be*, and he also wrote a three-volume *Systematic Theology*, several collections of lectures and sermons, works of art criticism, and two autobiographies: *On the Boundary* and *My Search for Absolutes*. Tillich's ashes are scattered in Paul Tillich Park in New Harmony, Indiana.

Bibliography

Anselm. *Proslogion, with the Replies of Gaunilo and Anselm.* Translated by Thomas Williams. Indianapolis: Hackett: 2001.
Armstrong, Karen. *The Case for God.* New York: Anchor, 2010.
Augustine. *Confessions.* Translated by Henry Chadwick. Oxford World's Classics. New York: Oxford University Press, 2009.
———. "Sermon 117." In Augustine, *Sermons*, vol. 2. Translated by Mary Magdalene Mueller, 177–82. Fathers of the Church 47. Washington, D.C.: Catholic University of America Press, 1964.
Blake, William. *Blake's Illustrations for the Book of Job.* Mineola, New York: Dover, 1995.
Bowler, Gerald. *Santa Claus: A Biography.* Toronto: McClelland & Stewart, 2005.
"The Buddha's First Sermon: Setting the Wheel of the Dharma in Motion (The Dhammachakkappavattana Sutta)." In *Buddhism*, edited by Donald S. Lopez, Jr., 177–81. The Norton Anthology of World Religions, edited by Jack Miles. New York: Norton, 2015.
Bultmann, Rudolf. "On the Problem of Demythologizing." In Rudolf Bultmann, *New Testament & Mythology and Other Basic Writings*, edited and translated by Schubert M. Ogden, 95–130. Philadelphia: Fortress, 1984.
Calvin, John. *Institutes of the Christian Religion.* Edited by John T. McNeill. Translated by Ford Lewis Battles. 2 vols. The Library of Christian Classics 20–21. Philadelphia: Westminster, 1960.
Campbell, Joseph. *The Hero with a Thousand Faces.* 3rd ed. The Collected Works of Joseph Campbell. Novato, CA: New World Library, 2008.
Camus, Albert. *The Myth of Sisyphus and Other Essays.* Translated by Justin O'Brien. New York: Vintage International, 1991.
Caputo, John D. *On Religion.* Thinking in Action. New York: Routledge, 2001.
———. *The Insistence of God: A Theology of Perhaps.* Indiana Series in the Philosophy of Religion. Bloomington: Indiana University Press, 2013.
———. *Philosophy and Theology.* Horizons in Theology. Nashville, TN: Abingdon, 2006.
———. *Truth.* Philosophy in Transit. New York: Penguin, 2014.
Clifford, William. "The Ethics of Belief." In William Clifford, *The Ethics of Belief and Other Essays*, 70–96. Great Books in Philosophy. Amherst, NY: Prometheus, 1999.
Descartes, René. *Discourse on Method and Meditations on First Philosophy.* Translated by Donald A. Cress. 4th ed. Indianapolis: Hackett, 1998.

———. *Meditations on First Philosophy.* Translated by Donald A. Cress. 3rd ed. Indianapolis: Hackett, 1993.

Dostoevsky, Fyodor. *The Grand Inquisitor and Related Chapters from "The Brothers Karamazov."* Edited by Charles Guignon. Translated by Constance Garnett. Indianapolis: Hackett, 1993.

Dreyfus, Hubert, and Sean Dorrance Kelly. *All Things Shining: Reading the Western Classics to Find Meaning in a Secular Age.* New York: Free Press, 2011.

Forster, Marc, dir. *Stranger than Fiction.* 2006; Culver City, CA: Sony Pictures Home Entertainment, 2007. DVD.

Freud, Sigmund. *Civilization and Its Discontents.* Translated and edited by James Strachey, with an introduction by Peter Gay. New York: Norton, 1989.

Friedman Richard Elliott. *Who Wrote the Bible?* New York: HarperOne, 1987.

Galilei, Galileo. "Letter to Madame Christina of Lorraine, Grand Duchess of Tuscany." In *Discoveries and Opinions of Galileo*, edited by Stillman Drake, 173–216. New York: Anchor Doubleday, 1957.

Geertz, Clifford. "Religion as a Cultural System." In Clifford Geertz, *The Interpretation of Cultures*, 93–135. 3rd ed. New York: Basic, 2017.

Gilkey, Langdon. *Creationism on Trial: Evolution and God at Little Rock.* Studies in Religion and Culture. Charlottesville: University of Virginia Press, 1998.

Goethe, Johann Wolfgang von. *Faust: Part One.* Translated by David Luke. New York: Oxford University Press, 2008.

Goodman, James. *But Where Is the Lamb? Imagining the Story of Abraham and Isaac.* New York: Schocken, 2013.

Gould, Stephen Jay. "Nonoverlapping Magisteria." *Natural History* 106 (March 1997) 16–22.

Hege, Brent A. R. "Contesting Faith, Truth, and Religious Language at the Creation Museum: A Historical-Theological Reflection." *Theology and Science* 12, no. 2 (2014) 142–63.

Heidegger, Martin. *Being and Time.* Translated by John Macquarrie and Edward Robinson. Harper Perennial Modern Thought. New York: Harper Perennial, 2008.

Hume, David. *Dialogues concerning Natural Religion.* Edited by Richard H. Popkin. 2nd ed. Indianapolis: Hackett, 1998.

Ignatius of Loyola: Spiritual Exercises and Selected Works. Edited by George E. Ganss. Classics of Western Spirituality. Mahwah, NJ: Paulist, 1991.

Jefferson, Thomas. "Letter to Peter Carr, August 10th 1787." In *The Life and Selected Writings of Thomas Jefferson*, edited by Adrienne Koch and William Peden, 397–401. New York: Modern Library, 2004.

Kant, Immanuel. "Answer to the Question: What Is Enlightenment?" In *Basic Writings of Kant*, edited by Allen W. Wood and translated by Thomas K. Abbott, 133–41. Modern Library Classics. New York: Modern Library, 2001.

Keller, Catherine. *On the Mystery: Discerning Divinity in Process.* Minneapolis: Fortress, 2008.

Kierkegaard, Søren. *Fear and Trembling/Repetition.* Edited and translated by Howard V. Hong and Edna H. Hong. Princeton, NJ: Princeton University Press, 1983.

———. *Papers and Journals: A Selection.* Translated by Alastair Hannay. Penguin Classics. New York: Penguin, 1996.

King, Martin Luther, Jr. "I See the Promised Land." In *A Testament of Hope: The Essential Writings and Speeches of Martin Luther King Jr.*, edited by James M. Washington, 279–86. New York: HarperOne, 1986.

———. "Letter from Birmingham City Jail." In *A Testament of Hope: The Essential Writings and Speeches of Martin Luther King Jr.*, edited by James M. Washington, 290–302. New York: HarperOne, 1986.

Kuhn, Thomas S. *The Structure of Scientific Revolutions: 50th Anniversary Edition*. 4th ed. Chicago: University of Chicago Press, 2012.

Lamott, Anne. *Plan B: Further Thoughts on Faith*. New York: Riverhead, 2006.

Larson, Edward J. *Summer for the Gods: The Scopes Trial and America's Continuing Debate over Science and Religion*. New York: Basic, 2006.

Le Guin, Ursula K. "The Ones Who Walk away from Omelas." In Ursula K. Le Guin, *The Wind's Twelve Quarters and The Compass Rose*, 254–62. SF Masterworks. London: Gollancz, 2015.

Long, Eugene. "Suffering and Transcendence." *International Journal for Philosophy of Religion* 60 (2006) 139–48.

Luther, Martin. "The Heidelberg Disputation." In *Martin Luther's Basic Theological Writings*, edited by Timothy F. Lull and William R. Russell, 14–25. 3rd ed. Minneapolis: Fortress, 2012.

———. "The Large Catechism." In *The Book of Concord: The Confessions of the Evangelical Lutheran Church*, edited by Robert Kolb and Timothy J. Wengert, 377–480. Minneapolis: Augsburg Fortress, 2000.

Mackie, J. L. "Evil and Omnipotence." *Mind*, N.S. 64, no. 254 (Apr. 1955) 200–212.

MacLeish, Archibald. *J.B.: A Play in Verse*. New York: Houghton Mifflin, 1989.

Marlowe, Christopher. *Doctor Faustus*. Edited by Paul Menzer. New Mermaids. New York: Methuen Drama, 2019.

Merchant, Carolyn. *The Death of Nature: Women, Ecology, and the Scientific Revolution*. New York: Harper & Row, 1990.

Montaigne, Michel de. *Essays*. Translated by John M. Cohen. New York: Penguin, 1993.

Nagel, Thomas. "The Absurd." *The Journal of Philosophy* 68, no. 20 (Oct. 1971) 716–27.

———. "Death." *Noûs* 4, no. 1 (Feb. 1970) 73–80.

Nietzsche, Friedrich. *Beyond Good and Evil: Prelude to a Philosophy of the Future*. Translated by Walter Kaufmann. New York: Vintage, 1989.

———. "Ecce Homo." In *Basic Writings of Nietzsche*, edited and translated by Walter Kaufmann, 655–792. Modern Library Classics. New York: Modern Library, 2000.

———. "On Truth and Lie in an Extra-Moral Sense." In *The Portable Nietzsche*, edited and translated by Walter Kaufmann, 42–47. Portable Library. New York: Penguin, 1982.

Pascal, Blaise. *Pensées*. Edited and translated by Roger Ariew. Indianapolis: Hackett, 2005.

Plato. "Apology." In Plato, *Five Dialogues: Euthyphro, Apology, Crito, Meno, Phaedo*, translated by G. M. A. Grube, 21–44. 2nd ed. Hackett Classics. Indianapolis: Hackett, 2002.

Segal, Robert A. *Myth: A Very Short Introduction*. 2nd ed. New York: Oxford University Press, 2015.

Solzhenitsyn, Aleksandr. *The Gulag Archipelago*. Vol. 1, *An Experiment in Literary Investigation*. Translated by Thomas P. Whitney and Harry Willetts. Harper Perennial Modern Classics. New York: HarperCollins, 2007.

Taylor, Charles. *A Secular Age*. Cambridge, MA: Belknap, 2007.
Throckmorton, Burton H. Jr., ed. *Gospel Parallels: A Comparison of the Synoptic Gospels*. 5th ed. Nashville, TN: Thomas Nelson, 1992.
Tillich, Paul. *The Courage to Be*. 3rd ed. New Haven, CT: Yale University Press, 2014.
———. "The Depth of Existence." In Paul Tillich, *The Shaking of the Foundations*, 52–63. New York: Scribner's, 1948.
———. "The Eternal Now." In Paul Tillich, *The Eternal Now*, 122–32. New York: Scribner's, 1963.
———. *Dynamics of Faith*. Perennial Classics ed. New York: HarperCollins, 2001.
———. *Love, Power, and Justice: Ontological Analyses and Ethical Applications*. Oxford: Oxford University Press, 1960.
———. *Systematic Theology*, vol. 1. Chicago: University of Chicago Press, 1973.
Vicchio, Stephen J. *Ivan & Adolf: The Last Man in Hell*. Eugene, OR: Wipf and Stock, 2011.
Vonnegut, Kurt. "Tomorrow and Tomorrow and Tomorrow." In Kurt Vonnegut, *Welcome to the Monkey House*, 284–98. New York: Dell, 1973.
Ward, Keith. *God: A Guide for the Perplexed*. London: Oneworld, 2002.
Ware, Kallistos. *The Orthodox Way*. 2nd ed. Crestwood, NY: St. Vladimir's, 1995.
Wiesel, Elie. *The Town beyond the Wall: A Novel*. New York: Schocken, 1995.

www.ingramcontent.com/pod-product-compliance
Lightning Source LLC
Chambersburg PA
CBHW062042220426
43662CB00010B/1612